EUROPEAN MONETARY UNION SINCE 1848

EUROPEAN MONETARY UNION SINCE 1848

A POLITICAL AND HISTORICAL ANALYSIS

Wim F.V. Vanthoor

Assistant Manager of the Econometric Research and Special Studies
Department and Head of the Historical Section, De Nederlandsche Bank

Edward Elgar
Cheltenham, UK; Brookfield, US

Published by
Edward Elgar Publishing Limited
8 Lansdown Place
Cheltenham
Glos GL50 2HU
UK

Edward Elgar Publishing Company
Old Post Road
Brookfield
Vermont 05036
US

A catalogue record for this book
is available from the British Library

Library of Congress Cataloging-in-Publication Data
Vanthoor, W. F. V. (Wim Frans Victor)
    [Europese monetaire eenwording in historisch perspectief.
English]
    European Monetary Union since 1848 / Wim F. V. Vanthoor.
    Rev. translation of: Europese monetaire eenwording in historisch
perspectief.
    Includes bibliographical references.
    1. Monetary policy—Europe—History. 2. Europe—Economic
integration. I. Title.
HG925.V3613   1997
332.4'94—dc20
                                                            96–31270
                                                            CIP

ISBN 1 85898 461 0

Printed and bound in Great Britain by
Hartnolls Limited, Bodmin, Cornwall

CONTENTS

LIST OF ABBREVIATIONS

BIS	Bank for International Settlements
BLEU	Belgo–Luxembourg Economic Union
BNR	Banca Nazionale nel Regno d'Italia
EBRD	European Bank for Reconstruction and Development
EC	European Community
ECB	European Central Bank
ECE	Economic Commission for Europe
ECSC	European Coal and Steel Community
ECU	European Currency Unit
EDC	European Defence Community
EEA	European Economic Area
EEC	European Economic Community
EFTA	European Free Trade Association
EMA	European Monetary Agreement
EMCF	European Monetary Cooperation Fund
EMF	European Monetary Fund
EMI	European Monetary Institute
EMS	European Monetary System
EMU	Economic and Monetary Union
EPU	European Political Union
ERM	Exchange Rate Mechanism
ESCB	European System of Central Banks
EU	European Union
EUA	European Unit of Account
Euratom	European Atomic Energy Community
GDP	Gross Domestic Product
IGC	Intergovernmental Conference
IMF	International Monetary Fund
LMI	Luxembourg Monetary Institute
LMU	Latin Monetary Union

MCA   Monetary Compensatory Amount
NATO   North Atlantic Treaty Organization
OECD   Organization for Economic Cooperation and Development
OEEC   Organization for European Economic Cooperation
SDR   Special Drawing Right
WEU   Western European Union

LIST OF CHART AND TABLES

PREFACE

This book is based on the Monetary Monography *De Europese monetaire eenwording in historisch perspectief* published in Dutch by De Nederlandsche Bank, in spring 1992, on the occasion of the Treaty of Maastricht signed in February of the same year. By comparing the nineteenth-century monetary unions with monetary integration in Europe after World War II some interesting conclusions could be drawn with regard to the relationship between EMU and political union.

The English volume is published in view of the 1996 Intergovernmental Conference. In principle, the outline from the Monography is followed though the description of monetary unions in the past century has been revised where necessary as a result of further historical research. Furthermore, Part II, dealing with the European integration in the twentieth century, has now been extended with a paragraph on plans about and developments of monetary integration during the Interbellum. Finally, monetary integration in Western Europe after World War II has been placed in a more political framework. Looking at the Treaty of Maastricht it tries to answer the question how far that agreement is in accordance with what the founding fathers of the post-war European integration had in mind.

In this work I used various quotations from authors and politicians of different nationalities. For those which were not written in English, the author thought it useful to translate them or to describe their meaning instead of using the text literally. Another point to be made is that in some cases the view of Dutch economists, bankers or politicians has been accentuated because of the Dutch-based version of my Monography mentioned above. This holds also for Appendix 2 in which for instance the ECU-central rate for the Dutch guilder is given each time when a realignment within the EMS has taken place.

I am particularly grateful to Professor Dr. Martin M.G. Fase for his initiative and stimulating force to publish the extended and partly revised version of the Dutch Monography. I also want to thank especially Dr. Joke Mooij for her valuable advice and constructive ideas during her reading of the manuscript. Many thanks go also to Idian Bocken and Liesbeth Klein for their English translation. It goes without saying that the responsibility for errors in the final version including the quotations used remains fully with the author. The same holds true for the views expressed in this book which are strictly personal and therefore need not necessarily be in accordance with the opinions held by De Nederlandsche Bank on this matter.

This book could never have been published without the assistance of Carolien Verhoeven and Gita Gajapersad who typed the manuscript and of Rob Vet who converted it, with endless patience, in the required style of the publisher. Finally I thank the staff of the library of De Nederlandsche Bank for their help in tracing down much of the published literature. From that it soon became clear to me that there is a long way to go before Coudenhove-Kalergi's ascertainment of nearly 75 years ago, that each change of great historical value began as an utopia and has ended as a reality, becomes true for the monetary integration in Europe.

Wim F.V. Vanthoor

INTRODUCTION

Two thousand years of European history bear witness to continual attempts to convert Europe, united as it had been in terms of culture and civilization since the very beginnings of our era, into a political and economic union. Philosophers and poets alike sang the praises of a united Europe. All favoured a federation of European states with representation in a single parliament. The most revolutionary ideas were launched by a Frenchman, Charles Irénée Castel, Abbé de Saint-Pierre who, in 1712, published a book called *Projet de traité pour rendre la paix perpétuelle entre les souverains chrétiens, ou projet de traité pour la paix perpétuelle en Europe.* In it he advocated an alliance of European states, to be represented in a European senate. Its Member States would have to contribute towards common expenditures and it would have a collective army to repel any attacks on the alliance.

Although the advocates of a league of nations met with some sympathy among the citizenry, they found little response among governments. For that the idea had to be carried by a State, even if the subjects of the envisaged European federation often had to be persuaded by force to believe in it. In Caesar's Rome, for instance, everything turned on the army, as it also did under the rule of Charles V and the Habsburg Emperors of the Holy Roman Empire of the German Nation. Things were no different in the new European order following the French Revolution. After all, the French Emperor Napoleon — who incidentally brought the Holy Roman Empire to an end in 1806 — was a military strategist before all else. In recent history, Hitler and Mussolini tried to create a Europe which would be united in a common ideology. Their efforts belonged to the same category of endeavours to restore political unity by conquest. Nevertheless, Europe never did succeed in creating a political unity. The reason for this failure was mainly due to the various humanistic and religious traditions, to the entirely different political ideologies of the responsible leaders, and last but not least to the multitude of economic and monetary particularisms.

Economically, the European landscape was rarely more than a reflection of ancient regional and national interests which occasionally coincided and sometimes conflicted. That was also the case in the monetary field, where the issue of coins had always been regarded as an important way of demonstrating national sovereignty. Nevertheless, attempts were continually made from that quarter to have a certain currency circulate — through monetary union or otherwise — within the largest possible area. Famous cases in point are the Byzantine *solidus*, also known as the 'dollar of the Middle Ages' and the Carolingian pound, with the aid of which Charlemagne succeeded in bringing about monetary union within his empire. Later down the ages there were the French *Ecu d'or*, the Dutch *Lion daalder*, the Austrian *Maria Theresia Thaler* and the Spanish *Real*, each and every one of them coins constituting an important medium of exchange or trade currency outside their territory, only to disappear again as soon as the State of issue fell into a decline. It is true that since the middle of the nineteenth century, the growing volume of international economic intercourse brought the idea of an international currency within the realm of international action. A two-thousand year history, nevertheless, shows that Europe has never had a single currency.

In this light, the Maastricht Treaty which became operative in November 1993 could be interpreted as a modern version of that age-old dream of a united Europe with a single currency, modern in the sense that faith in political union can and will no longer be imposed by armies. The Treaty turns on Economic and Monetary Union (EMU). It is this Treaty which raised the question, discussed in this book, to what extent the historical pessimism surrounding a single European currency is justified or whether the idea of unification as contained in the Treaty may be viewed with greater optimism. On the basis of a study of literature on this subject, the author looks at the experience gained with certain forms of economic and monetary integration, which have at some time been operative in Europe since the middle of the nineteenth century. Looking at this period may be useful in order to see if a historical parallel can be drawn from monetary unions in the past for the present development towards European monetary unification.

The present study is made up of three parts. Part I deals with the monetary unions which came into being from the 1850s onwards, against the background of the then metallic monetary system. In Chapter 1 the characteristics of that system are reviewed within the context of the general economic and political constellation of the time. Chapter 2 goes into the definition of a monetary union underlying the classification of unions in operation in the nineteenth century. A distinction is made between unions born of a process of political unification and unions concluded by politically autonomous nations. Attention is also paid to the features of the issuing bank as precursor of the central bank. Chapters 3 and 4 go into the birth and development, respectively, of the two categories of monetary unions. It turns out that monetary tensions, usually generated by economic and/or political conditions, manifested themselves not so much in coins as in the fiduciary paper money, so that, in spite of political unity, monetary unification often took a long time to be rounded off. However, where monetary union was no more than the outcome of an agreement concluded between autonomous nations, these same tensions sooner or later heralded the demise of the union. This leads to the conclusion, set out in Chapter 5, that in the nineteenth century political union was a prerequisite not only for the sustainability of the monetary union, but also and especially for its irreversibility.

Against this background, Part II takes a look at monetary integration as it has taken shape in Europe in the twentieth century. Chapter 6 deals with the Interbellum. Following a short-lived recovery, the gold standard went under for good during that period, while in the political arena idealists promulgating the United States of Europe did not stand a chance against the upsurge of nationalism. It was these two factors which thwarted the attempts to reactivate existing monetary unions or to form new ones. Chapter 7 sets out the changes which took place after 1945 when integration in Western Europe became mainly economic in character after the conference of Messina. Chapter 8 starts with the establishment of the European Economic Community (EEC) in 1957. Although the Treaty establishing the EEC offered scope for the development of political union, stagnation set in as a consequence of the 1966 compromise reached in Luxembourg. Chapter 9 deals first of all with the 1969 conference of The Hague, and sets out the objectives of EMU. Under the impact of international developments and economic tensions within the Community, the quest for EMU made way for closer monetary integration in the 1970s. Chapter 10, therefore, discusses the period — still ongoing — of the European Monetary System (EMS) which became operative in March 1979. During this period the concept of a European Union (EU) has been worked out in the Single European Act. This Act was followed by the Delors Report, discussed in Chapter 11, which was in turn given its final shape in the Maastricht Treaty. An evaluation of the post-war quest for integration can be found in Chapter 12, which concludes, among other things, that the EU, as formulated in the Maastricht Treaty, insufficiently guarantees the irreversibility of economic and monetary unification.

Part III takes a look at the lessons which can be learnt from the past as described in the preceding chapters. Chapter 13 begins by comparing the monetary unions of the nineteenth century and the broader quest for European integration manifest since the Second World War, discussing the differences and similarities between the two processes. The question of what EMU is really meant to achieve, or in other words, what the relationship is between EMU and political unification, as embodied in the term European Political Union (EPU), is discussed in Chapter 14. The answer to that question given in the summary and conclusions in Chapter 15 finally prompts an outline of the conditions which a united Europe, as worded in the Maastricht Treaty, will have to meet.

The book ends with two appendices. The first contains a chronological overview of the relevant measures which led to the establishment of the nineteenth-century monetary unions. The second is made up of a calendar of relevant monetary, economic and political events and the measures taken with a view to Western European integration in the period 1945–1995.

Part I

19TH-CENTURY MONETARY UNIONS

'A monetary union between countries, even if they are not united in a political union, makes sense provided that the participating central banks conduct a fully harmonized monetary policy.'

(Alfred Lansburgh, 1928)

1 GENERAL CHARACTERISTICS

1.1 Economic and political constellation

In nineteenth-century Europe, economic conditions were characterized by industrialization, modernization and internationalization boosting in equal measure the establishment of nation states and the formation of larger political units. This development was the result of the emergence of liberalism in political thought and the attitude of *laisser-faire* dominating economic thinking. Both these movements held that the interests of all peoples would become intertwined as a matter of course, leading to ever larger cooperative groups.

Although, as noted in the Introduction, ideas to shape Europe into a political and economic unit were not novel, they were given a new impetus with the advent of the Industrial Revolution. In the wake of philosophers such as Jeremy Bentham and Immanuel Kant whose contemplation of peace at the end of the eighteenth century had come up with the idea of a united Europe, the German philosopher Karl Krause published a plan for a European League of Nations in 1814, in which the European peoples would, in stages, voluntarily unite themselves into a federal state. In that same year, Count Henry de Saint Simon wrote his *Mémoires sur la réorganisation de la société européenne*, where he, too, advocated a liberal European federation whose cornerstone was to be political cooperation between France and the United Kingdom. His ideas found favour among people like the Italian Carlo Cattaneo, who insisted in the 1850s that 'we shall have peace, when we have the United States of Europe'.[1] The French poet Victor Hugo even demanded unification during the Peace Conference of August 1849. A more belligerent proposal was put forward by the Italian Giuseppe Mazzini who felt that a united Europe could be achieved only if the monarchies of the various countries were overthrown by revolutionary movements (Anton Zottman, 1963).

Following the revolutions of 1848, the concept of a united Europe was crowded out by nationalist movements which stressed the importance of their own nations. As had been the case in preceding centuries, their ideas

3

often had to be rammed down people's throats. This was so notably in Italy and Germany, where wars and insurgences were ultimately aimed at setting up a politically unified state. A true federation was established in Switzerland, where the 1848 constitution laid the foundation for a political structure similar to that which the advocates of a united Europe had had in mind.

1.2   The monetary system

It is characteristic of nineteenth-century monetary systems that they were based mainly on precious metals (gold and silver). The unit of account was the standard coin which was usually also legal tender, and could be issued without restriction. In practice, the metallic system operated in various forms. The most prevalent were monometallism, where either gold or silver served as the standard, and the double or bimetallic standard, where both gold and silver, whose exchange ratio was fixed by law, functioned as the standard metal within a certain area. In most European countries the single standard was based on silver. Only the United Kingdom had adopted the gold standard, by law of 1816, legalizing a practice that had existed since the early eighteenth century. France was a prominent representative of the double standard, even though the Coinage Act of 1803 was not explicit on this point.[2]

The double standard, in particular, often gave rise to problems. These arose whenever the market value of gold or silver underwent a development that caused the exchange ratio of the two metals to deviate from that laid down by law. The metal which rose in value became undervalued in the country concerned, and was then either hoarded or taken abroad, where it could be sold at higher market prices. Here Gresham's law played a role which observes that, when the double standard is applied at a ratio for the two metals which does not make allowance for their true values, the overvalued metal will crowd out the undervalued metal. As a result, usually only one of the two metals was actually being circulated, a situation contrary to the aim of bimetallism. For that reason, the double standard may also be called the alternating or alternative standard.[3] It goes without saying that, with the alternating use of silver and gold, application of the double standard was on occasion an exceptionally complicated business.

In most countries circulating both gold and silver coins, the weight and content of the coins was determined so that one kilogramme of gold equalled 15.5 kilogrammes of silver. This ratio corresponded with the market ratio existing between the two metals since around 1800. The chart below presents the movements in that ratio until the end of the nineteenth century, showing that gold was on the decline from about 1850 to around 1870.[4] Nevertheless that decline was limited in scope. The difference between the market ratio and that fixed by law was never more than 2 per cent. The discovery of gold in Russia, California and Australia in the middle of the century exercised a downward pressure on the value of gold, which consequently tended to drive out silver. The fact that the ratio nevertheless stopped going down can be ascribed in part to the more or less spontaneous absorption of the silver outflow by the increasing demand for this metal on the part of India and China, traditionally accumulators of silver.

The ratio between the two metals underwent a clearly discernible change roundabout 1870 for two reasons. The first reason was that in the 1860s considerable amounts of silver had been discovered in the United States, which depressed the price of silver. The other reason was the gold price in Europe, which became subject to upward pressure when the newly united State of Germany adopted the gold standard, boosting demand for gold.

Chart 1.1 Ratio of gold/silver market values, 1800–1895*

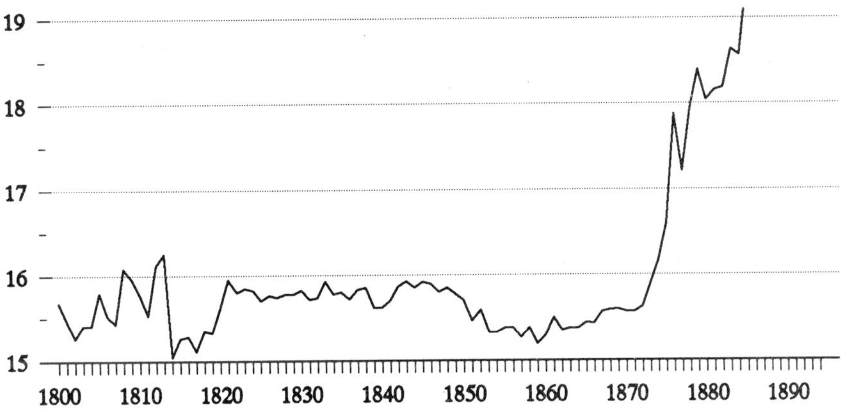

* Prices in Hamburg (until 1833) and London. Source: *The Bimetallist*, II, 1896, p. 52.

The proponents of bimetallism supported the view that a bimetallic standard would always yield a steadier price level than at least one of two alternative monometallic standards and might yield a steadier price level than either. The rationale was that if only the double standard were applied in the largest possible area, the dearer metal could not be crowded out. After all, there would then be little scope for taking the more expensive metal 'abroad' where it could be sold at a profit. There was the added advantage that the value of money would not be dependent on the value of just one of the two metals, but on the production of both of them. It was hoped that excessive veins of the one metal would be compensated for by depletion of mines of the other and *vice versa*.

In this context, the history of France, notably during the period 1803–1873, shows that, under favourable circumstances, it was indeed possible to maintain both gold and silver as standard metals under the bimetallic system. Between 1803 and 1850, silver tended to drive out gold in France (Irving Fisher, 1911). Normally bimetallism would then have been replaced by the monometallic standard, were it not that new veins of gold were discovered in California roundabout that time. The increased production of gold resulted in a contrary development, and it seemed as if silver would disappear altogether from France, making way for gold. However, the new gold mines were gradually depleted, while the production of silver expanded, and the situation was again reversed. France's success in keeping both gold and silver coins in circulation is ascribed by Milton Friedman (1990) to various factors, the most important one being France's economic prowess *vis-à-vis* the rest of the world. In addition, the French were unusually predisposed to use metal for minting coins and indirectly for building up reserves as a cover for paper money and deposits. These two factors helped to make France a major party in the market for gold and silver, of sufficient import to maintain a more or less constant price relationship between gold and silver, in spite of the considerable changes taking place in the production of the two metals.

The French situation is aptly illustrated by the Dutch economist and banker Nicolaas Gerard Pierson (1912): 'Silver was sold in great quantities, and gold purchased. Thus France propped up the value of gold, whose production had expanded, selling large quantities of the other metal. The greater production of gold could consequently not but lead to a lower value not only for this metal, but also for silver. In unison, however, the two metals did not decline as much as gold would have done on its own if France had not operated the double, but the single silver standard. And thus it came about that in the years 1867–1870 the ratio of the two metals again reached the medium which had been in force in the period 1803–1820: 15.85.'[5]

Another characteristic of the nineteenth-century monetary systems was the often highly heterogeneous composition of the money circulation. It comprised not only coins indigenous to the country in question, but also high-grade as well as inferior foreign coins, which, though not legal tender there, were accepted as a means of exchange. Domestically, the authorities were held to ensure that the weight and metal content of the coins issued by them were in conformity with their face value. In practice, this boiled down to a guarantee that debased coins could be exchanged for new ones to the same value at all times. Tensions arose whenever the authorities fought shy of this responsibility, tensions which were often exacerbated by war, fought on various occasions with a view to political unification. These wars made heavy inroads on public budgets, forcing governments to issue notes with forced currency, which meant that State cashiers were under the obligation to accept them as a means of payment. This paper was not covered by metal and usually served as money on a temporary basis. Finally, the currency system was, from time to time, seriously disturbed by excessive issue of paper money by banks as a result of which banknotes began to depreciate ensuing speculative capital outflows in the form of gold or silver money. Obviously in many countries the circulation of inconvertible state-issued notes and depreciating banknotes led to monetary chaos sooner or later. It was these circumstances which usually gave a major impetus to unification of coinage systems.

Notes

1. Duroselle (1957), p. 20.
2. See chapter 4.2.1.
3. Another variant of the double standard emerged in countries wishing to adopt the gold standard without making their stock of silver worthless. The mintage of silver was then stopped, but the existing silver coins continued to circulate. This is known as a limping standard.
4. A silver coin weighing five grammes of 90 per cent fine silver equalled 4.5 grammes fine which corresponded with 222.2 francs per kilogramme of silver. As the French gold twenty franc coin contained 6.5 grammes with a metal content of 90 per cent fine gold, the gold price came out at 3.445 francs, so that the gold/silver ratio corresponded with 1:15.5. When the market ratio fell to, for instance, 1:15 (gold consequently being overvalued), the price of 1 kilogramme silver then came out at 229.7 francs. In that case it became more lucrative to export silver or to sell it on the free market instead of using it as medium of exchange at the legally lower rate of 222.2 francs per kilogramme.
5. Pierson (1912), p. 463.

2 MONETARY UNION

In this chapter attention will be paid to the definition of monetary union, the various categories of unions on the basis of this definition as well as to the characteristics of the nineteenth-century banks of issue.

2.1 Definition

In 1933, Axel Nielsen defined a monetary union as 'an agreement between two or more states to adopt some form of common regulation of their respective currencies'.[1] The most essential objective on which the nineteenth-century monetary unions made agreements — institutionalized or otherwise — was the unhindered circulation of the standard coins in the various regions. According to Nielsen, the least far-reaching arrangement was that where national coins were simply legalized in border areas by compelling the State cashiers there to accept coins from the neighbouring country. At the other extreme, he sees the transfer of the competence to mint coins between nations. Between these two extremes, he distinguishes three forms: unions where the coins of the Member States were circulating at a fixed exchange rate within the entire union, unions with a common currency, and unions which operated a kind of parallel currency in addition to their own.

A more contemporary definition is wielded by Theresia Theurl (1992) who avers that a monetary union is characterized by either a uniform or a common monetary agreement.[2] She holds that a uniform arrangement is in operation when national bodies are subjected to carefully formulated rules as to how they should behave in certain concrete situations. Under a common arrangement, national monetary competences are transferred to a supranational authority. In both cases the establishment of a monetary union is always attended by limitation of the participating countries' monetary sovereignty. According to Theurl, any description of a monetary union should turn on the elements which underlie the agreement. These include, first of all, the area where the monetary medium serves as legal tender in its various forms (coins and banknotes). Of no lesser importance is the

8

manner in which the ratio between the national currencies is determined. This cannot be viewed in isolation from the agreements made among Member States about the issue of coins and banknotes, about the manner in which they will conduct their monetary policy on this point, and about the policy objectives envisaged by the Member States. Thus monetary integration in the nineteenth century boils down, according to Theurl, to complete liberalization of international capital transactions, the unification of monetary systems, a partial inter-circulation of coins, sometimes fixed exchange rates between the currencies of various monetary systems, and cooperation between the participating central banks.

2.2 Categories of monetary unions

The monetary unions which sprang up in the nineteenth century may be divided into two categories:

(a) supraregional monetary unions: these were more or less imposed as the outcome of a process of political unification. This category includes the monetary unions forming part and parcel of the federations, mentioned in Chapter 1.1, which were set up in Switzerland (1848), Italy (1861) and Germany (1871).

(b) inter-European monetary unions: they consisted of agreements between sovereign nations about their mutual rates of exchange. Such an agreement ceased to exist as soon as one of the parties announced that it would no longer abide by its provisions. Examples of these unions are the German–Austrian Monetary Union of 1857, the Latin Monetary Union of 1865 and the Scandinavian Monetary Union of 1872.

The characteristic feature of the first category of monetary unions was the standardization of the coinage system. Hence, that is why they are called currency unions which provided for a common unit of account as well as for the free circulation of coins as a means of payment among the regional states. In itself, installing a common unit of account and a common currency as means of payment would constitute the completion of monetary union, were it not that another typical phenomenon of these unions was the circulation of paper money by the banks of issue of the regional states themselves. Another feature, of no lesser importance, was the fact that the monetary union was irreversible because it was embedded in a political union.

Typical for the second category of monetary unions was the link between the participating currencies. The principle of fixed exchange rates was

applied between the Member States of the Scandinavian Monetary Union
and those of the Latin Monetary Union. As in both unions the exchange
rates entailed a one-to-one ratio, a common unit of account was in fact in
operation, *viz.* the crown in the Scandinavian Monetary Union and the
franc in the Latin Monetary Union. A partial inter-circulation of coins —
in fact a parallel currency — was in evidence within the German–Austrian
Union.

2.3   Function of the banks of issue

With regard to the supraregional monetary unions, it should be pointed out
that the banks of issue in the nineteenth century fulfilled a totally different
function from today's central banks. Most of them were no more than
profit-seeking private companies whose lending activities were much like
those performed by the commercial banking system. Monetary policy was
part of the general economic policy, with the task of the issuing banks being
mainly to stimulate lending, so as to boost the development of the payment
system (Valeria Sannucci, 1989). The role played by banknotes within the
nineteenth-century monetary systems was consequently very different from
that which they have in our time. Banknotes were issued by private banking
institutions, and they were used only for certain transactions. They were
not legal tender and were usually used only in a local or regional context.
The reason why they came to be used as a means of payment was that it was
less expensive to settle debt with the aid of banknotes than by transporting
huge quantities of coins. From this viewpoint, banknotes fulfilled a role very
similar to that of today's giral bank deposits.

As for the issue of banknotes, the authorities of the unified countries
were faced with the choice between a single issuing bank and a limited
number of regional banks, which had issued banknotes in their region prior
to political unification. Among both economists and politicians, there was
no consensus on whether preference should be given to a pluralistic or to a
centralized system of issuing banknotes. Although the emerging principle
of laisser-faire was contrary to every form of monopoly, and thus clearly
favoured the principle of free banking, the Governments of Switzerland,
Italy and Germany felt an immediate or gradual need, following political unification, to award the right to issue banknotes to a single agency.
That institution would not be led by profit-making motives, but handle
the money supply in conjunction with, and under the supervision of, the
Government. It was this issuing agency which would eventually evolve into
the central bank as it exists in our day and age.

The choice between a plural or centralized system of note issuance was keenly debated in the nineteenth century, evolving into the Free Banking versus the Central Banking controversy which found its theoretical foundation in the theories of the Banking versus the Currency Principle. It is beyond the scope of this book to deal with the rival theses of these theories. The relevant question is whether a central bank of issue needed to be a necessary complement to the completion of monetary unification in the supraregional monetary unions. Disturbances of the coin circulation could be countered by means of strict agreements with regard to the issue of banknotes so as to prevent excessive lending. The fact that the countries concerned, nevertheless, felt a need for a central bank is explained by Charles Goodhart (1989) in terms of the need to protect the base money consisting of gold and/or silver. The concentration of metal within one central bank would have a stabilizing effect on credit expansion so that business cycles would be dampened. Furthermore, the central bank was expected to vary interest rates in a non-competitive way in order to protect the gold and/or silver stock. Goodhart is right to point out that these typical central bank functions do not necessarily require a monopoly on the issue of banknotes. The objective was to concentrate this metal at a certain agency. This would constitute a sufficient guarantee for the other issuing banks that the convertibility of their banknotes would be warranted.

According to Goodhart, one of the main reasons for the centralisation of note issuance is the advantage of having seigniorage concentrated in a single institution, 'where it could be most easily taxed by the political authorities'.[3] A second reason is the growth of deposits, which put a new source of funds at the disposal of the commercial banks and hence made them put up less resistance to the establishment of a central bank. Here Goodhart seems to deviate somewhat from the stance of Vera Smith (1936) who refers primarily to political arguments for establishing central banks: 'looking at the circumstances in which most of them were established, we find that the early ones were founded for political reasons connected with the exigencies of State finance, and no economic reason for allowing or disallowing free entry into the note-issuing trade was, or could have been, given at that time, but once established the monopolies persisted up to and beyond the time when their economic justification did at last come to be questioned'.[4]

No matter how valid these two points of view may be, the next chapter will show among other things that, in times of cyclical and political tensions, it was especially the competition between the banks of issue which often led to an excessive expansion of lending in the form of the issue of banknotes. In addition to political considerations, this constituted a major factor calling for the establishment of a single bank of issue. Although

Sannucci concludes that 'the inadequate coordination, and sometimes competition, between the banks of issue were not the only cause of the excessive money creation', she also points out that 'they certainly contributed to make the money supply less flexible and to the virtual abandonment, even in the periods of inconvertibility, of the discount rate as an instrument for the control of credit and money'.[5]

In the following discussion of monetary unions, the final objective is considered to have been reached with the establishment of a central bank having the monopoly to issue banknotes within the union. From that point of view, the development runs from the nineteenth-century monetary unions to the monetary unification set in motion after the Second World War, which will reach its definitive form in the envisaged Economic and Monetary Union turning on the European Central Bank (ECB) as the sole issuer of banknotes with legal tender status in all Member States of the Union.

Notes

1. Nielsen (1933), p. 595.
2. In 1992, the history of the nineteenth-century monetary unions was analysed in detail by Theresia Theurl from the University of Innsbruck. In her book *EINE gemeinsame Währung für Europa, 12 Lehren aus der Geschichte* the author deals with the political, cultural, social and economic aspects of these unions and the lessons which can be drawn from them for the Economic and Monetary Union formulated in the Treaty of Maastricht. The approach followed here is of a more overall nature. It focuses primarily on those aspects of the former monetary unions which are considered to be relevant in view of the decision to establish the European Central Bank in 1999, making the Economic and Monetary Union irreversible.
3. Goodhart (1989), p. 284.
4. Smith (1936), p. 147.
5. Sannucci (1989), p. 266.

3 SUPRAREGIONAL MONETARY UNIONS

This chapter looks at the ways in which monetary unification was realized within the politically unified countries of Switzerland, Italy and Germany.

3.1 Switzerland

3.1.1 Single currency

Switzerland's political unification (1848) was attended by large-scale currency reform. At that time, the introduction of a common currency was not considered a viable option in the new Confederation, owing to the lack of unity felt among the different regions whose languages, origins and trade relations diverged markedly. Theurl refers in this connection to Kurt Blaum who, in 1908, wrote that above all, the new Federal State had to draw the twenty two provinces (cantons) more closely together by creating a specific Swiss national feeling.[1] The Government consequently had to choose between the French franc and the South German *Gulden*. This choice was dictated by differences in geographical trade patterns. The North and the East of Switzerland traded with the countries of the German *Zollverein*, or customs union, and Austria, while the West and the South were focussed mainly on France and the Italian Piedmont. The French franc, with its status of an international currency, won the day.

The French-franc-based monetary system came into operation by the Act of 7 May 1850. The unit of account was the silver franc, whose size, weight and content coincided exactly with that of the French franc which consisted of five grammes with a metal content of 90 per cent fine silver. The standard coins of five, two, one and half francs functioned as legal tender. Private companies were not permitted to mint coins. The Act left it to the Federal Government to determine the quantity and types of coins. However, to cut its costs, the Confederation issued coins on no more than

13

a limited scale. Coins were supplied mostly from Paris, with the result that soon nearly 80 per cent of the Swiss coins in circulation originated in France. In addition, there circulated silver and copper subsidiary coins which were legal tender up to a certain amount. These had to be Swiss in origin.

The strict link to the French monetary system made Switzerland dependent on the provision of coins by France. The problems began soon after the reform. In France the depreciating gold began to crowd out silver, so that it was no longer able to supply Switzerland with the necessary silver francs. As a consequence, the general public in Switzerland adopted the French *Napoleon d'or*, which was not legal tender in Switzerland. Following a turbulent parliamentary discussion, the Act of 31 January 1860 laid down the legal rate of French gold coins with face values of one hundred, fifty, forty, twenty, ten and five francs. By contrast with the French Coinage Act of 1803, the Swiss Act explicitly acknowledged the double standard, on the basis of a ratio between the two metals of 15.5:1.

One of the most pressing problems confronting Switzerland at that time was the outflow of silver which brought about a lack of coins for paying small transactions. To meet that need, the Act of 1860 allowed the authorities to reduce the metal content of silver standard coins, with the exception of five franc pieces, to 80 per cent. This made the fractional into token or subsidiary coins.[2] Only the five franc coin continued to be legal tender. Tensions consequently arose, in France, as well as in Belgium and Italy, whose coin systems were also organized along French lines. These three countries were now confronted with an inflow of inferior Swiss subsidiary coins, whose issue and the consequent seigniorage made fell to an alien power, in this case Switzerland. The ensuing tensions prompted Switzerland to join the negotiations on the Latin Monetary Union (LMU) which was set up in 1865 and ratified by Switzerland on 5 March 1866.[3]

The prohibition to export gold imposed by France in 1870 in connection with its war against Germany eventually compelled Switzerland to begin minting its own coins. The Act of 22 December 1870 authorized the Federal Council to mint gold coins either for account of the Confederation, or for account of third parties in accordance with the provisions of the LMU. The weight of the gold franc was 0.32258 gramme with a metal content of 90 per cent fine gold. The implementing rules of 15 January 1873 provided for the conditions under which private companies were permitted to mint gold coins. Owing to the high costs involved in minting, which more than doubled those in France, there were no private companies which availed themselves of this right. The first gold coins were minted for account of the Confederation in 1883. A limited number of twenty franc pieces was brought into circulation. Demand for coins was, however, amply met by those of other Member States of the LMU. In addition, gold coins of English, American and Austrian origin were accepted in payment. In subsequent years, the functioning of the currency system was highly influenced by speculative capital flows to and from Switzerland as a result of the participation of Switzerland in the LMU. Apart from that, in the last decades of the nineteenth century, the country was confronted with heavy outflows of silver known as the 'silverdrainage' (see next paragraph).

In December 1926, the Federal Council informed the Member States of the LMU that Switzerland considered the Union as disbanded as from 1 January 1927. This entailed that, in addition to the silver coins, the gold coins from the other Union States also ceased to be legal tender in Switzerland. From then onwards, the Swiss coinage system became subordinate to the national authorities. The Coinage Act of 3 June 1931 provided that gold would be the only standard metal. The new unit of account was the Swiss franc with a parity of 0.29032 gramme fine gold.[4] The Act provided for the minting of gold coins of one hundred, twenty and ten francs, which were all legal tender. The previous silver five franc coins gained the character of subsidiary coins. The Act also stipulated that anyone taking gold to the Federal Mint at the conditions set by the Federal Council, was permitted to have twenty and ten franc coins minted. Coins of one hundred francs were allowed to be minted only for account of the Confederation. Switzerland had thus formally adopted the gold standard.

3.1.2 Unity of note issuance

The 1848 monetary reform had not included paper money. Its issuance was the express prerogative of the cantons, which wielded rules of their own with regard to the volume to be issued and the metal cover required. The banknotes were not legal tender. Acceptance by the general public was at first tenuous, being highly dependent on whether or not the currency figuring on the notes was in circulation in the canton concerned. The crisis resulting from the Franco-German War forced the general public to use banknotes as a substitute for coins, after which the issuance of banknotes expanded materially, as can be seen from Table 3.1.

A stimulating factor in this respect was the *Konkordat* concluded in 1876 between the major banks of issue. According to this agreement the banks accepted each other's banknotes for which the bank of Zürich should act as the central clearing institute. On 1 July 1882, an act came into force (*Banknotengesetz*) enabling the Confederation to make arrangements for the issuance and redemption of banknotes, without detracting from the principle of competition. It was this competition which put one of the main functions of the classic currency standard, *viz.* the automatic regulation of

Table 3.1   Banks of issue and banknotes in Switzerland, 1850–1900

Year	Number of banks of issue	Banknotes in circulation (millions of francs)
1850	8	7.6
1860	17	13.8
1870	28	19.0
1900	35	216.7

Source: Theurl (1992), Table 8.

the exchange rate, out of action. The strongly growing number of issuing institutions thwarted control of the money supply, especially because each institution attempted to issue as many notes of its own as possible by offering attractive credit rates. When, in the 1880s and especially in the 1890s, the Swiss franc depreciated, notably against the French franc, the Swiss banks of issue were confronted with a drain of their silver reserves which they had — for reasons of profitability and liquidity — reduced to a minimum. The banks tried to compensate for this drain by repurchasing the exported silver coins at higher prices, thereby incurring heavy losses. As these repurchases had to be financed with French money, the Swiss banks of issue themselves brought about a continuing upward pressure on the exchange rate of the French franc. For years, this mechanism caused a steady silver flow towards Switzerland without fundamentally changing the exchange rate of the Swiss franc. At the end of the century, this flow was estimated at 110 millions of francs of which the exchange rate losses had to be borne for more than fifty percent by the *Banque du Commerce* in Geneva. The Swiss monetary system as a whole very much resembled a central bank which, for lack of disposable reserves, at the same time sold foreign currency at parity and repurchased it at higher market prices (Franz Ritzmann, 1964). In other words, the banks did nothing more than to pay out the exchange rate difference to speculators who did not take any risk.

Control of the money supply and stabilization of the exchange rate called for centralization of banknote issuance. By Act of 6 October 1905, the Swiss National Bank was established, which obtained the monopoly on issuing banknotes. Until 1914, however, banknotes were not legal tender. They could only be accepted in payment by State cashiers and the National Bank. When the First World War broke out in August 1914, the Federal Council gave the banknotes issued by the National Bank forced currency, so that the convertibility of paper money provided for by the Swiss Bank Act of 1905 was abolished. It was only when the Act was amended in 1929 that convertibility was restored, which meant that the forced currency of the banknotes was abolished as from 1 April 1930. This stipulation was formally incorporated in the 1931 Coinage Act.

In conclusion it may be noted that the envisaged Swiss monetary reform following the establishment of the Confederation was seriously hampered by Switzerland's participation in the LMU. This made Switzerland's monetary system *de facto* dependent on France, and it was soon infected with the latter's problems with the bimetallic standard. It was only after the LMU was disbanded that Switzerland gained monetary autonomy, a development which, combined with the transition to the single gold standard, paved the way for unity of currency. Although banknotes were not included in the monetary reform, the cantonal issuing banks' regularly resurgent zeal to issue banknotes called for strict management which ultimately compelled the authorities to award the monopoly to the National Bank. The establishment of this institution was, however, in no way the fruit of consultations based on sound economic and monetary grounds. In this respect one can fully agree with Ritzmann (1973) who concludes that the experiment of the free note issuance was continued to the bitter end and it was only after the issuing banks completely resigned that the first step towards a national institution with a monopoly on the issue of banknotes was taken.

3.2   Italy

3.2.1   Single currency

In Italy, too, the political unification attained in 1861 began with monetary reform. By contrast with Switzerland, that reform sought to bring about unity of both coins and banknotes. In view of the leading position of the Kingdom of Sardinia, which had formerly been French-oriented, and which had played a central role in the quest for political unification, the French double standard was adopted. It had the added advantage of constituting a suitable compromise between the mostly gold-coin circulation in the North and the use of silver in the South of Italy. The new monetary unit was the silver *Lira Italiana*, whose weight corresponded with 4.5 grammes of silver or 0.290322 gramme of fine gold. Thus the lira's parity equalled that of the French franc. The Act of 24 August 1862 permitted the unrestricted issue of gold coins of one hundred, fifty, twenty, ten and five lira, as well as, for private account, of silver coins of five lira. Gold and silver coins were issued without restriction, the official ratio amounting to 1:15.5. The subsidiary coins were bronze and silver two and one lira coins and fifty and twenty centime coins, whose metal content was 83.5 per cent.[5] As in Switzerland, the number of these coins issued per head of the population was limited. With Italy taking part in the LMU, the new Italian constitution stipulated that the gold and silver standard coins of the other Member States of the LMU could also serve as legal tender. The stipulation that silver five lira coins could only be issued at the request of private companies was consequently withdrawn domestically. In April 1876, the unrestricted issue of silver coins was suspended in line with the monetary agreement concluded between the Member States of the LMU on 5 February 1875. Italy thus adopted the limping standard. The five lira coins in circulation remained so and were accepted without restriction for transactions among private individuals. This situation continued until the end of 1927, when Italy adopted the gold standard by Act of 21 December.

3.2.2   Unity of note issuance

By contrast with the introduction of a single coin, the unification of paper money proved a highly laborious and complicated process. Although in 1861 the bank of issue of Sardinia had already been designated by the authorities to take upon itself the role of national note-issuing bank, changing its name to *Banca Nazionale nel Regno d'Italia* (BNR), seventy years were to pass before this objective was realized. In part this was due to the Government's indecisiveness in a climate which, under the influence of a policy of laisser-faire, resisted every form of monopoly, especially where money issuance was concerned. An equally serious obstacle was constituted by the divergent structure, in terms of origin and activities, of the note-issuing banks in operation. The BNR was a private institution whose close credit links with the government of the former Kingdom of Sardinia gave it a wide experience with the issue of inconvertible paper money. The Tuscan private note-issuing banks were heavily engaged in credit business with landowners and small tradesmen. In the South, the issuing banks were public institutions raising funds by issuing so-termed deposit certificates which served as a means of payment. For a long time past, the money circulation there had been made up largely of this paper, which is why there was fierce resistance to any attempts on the part of the new State to stimulate the geographical spread of the BNR's issuing activities.

Relations between the issuing banks did not improve when in 1866 Italy, taking part in the Austrian-German War, again had to resort to BNR issuance of banknotes which could not be exchanged for metal. The depreciating paper drove out high-grade metal money, leading to a serious shortage of small-denomination coins. As a result, many unauthorized banks began to issue notes of their own. In 1874 an act saw the light which, though maintaining the principle of pluriformity with regard to the

Table 3.2   Banknotes in circulation in Italy, 1861–1884
(percentage shares)

Bank of issue	1861	1874	1884
Banca Nazionale	28	57	65
Banco di Napoli	48	25	21
Banca Nazionale Toscana	11	10	8
Banca Toscana di Credito	–	2	2
Banco di Sicilia	13	6	4

Source: Sannucci (1989), Table 9.8, excluding the *Banca Romana.*

issue of banknotes, nevertheless ruled out complete freedom of issuance.[6] Regional banknotes acquired the status of legal tender.

The regional nature of the issuing operations prevented active use of the discount instrument. Insofar as discount rate adjustments were not dictated by interest rate movements abroad, the BNR attempted, until 1866, to counter deterioration of its liquidity position through imports of gold or silver — in order to raise its metal cover — rather than through a self-imposed increase of the discount rate, a step which it feared other issuing institutions would not follow. When inconvertible government paper money was introduced, discount policy became the concern of the State, which prevented discount rate rises for budgetary reasons.

The Bank Act of April 1874 was the first attempt to unify the paper money of the banks. The right to issue banknotes was granted to no more than six institutions. An unduly large money circulation was to be prevented by imposing on the banks a quota on the issuing volume, amounting to three times the size of their capital and reserves. The way in which these developments influenced the issuing activities of the BNR and the other issuing banks is shown in Table 3.2.

After convertibility was restored in April 1883, the monetary situation continued to give rise to concern. The upturn in economic activity boosted competition among the issuing banks in the private credit market. Competition of this nature was more or less induced when, in 1885, the quota directive was changed to the effect that the permissible issuance level could be exceeded, so long as all of the excess was covered by metal. This move led the banks to take up funds abroad with a view to strengthening their reserves. Fierce competition ensued, with each institution trying to maintain or expand its market share in the banknote circulation via its lending operations. With the Government's budgetary position soon deteriorating again, this behaviour kindled an unbridled monetary expansion, which was attended over the next few years by stock exchange crises, speculative capital outflows and unabated pressure on the lira. The 1891 bank crisis resulted in liquidation of a bank of issue (Banca Romana) and in a merger of the two Tuscan banks with the BNR, together forming the Banca d'Italia. When in 1894 the convertibility of paper money was again abandoned, the lira's exchange rate against sterling and the French franc had fallen by 12 per cent on ten years earlier.

The new Bank Act of 10 August 1893 provided the three remaining banks of issue, viz. the *Banca d'Italia*, the *Banco di Napoli* and the *Banco di Sicilia* with the right to issue banknotes. The Act laid down the permissible level of issuance, depending on the size of the capital of the institution involved. The Banca d'Italia was consequently assigned nearly three-quarters of the total quota. The banknotes of the three issuing banks were declared legal tender throughout the country. They could be exchanged for government paper money or metal at market rates, an arrangement which remained in force until after the First World War. However, the monetary situation continued to give rise to concern, not the least because the excessive money circulation generated by that War considerably exceeded the growth of output. The Banca d'Italia's lender-of-last-resort function during the financial crises of 1907–1908 and 1921–1922 was the last step towards monetary unification. In 1926, the process was crowned with the establishment of a single central bank, the Banca d'Italia, which was given the monopoly to issue banknotes. A general monetary reform took place, entailing among other things that the Banca d'Italia was also given the authority to exercise supervision on banks subject to a reserve obligation and to liquidity and solvency requirements. Italy had achieved monetary union. By the Act of 21 December 1927 the gold exchange standard was introduced with the parity of the lira being fixed at 7.919 grammes of fine gold per hundred lira.

Overlooking the Italian situation since 1861, one may conclude that the unification of paper money issuance failed in spite of political unity. The lack of a sufficiently strong political will on the part of the Government and the strongly regional structure of the issuing banks with their different legal statuses were the main reasons for the continued existence of more than one bank of issue. Sannucci (1989) suggests that the instability of the Italian financial system was primarily due to the inability of the Government to compel the banks to respect 'the rules of the game' on an inter-regional basis. Consequently, the lack of monetary control was the result of the absence of effective mechanisms of cooperation rather than of there being more than one bank of issue. It was the way in which the system worked which was, in her opinion, to the advantage of the more unscrupulous of the issuing banks. Nevertheless, it cannot be denied that only after the establishment of the Banca d'Italia, the stability of the monetary system in Italy significantly improved. This view is shared by Gianny Toniolo

(1989) who points out that in times of political instability an authoritative and independent central bank may take correct and timely decisions that will offset some of the dangers deriving from the lack of political leadership.[7]

3.3 Germany

3.3.1 Prehistory

For a proper understanding of the process of monetary unification in Germany, a short review of its prehistory is called for. The establishment of the German Zollverein, in 1834, supplied the basis for economic integration of North and South Germany, even though these were dominated by the antipoles of Prussia and Bavaria. In both parts of Germany a common currency was in circulation: the *Thaler* in the North including Prussia and the Gulden in the South including Austria.

The founders of the Zollverein realized very well that the diversity of monetary conditions was an impediment to the free exchange of goods, an impediment which ought rapidly to be removed (Carl-Ludwig Holtfrerich, 1989). The Treaty, therefore, contained the stipulation that the Governments of the Member States should take action in order to bring their coinage systems on to a common standard. In 1837, the Munich Coinage Treaty was signed introducing coinage standards for the Gulden in the South German States. The silver content of that coin was prescribed at 9.5 grammes of silver, after which one and later two Gulden coins came to serve as a means of exchange in that area. A year later, on 30 July 1838, the Dresden Coinage Convention was signed. Under this Treaty, each Member State of the Zollverein had to choose either the Thaler or the Gulden, the ratio of the two currencies being fixed at 1 Thaler = 1.75 Gulden. The Member States were not obliged to accept each other's coins as legal tender. That was, however, the case for the so-termed *Vereinsmünze* or union coin with a value of 2 Thaler or 3.50 Gulden. Because of its weight (33.4 grammes of silver), this coin never really became accepted as a medium of exchange, so that it became known as *Champagnethaler*.

The Treaty of Vienna concluded in 1857 linked Austria to the two monetary systems of the German Zollverein. It provided for a fixed ratio between the Prussian Thaler, the South German Gulden and the Austrian Gulden as well as for the introduction of the one Thaler Vereinsmünze (16.7 grammes of silver) which was equated with the Prussian Thaler.[7] The success of the new union coin as a parallel currency was evident from the fact that in the period 1851–1871 more than 90 per cent of the coins minted in the South German area were *Vereinsthaler*. The war between

Table 3.3   Circulation of banknotes in the German States, 1850–1870

Year	Total	Prussian Bank	As percentage of total issue
1850	31	19	61.3
1860	126	88	79.8
1870	281	195	69.3

Derived from Sprenger (1991), Table 24.

Prussia and Austria put paid to the Treaty of Vienna. Annexation of German States (including Hanover, Schleswig and Holstein) by Prussia in 1866 made for a further expansion of the Thaler's area of operation and it became the common coin for all practical purposes.

As a result of the fiasco with the French *assignats* and other disastrous experiments with debt instruments, German citizens were long reluctant to accept paper money. Virtually all paper being circulated came in the form of government-issued notes which were accepted as a means of payment by the State cashiers. Around 1840 nearly 80 per cent of the notes in circulation had been issued by Prussia. The start of the Prussian Bank, in 1846, laid the foundation for the emergence of the banknote that was to gain definitive pride of place among paper money when in 1856 the issue quota fixed for this bank was abandoned. As can be seen from Table 3.3, the Prussian Bank accounted for two-thirds of the banknote circulation.

All the same, no less than nineteen new issuing banks (*Zettelbanken*) were set up in the years 1853–1856, most of which specialized in the issuance of very small denominations (up to one mark). The trade and banking crisis of 1857 put an end to this proliferation, although in the early 1860s there were still about thirty note-issuing banks operating in twenty German States. The banknote was a substitute for coins. If the holder so requested, banknotes had to be exchanged for metal.

In the years following 1860, the debate in Germany came to centre on the question as to what the most appropriate standard metal should be. Commercial and industrial circles pleaded for the introduction of the gold standard. With the money circulation in countries such as France, the United Kingdom and the United States, too, made up mainly of gold coins, the German States increasingly came to fear isolation on account of their silver standard. At the national economic congress of 1867, a case was made out for joining the French franc system and hence for a transition to gold. The discussions also focussed on the establishment of a German Monetary Union, encompassing the North German Confederation,[8] the United Kingdom and the United States.

During the 1860s it was, however, Ludwig Bamberger — the father of German monetary unification — and Adolf Soetbeer who became the main promoters, in politics and in the public media, of the idea of the gold standard in order to link the German currency area to sterling, which was the most important transaction currency in international trade and finance. They argued that for the preservation and defence of the gold standard Germany would need a strong central bank like the Bank of England. In 1868, the new Federal Parliament adopted a resolution which was unequivocally in favour of a centralized currency system, the monetary sovereignty of the formerly autonomous German States being transferred to the central authority.

3.3.2 Single currency

The German *Reich* was founded in early 1871, when the South German States were joined with the States of the North German Federation. The outcome of the Franco-German War implied for France reparation payments amounting to five billion gold francs in favour of Germany, the bulk of which (over four billion francs) was in the form of trade bills. This reparation facilitated the adoption of the gold standard, even though the decision to that effect was no foregone conclusion. Pursuant to the (provisional) Act of 4 December 1871, the so-termed *Reichsgoldwährung* was introduced as the standard coin, of which one-tenth, the mark, served as the new unit of account. Standard coins of ten and twenty marks were to serve as medium of exchange. This Act did not, however, provide for a decision as to a double or a single standard. The second Coinage Act of 9 July 1873 was also a provisional measure — speaking of *Reichswährung* — with the gold standard coins being supplemented by a five mark coin. The series of official coins would also encompass copper and nickel coins, as well as silver mark coins with denominations of five, two, one, a half and two-tenths, whose metal content was about 10 per cent less than that corresponding with the 15.5:1 ratio vis-à-vis gold. These coins consequently had the character of subsidiary coins, whose number was limited per capita. In fact a limping standard was in operation because the old silver Thaler, which had been brought into circulation by the individual States at the time of the Zollverein, continued to be legal tender without restrictions next to the new gold marks. By Imperial Decree of 1 January 1876 — also the date of establishment of the *Reichsbank* pursuant to the Bank Act of 14 March 1875 — the new official coins were introduced throughout Germany.

The transition to the new monetary system confronted the Government with the problem of how to withdraw the old silver coins from circulation. Here an impediment was the shortage-induced demand for gold in Belgium,

France and the United Kingdom, which made the exchange rate against Germany go up in 1873. The premium on German gold coins rose to 5 per cent, with the result that they were hoarded and the banks had to meet the existing need for coins by running down their stocks of silver. It was only when in July 1875 the Reichsbank precluded a premium on gold by announcing the convertibility of its banknotes, that the situation changed. At the end of the 1870s, gold coins made up more than 60 per cent of total coins in circulation, as compared with barely 13 per cent at the beginning of that decade. On 1 October 1907, the silver Thaler coins lost their status of legal tender. That in fact marked the end of the limping standard, whose practical effect had already declined because, in the period July 1875 to October 1907, the central bank exchanged its notes for gold on request, eschewing the possibility to use silver to that same purpose. The silver Thaler still circulating were now withdrawn, but it was another two years before the old silver coins had been completely removed from circulation. With the introduction of the Coinage Act of 1 July 1909, Germany adopted the gold standard *de jure*. Under paragraph 1 of that Act, the German Reich became subject to the *Goldwährung* system centring on the *Mark* as unit of account which contained 1/2790 kilogramme fine gold.

3.3.3 Unity of note issuance

In the new German State, as in Italy, monetary reform entailed not just the standardization of coins, but also the centralization of the issue of paper money. There was, however, no agreement about the way in which to achieve that goal among, on the one hand, those favouring and those opposing monetary union, and, on the other hand, Prussia and the rest of Germany. Although the unification process consequently progressed only gradually, the discussion about how issuing was to be organized was attended by less tension than elsewhere. Smith (1936) attributes this to the circumstance that Germany 'at no time adopted true laisser-faire principles in her commercial policy',[9] with the result that Government interference was more common there than in other countries. Once the gold standard had been introduced, the conviction soon gained ground that a strong central bank modelled on the English Act of 1844 was needed to maintain a stable gold coin. Germany's preference for a strong central bank was, however, not only based on ideological motives. Reference can be made to the outflow of gold after 1871 which called attention to the role the discount policy should play in the economy. People believed that an effective discount policy could only be managed by a specially constituted central bank taking the responsibility of controlling capital flows. This argument, combined with an appeal to nationalist feelings by the political authorities undermined the resistance of those who had advocated the pluriform system of banknote issuance. Thus the way was paved for the establishment of a single note-issuing bank with monopolistic competences.

Where banknotes are concerned, the second Coinage Act of 1873 stipulated, among other things, that, by 1 January 1876, all banknotes not denominated in marks had to be withdrawn and that the lowest denomination for future banknotes would be one hundred marks, so as to prevent competition with the golden mark coins. It was notably the size of this denomination which made it easier for the Reichsbank to gradually evolve into a central note-issuing institution. After all, the banks were compelled to accept these banknotes, which circulated mainly in the world of business, at their counters from customers wishing to repay their debts. It goes without saying that these notes were accepted more readily to that end in the economically booming Prussia than in the other, less prosperous States. The Reichsbank was charged with the task to regulate the money circulation in the entire country, and also took upon itself the obligation to purchase and sell gold at a fixed price of 1392 marks per half kilogramme of fine gold. Although the Reichsbank was subordinate to the Government,[10] it enjoyed a large measure of autonomy in practical matters, due in part to the fact that its notes were covered mainly by precious metals and trade bills.

The central authorities were reluctant to do away with the issuing banks altogether, owing to the political resistance which the Governments of the Federal States were expected to put up. However, the Bank Act was formulated so as to ensure a central role for the Reichsbank in the future. It stipulated that issuing banks could either continue their banking operations as before, but then only within the boundaries of their own region, or engage in the same activities as the Reichsbank, but then in the entire country. In the latter case, investments and mortgage lending were not permitted, while issuing activities were subject to the same rules as those applicable to the Reichsbank. In 1899, the Bank Act was amended to the effect that, when fixing their discount rates, private issuing banks were permitted to deviate from that of the Reichsbank only fractionally. Under the influence of this restriction, the private issuing banks gave up their struggle one by one. Of the thirty three banks which made use of their right to issue banknotes in 1871, no more than four remained in 1906. Although, under the Bank Act of 1 June 1909, the Reichsbank's notes were officially declared legal tender effective on 1 January 1910 it was only in 1935 that the other institutions definitively lost their right to issue banknotes.[11] Their competition initially manifested itself in the field of discount policy. When this facility was abolished in 1899, they had in fact become mere branches of the Reichsbank, so that it would seem justified

Table 3.4   Development of the money supply in Germany, 1875–1910
              (in millions of marks)

Year	Coins	Banknotes	Notes and coins	Demand deposits	Total
	(1)	(2)	(3) (1)+(2)	(4)	(5) (3)+(4)
1875	1.913	1.022	2.935	3.975	6.910
1880	1.662	964	2.626	4.757	7.383
1890	1.382	1.110	2.492	8.809	11.301
1900	2.049	1.292	3.341	16.126	19.467
1910	3.118	1.640	4.758	33.825	38.583

Derived from Sprenger (1991), Table 28, excluding cash reserves with the banks.

to regard the process of monetary unification in Germany as completed by around 1910.

It should be noted that Germany's introduction of the gold standard did not guarantee monetary stability in terms of price stability. Table 3.4 indicates that after unification the composition of the money supply structurally changed in favour of demand deposits. In 1910 coins and notes together had nearly doubled while the amount of outstanding deposits was gone up to a tenfold of that in 1875. As demand deposits were not covered by gold, money creation was independent of the gold stock. Consequently, the increase in the money supply accelerated at the end of the nineteenth century resulting in a price increase of nearly 30 per cent between 1900 and 1910.

In summary, German monetary unification was a process in which the standardization of the coinage system was already nearly completed before the foundation of the united German State in 1871, in other words, the monetary system had already been put in order before the gold standard was introduced. Where the issuing banks were concerned, Germany was also in a more favourable position than Switzerland and Italy, for one, because Prussia, being a major economic power, dominated the unified country, and for another, because the German authorities had clearly opted to have the Reichsbank function as the leading bank of issue from the outset. Another factor of importance was public opinion, which had been prepared, even before political unification was achieved, for the establishment of a powerful central bank. This was in contrast with what happened in for instance Switzerland, where the citizenry still had to be persuaded to adopt a national identity, which only gradually culminated in the acceptance of a national central bank, after political union had been achieved.

Notes

1. Blaum (1908), p. 21, cited by Theurl (1992), p. 63.
2. As a result of the reduction of the metal content to 80 per cent, 5 grammes of silver now came to contain 4 grammes of fine silver, so that the price per kilogramme of such coins rose to 250 francs and the gold/silver ratio dropped to 13.8 (3445/250). The export of subsidiary coins became lucrative as soon as the market ratio of gold to silver dropped below 13.8.
3. The participating states in the Latin Monetary Union were Belgium, France, Italy, Switzerland and Greece. See Chapter 4.2.
4. In its annual report, the Bank for International Settlements still expresses it balance sheet and profit and loss account in gold francs.
5. This corresponded with a price of 239.5 francs per kilogramme of silver for subsidiary coins.
6. In April 1874, the six issuing banks formed a consortium that issued one billion lira worth of notes on behalf of the State. The proceeds were meant for the repayment of war debts. In all regions, the banknotes circulating there could be exchanged for that government paper which was legal tender throughout the country.
7. See Chapter 4.1.
8. After the war with Austria in 1866, the *Deutsche Bund* was split up in the *Norddeutsche Bund*, the Southern German States and Austria.
9. Smith (1936), p. 49.
10. The Reichsbank was a legal entity subject to supervision by a Board of Trustees. This body included the Chancellor and four representatives of the countries making up the Confederation. Pursuant to the law, the Chancellor had overall responsibility for the Bank's administration, and gave instructions to the Governing Board. Under the law, the Bank's Governing Board, headed by a Governor, was no more than an executive body. Its members were appointed for life by the *Kaiser*, on the recommendation of the Federal Council.
11. As from February 1906, the Reichsbank issued banknotes with denominations of twenty and fifty marks.

4 INTER-EUROPEAN MONETARY UNIONS

This chapter looks into the birth of the three nineteenth-century inter-European monetary unions, their functioning in practice, and the reasons for their demise.

4.1 The German–Austrian Monetary Union, 1857–1867

4.1.1 Objective

The attempts made by Austria on political grounds in 1848[1] to take part in the German Zollverein eventually resulted in a trade treaty with Prussia, to which the South German States became a party more or less willy-nilly in 1853. However, the ensuing trade advantages in the form of lower customs duties threatened to largely pass Austria by because of its currency problems. In order to finance its budget, the Government resorted to the issue of inconvertible paper money, a method it had already applied on several occasions in the eighteenth century. As the depreciating banknotes made the import of products from the partner States more expensive, Austria sought a way to stabilize its currency. In 1854 a monetary conference was held in Vienna. Austria urged Prussia to abandon the silver standard. By switching to gold, whose value had meanwhile begun to decline, Austria hoped not only to be able to repay its war debts with cheaper funds, but also to prevent the Prussian Thaler circulating within the Zollverein from coming to function as the common currency in Austria as well. Negotiations were suspended in 1855 owing to resistance on the part of Prussia, but resumed a year later, after it had become clear that Austria would acquiesce in the wishes of its political rival. The German–Austrian Monetary Union was concluded on 24 January 1857.[2]

28

4.1.2 The monetary Treaty

As noted in Chapter 3.3, the Treaty provided for the introduction of the silver one Thaler Vereinsmünze as the double or parallel currency whose value corresponded with that of the Prussian Thaler. Its exchange rate was set at 1.75 South German Gulden and 1.5 Austrian Gulden. Use of the Vereinsthaler was meant to underpin the Treaty by way of the stipulation that debts in national currencies could be paid in Vereinsthaler, but obligations denominated in the Vereinsthaler could not be settled in national currencies. This provision was at the root of the problem that arose when the Treaty was undone. Irrespective of the country of origin, the Union coin was legal tender throughout the Union, whereas the national currencies were so only within their own territory. The Vereinsthaler was, in other words, superior to the Austrian Gulden (Helfferich, 1894). The circulation of the Vereinsthaler was supervised by the combined governments. Problems relating to the minting instructions had to be brought before an arbitration committee. Under the Treaty the issuing states were responsible only for minting the Vereinsthaler and for safeguarding their metal content. Whether the Thaler had been minted in Berlin or Vienna was irrelevant from the point of view of its status as legal tender.

Gold was allowed to be used only to mint the so-termed *Vereinshandelsmünze* (one and half *Krone* coins with a weight of ten and five grammes of fine gold, respectively), which were not legal tender domestically but which served, as the name indicates, solely to finance external trade. The ratio between gold and silver was left to market forces. The Treaty was to remain in force until 1878, after which it was to be tacitly extended for five-year periods. It did not contain a liquidation clause, which was in fact not needed because the value of the Vereinsthaler was identical to that of the North German Thaler, so that the two coins could, in case of dissolution, be exchanged for each other without problems.

The Treaty of 1857 was the only international Treaty concluded in the nineteenth century which contained provisions on the issuance of paper money. Article 22 of the Treaty prohibited the issue of paper money with forced currency so long as no arrangements had been made to exchange this paper for high-grade silver coins, providing, in other words, for coin convertibility. The existing exceptions needed to be cancelled before 1 January 1859. Apart from stipulations regarding the Vereinsthaler and paper money, the monetary Treaty did not contain directives as to the monetary policies to be pursued by the Member States, which continued to be their responsibility.

4.1.3   The Treaty in practice

For Austria, the Treaty entailed the introduction of the silver Gulden as
the new national currency unit. The issue of banknotes remained the
prerogative of the *Priviligierte Oesterreichische Nationalbank*, established
in 1816. Under the Treaty, banknotes had to be exchanged for silver coins
at the request of the holder. This meant that the Union could work only if
Austria were prepared to scrap the inconvertibility of its paper money. It
did so for a short while, viz. in the period from 6 September 1858 until 21
April 1859, after which it again resorted to the issue of inconvertible paper
money because of its war against Italy (Magenta and Solferino). The second
attempt to restore convertibility failed when war broke out against Prussia
in 1866, and Austria left the Union. The Treaty was disbanded in Berlin
on 13 June 1867. Monetary union was hence short-lived, and had barely
any impact in Austria.

The Treaty's liquidation forms an important element in the history of
the German–Austrian Monetary Union. As Austria had not succeeded in
returning to the metal standard, Gresham's law had done its work in that
the silver coins had been driven out by inferior depreciating paper money.
When the Union was disbanded in 1867, the bulk of the Vereinsthaler
(estimated by Helfferich at the equivalent of fifty million marks) and silver
Gulden minted in Austria were circulating in the South German States.
No liquidation arrangements having been made, the former parties to the
Treaty agreed that the Thaler was to remain legal tender, unless one of
them was to adopt another monetary system before 1870.   When this
did not happen, the Vereinsthaler continued to be legal tender in Austria.
Germany, in the meantime, was saddled with a huge amount of Austrian
Vereinsthaler which could not be exchanged in the country of origin, simply
because Austria did not possess any German currency.

A new problem arose when in 1870 Germany adopted the gold standard.
This measure indirectly coupled the Vereinsthaler in Germany to gold,
whereas in Austria it remained based on silver. When around 1870 the price
of gold began to rise relative to silver, the German Vereinsthaler became
subject to a rising premium while the Austrian Vereinsthaler was traded at
par. Like a magnet, the profits to be made on this trade by Austrian holders
of Vereinsthaler lured the last Vereinsthaler to Germany. These capital
exports were boosted further by the flight of the Austrian Gulden. So long
as Germany had stuck to silver, the Austrian Gulden had been a currency
in its own right in Germany in that its value corresponded to 2/3 Thaler.
However, after Germany had adopted the gold standard, the increasing
value of gold led to a depreciation of the Gulden vis-à-vis the Thaler. As
a result, great masses of Austrian Gulden flowed to Germany where, for

some reason, the Gulden was still being accepted at an exchange rate of 2/3 Thaler. According to Helfferich, people could not understand that the Gulden continued to be a silver coin whereas the Thaler remained a silver coin but had, in practice, become a gold coin.[3] Although Germany had prohibited the import of Austrian Gulden in 1873, the problem persisted until 1892, when Austria, too, adopted the gold standard, committing itself to take back one-third of the Austrian money collected by the Reichsbank at par value. The remainder was melted down in Germany, which had to bear the expenses of the price fall of silver, to be used for the production of other coins.

In conclusion it may be noted that the German–Austrian Monetary Union had been doomed to failure owing to the underlying serious political tensions between the participating countries. But even apart from that, the use of the Vereinsthaler as the parallel currency in Austria would have stood little chance of success, as long as that country was incapable of bringing its economic development into line with that of Germany, and hence had to resort to inconvertible paper money which inevitably made the high-grade silver coins flow to its ally.

4.2   The Latin Monetary Union, 1865–1926

On 23 December 1865, the Treaty on the Latin Monetary Union (LMU) was signed between Belgium, France, Italy and Switzerland. It entered into effect on 1 August 1866. Three years later Greece also joined the Union.[4]

4.2.1   Objective

France played an important part in bringing about the LMU. In 1803, on the initiative of Napoleon, a Coinage Act had been adopted which stipulated that, from then on, the French franc would contain five grammes of silver of 90 per cent fine. France had thus in principle opted for a monometallic system based on the silver standard. However, an article later added to this Act permitted the minting of a certain amount of gold coins for the settlement of large goods transactions. When the price of gold began to drop around 1850, it turned out that the French citizens had little objection to the circulation of gold coins, because in the past creditors had, under certain circumstances, already shown a preference for payment in gold. It also turned out at that time that the 1803 Act had given neither gold nor silver coins the status of exclusive legal tender. This gave the general public the impression that the Act had been meant to introduce the double standard. A committee appointed in 1858 admittedly rejected bimetallism, but did not unequivocally choose between gold and silver. As a consequence, France operated the double standard, de facto if not de jure.

After its political independence, Belgium adopted, in its Coinage Act of 5 June 1832, the French monetary system, so that the content and value of the new Belgian franc corresponded to those of the French franc. The same happened in Italy and Switzerland which, as we have seen, also adopted the French monetary system when political unity was achieved. Although these countries cannot be said to have been economically integrated to any considerable extent, France formed the main trading partner for Belgium, Italy and parts of Switzerland within the LMU. The Belgian and Swiss economies were characterized by high capital intensity consequent on the process of industrialization which had set in early there. A different situation was in evidence in France and Italy, where industrialization had gained impetus only after the middle of the nineteenth century. Yet France, and Paris in particular, still played a central role in international payments because of its illustrious past. In spite of its relatively weak economy, it had evolved into the most prominent exporter of capital in Europe.

The disadvantages of bimetallism became tangible when the gold price began to fall around 1850. All four participants in the LMU were faced with vast imports of gold for minting purposes, and with equally massive exports of silver coins. In an attempt to meet its shortage of silver fractional coins, Switzerland decided, as noted earlier, to reduce the metal content of these coins to 80 per cent. Italy followed suit in 1862, France in 1864, with the proviso that these two countries brought the metal content down to 82.5 per cent. The disparity led to confusion and chaos because subsidiary coins of different contents had replaced the high-grade silver coins in all of the Union's Member States. The changed fineness hindered export of subsidiary coins, affecting Belgium, which had hardly any subsidiary coins of its own, most of all. For that reason, Belgium urged a uniform regime for subsidiary coins. At a conference initiated by France and held in Paris in November 1865, such a regime was set up in the form of the Latin Monetary Union.

The objective of the Union was twofold. In addition to the quest for a single large area where gold and silver coins could circulate freely, France in particular saw the LMU as the nucleus of an international — and preferably global — monetary system centring on the double standard. The negotiations in Paris, therefore, focused not so much on their *raison d'être* — viz. how to solve the subsidiary coin problem — as on the question what monetary system was to be introduced. The French Government fervently advocated the double standard, hoping, among other things, to expand its economic and political power beyond its borders. The other partners were in favour of the gold standard in the expectation that such a move would persuade other major countries, including the United Kingdom, to join the Union. Eventually the double standard was adopted, the other countries acquiescing because of their close financial ties with France.

4.2.2 The monetary Treaty

The 1865 Treaty provided solely for rules on coins. It stipulated that the Belgian franc, the French franc, the Swiss franc, the Italian lira and later the Greek drachme would serve as units of account. The official parity was 1 Belgian franc = 1 French franc = 1 Swiss franc = 1 Italian lira = 1 Greek drachme. In Article 2 of the Treaty the high contracting parties agreed not to strike, or allow to be struck, with their stamp, any gold coin of other kinds than pieces of one hundred, fifty, twenty, ten and five francs. To that list, Article 3 added the silver five franc coin. All these coins had a metal content of 90 percent fine silver. The parity between gold and silver was not explicitly laid down, following as it did from the traditional ratio of gold to silver, of 1:15.5. There were no restrictions on the minting of gold and silver coins. Additionally, silver subsidiary coins were brought into circulation which had the lower metal content applied by Italy and France (83.5 per cent). Switzerland was given twelve years to adjust the content of its small coins (80 per cent) accordingly. As a result of the reduction of the metal content of fractional coins, their face value came to exceed their intrinsic value. In order to prevent one Member State from enriching itself at the expense of another by issuing large quantities of subsidiary coins,[5] its circulation was limited to six francs per head of the population. Formally, the national standard coins — with the exception of those of Greece and Italy — were not legal tender within the Union. State cashiers were, however, under an obligation to accept them. To that end, the Treaty stipulated that not only the standard coins, but the silver subsidiary coins of each Member State, too, would be exchanged by State cashiers of the other Members of the Union at a rate fixed by law. Although this stipulation did not provide for an obligation to accept the coins for private transactions as well, it boiled down to practically the same thing. The Treaty did not contain any provisions as to the issue of paper money, the status of the note-issuing banks and their discount policies. They fell under the national monetary sovereignty of the Member States. Furthermore, no liquidation arrangement was provided for. The Treaty was valid for fifteen years, and was to be extended automatically by fifteen-year periods.

4.2.3 The Treaty in practice

The LMU started off under politically inauspicious circumstances. The Treaty had barely been signed when war broke out between Austria and Italy in 1866, with Italy resorting to the issue of inconvertible paper money. The hoarded coins could consequently be sold at a premium, and led to widespread speculation, a phenomenon that the Treaty had not foreseen. Italian coins were soon exported in great quantities to France and Switzerland, exchanged there at the official rates for their banknotes, which were subsequently exchanged for the inferior Italian paper money. The situation was aggravated considerably further when Greece joined, because there, too, inferior notes with forced currency were in circulation. Although as a result of the Franco-German War, France had also abandoned the convertibility of its banknotes. However, the exchange rate of these banknotes differed barely if at all from that of its coins because of the favourable development of its external trade and capital transactions. Apart from this, speculative capital flows revolved within the Union mainly around subsidiary coins, as, in the event of major exchange rate fluctuations, standard coins would soon have been melted down, and the metal sold in the market. It was not long before the trade in subsidiary coins confronted Italy and, at a later stage, Greece with a serious and persisting shortage of payment means.

In the meantime, France had failed in its attempt to use the LMU as a lever towards a global monetary system during the international monetary conference held in Paris in 1867. The twenty countries taking part in the consultations had admittedly professed a preference for the bimetallic monetary system used within the Union, but this proved no more than a hollow phrase when they opted virtually unanimously for the gold standard[6] on which the Union Treaty — like the French Act of 1803 — was not unequivocal. The preference for gold was one of the reasons why the LMU was never expanded. But within the Union, too, the desire for expansion had cooled after the foreign exchange problems arose. In 1874, it was decided that access to the Union would be conditional upon the approval of the Union Members. Thus the Union seriously undermined its own objective, viz. to eliminate the disadvantages of bimetallism by establishing a worldwide union.

The drawbacks of the bimetallic system manifested themselves in full around 1870 when the value of silver began to decline, and the 15.5 ratio was exceeded. It then became profitable to buy unminted silver in the market at the lower price, paying in gold and minting the silver purchased at the nominal rate. As a result, gold coins disappeared from circulation in the Union countries to make way for silver that was now being supplied in large quantities for minting five franc pieces. The greatest flow went to Belgium, where the unminted silver purchased in London could be sluiced into the Union in the cheapest manner. The ensuing danger of inflation prompted the Union Members in 1874 to decide on a temporary restriction of the production of silver coins. The next step was the new Treaty, concluded in 1878 for a mere six-year period, which put a full stop to the minting of silver coins, five franc pieces in particular. In fact the Union thus adopted the gold standard.[7]

After 1879, the LMU was again confronted with various tensions. Facing serious losses of gold in connection with its balance-of-payments deficits, France tried to rehabilitate the status of silver. A contrary movement was in evidence in Italy, which had recourse to the gold reserves of other countries (in the form of loans) in an endeavour to restore the convertibility of paper money. Italy thus definitively joined the countries favouring the gold standard. These countries put their stamp on the international monetary conference of 1881, which was also held in Paris.[8] Relations with France did not improve when Italy announced in that same year that it would no longer accept the silver coins of the other Member States once the Treaty had expired. In 1883 it issued a decree to the effect that at least two-thirds of the national reserves should consist of gold. This decision was generated by fears that France was about to demand that its partners withdraw any silver coins circulating within its borders. Italy received the immediate support of Belgium, which feared vast losses if the French plan materialized, owing to its relatively important role in the minting of these coins. In 1884, France announced that it would extend the Union Treaty only if an adequate liquidation arrangement were provided for.

The liquidation arrangement was laid down in the 1885 Treaty. This time it was underlain by tensions vis-à-vis Belgium, which fiercely resisted any attempts towards the exchange of the silver coins in circulation for gold. The remarkable fact was that this time Belgium stood alone in its protest. Switzerland had nothing to lose in this matter, while Italy no longer stood to benefit from the dissolution of the Union following the (temporary) abolition of the forced currency regime. These two countries accused Belgium of irresponsible behaviour, pointing out that it had invoked the original Treaty of 1865 in vain, because the Union had, in fact, already accepted the gold standard some time before, a situation which urgently called for a solution to the problem of silver. Under pressure of the partner countries, a liquidation clause was drawn up after numerous meetings, with each Member State committing itself to withdrawal of its silver five franc pieces circulating in the other Union countries at their face value should the Treaty be annulled. The silver coins were to be converted in gold coins, in the silver coins of the country making the exchange, or in trade bills. The new provisions were to be effective for five years, with possible one-year extensions after that.

Although the 1885 Treaty helped to stabilize exchange rates of the LMU-currencies vis-à-vis those of Germany, the United Kingdom and the United States, the Member States found it hard to put their own house in order. After Italy had gone back to issuing inconvertible paper money, again in the company of Greece, the Union became subject to heavy pressure as a result of vast speculative capital flows in the form of shifts in subsidiary coins. In subsequent years, these led to numerous revisions of and adjustments to the Treaty, which in fact further undermined what it had originally been intended to achieve. In 1893, Italy definitively undertook the nationalization of its subsidiary coins, so that these could no longer be exchanged at a fixed rate at the State cashiers of the other Union countries. Greece followed suit in 1908. These were the first steps towards total elimination of subsidiary coins from the Union.

Upon the outbreak of the First World War, most European countries left the gold standard.[9] The convertibility of their paper money was cancelled. The central banks of these countries made a deliberate effort to withhold gold coins so as to strengthen the metal base of their banknotes as much as possible. The public reacted immediately to this move with widespread hoarding, as a result of which the only coins in circulation were silver five franc pieces and subsidiary coins. In spite of all sorts of prohibitive measures, these coins flowed to Member States whose currencies showed the least depreciation. Problems first arose in France where coins were exchanged for banknotes which were sold on the exchanges for the depreciated notes of the other Member States. The coins which consequently flowed to France disappeared from circulation immediately there. On 13 March 1915, the Swiss Government introduced a law which prohibited all trade in coins issued by the other Union countries. This measure was, however, barely effective as the economic situation in France underwent a turnaround after 1915 which reversed the flow of capital, now directed at Switzerland. The situation was aggravated in 1919–1920 when the price of silver went up making it lucrative for speculators in France and Italy to collect silver five franc pieces which were exchanged in Switzerland being the country with the least depreciation of banknotes. After a futile attempt to curb this inflow via an import prohibition, Switzerland announced, in 1920, that it would no longer exchange the silver coins minted outside its territory at a fixed rate. In fact this measure was counter to the Treaty, but the situation was legalized retroactively by the agreement of 9 December 1921. When the Union countries agreed to this decision the Union had already been robbed of all its essential characteristics. Eventually, it was Belgium which took the initiative, at the end of 1925, of resigning from the Treaty as from

1927. Soon after that, Switzerland announced that it considered the Union terminated as at 1 January 1927.

In conclusion, it must be noted that the LMU did not live up to the expectations with which it had been set up. Although the bimetallic standard formed a major obstacle to the functioning of the LMU, that was not the core of the problem confronting the Union during its entire existence. That lay in the insufficient convergence of the policies conducted by the Member States. As a result, the country abiding by the rules most stringently was inevitably flooded by speculative capital flowing from Member States whose currencies felt the pressure of their expansionary spending policies. Though these flows of capital were initially fairly one-sided in nature, stemming as they did mainly from notoriously weak countries such as Greece and Italy, they became more diverse after the First World War when other Member States also came to contend with depreciating banknotes and outflows of coins to the country whose currency was depreciating the least. The Union only managed to survive until after the First World War because it offered France the opportunity to extend its political and economic influence to the other Member States, which in turn feared that by resigning from the Treaty, they would risk being cut off from French capital as well as incurring serious losses consequent on the introduction of the liquidation clause. This conclusion is corroborated by Erich Egner (1925) who points out that the dominance of France was the essential characteristic of the LMU without which its historical development cannot be understood. The danger that other Member States by leaving the Union would be confronted with the presentation by France of huge quantities of their own silver coins or would be excluded from the French capital market made them pliable Member States of the LMU.[10]

4.3   The Scandinavian Monetary Union, 1872–1931

4.3.1   Objective

Around the mid-nineteenth century, the so-termed Scandinavian Movement manifested itself in Sweden and Denmark. Its objective was to turn the Scandinavian countries into a political, economic and cultural unity. In a political respect, there had traditionally been close ties between these countries. Already since the end of the fourteenth century, Norway and Denmark had constituted a double monarchy, which came to an end in 1814, when Norway entered into a personal union with Sweden. The economies of the three countries showed a number of common elements. They were all characterized by an efficient agricultural system, a starting industrialization process and substantial external trade. In addition, monetary integration was already advanced. At an early stage, the public authorities of the three countries had learned their lesson from the consequences of a disorganized monetary system. That was why the pursuit of a stable and orderly monetary system dominated their policies. In addition, they all adhered to the silver standard and all accepted each other's coins and banknotes.

Around 1860, discussions arose about a reform of the monetary system. This was underlain directly by the international plans mentioned earlier to establish a global monetary system. During the negotiations on accession to the LMU conducted within this framework, Sweden pulled out for political and economic reasons. When Germany subsequently opted for the gold standard, fears arose in the Scandinavian countries that silver would become subject to downward pressure. In 1872, this resulted in the adoption of the gold standard in a treaty being concluded between Denmark and Sweden, with Norway joining by Treaty of 16 October 1875.

4.3.2   The monetary Treaty

The common unit of account opted for in the monetary Treaty was the Scandinavian crown (containing 1/2480 kilogramme gold). This meant that the mutual exchange rate between the Danish, Norwegian and Swedish crown (each 90 per cent fine gold) was 1:1:1. The standard coins were gold coins of ten and twenty crowns. In addition, silver and bronze subsidiary coins of two, one and smaller denominations were brought into circulation. Both the standard coins and the token coins of the three countries were completely identical; the only difference was the mint mark. Not only the gold coins were legal tender, but also the tokens and the silver coins which had already been in circulation in the three countries before the Treaty. This meant that the Union in fact accepted the limping standard. By contrast with the LMU, the Treaty did not impose a limitation on the production of silver subsidiary coins. In order to prevent an excessive amount of these coins from being brought into circulation, each State made them redeemable in gold, upon the holder's request without restriction. In 1879, this regulation was amended. As from 1 January of that year, coins of one and two crowns were only legal tender up to an amount of twenty crowns in the countries where they had not been issued. For even smaller coins, a limit of five crowns applied. The Treaty only applied to coins. Banknotes were not taken into account.

4.3.3 The Treaty in practice

During the first few decades of its existence, the Union functioned successfully. The choice in favour of the gold standard ensured that the difficulties of bimetallism witnessed elsewhere were avoided, while the mutual exchange of coins and banknotes went smoothly. The latter was related in part to two agreements, which were not included in the Treaty, but nevertheless contributed strongly to the Scandinavian Monetary Union's prominent place in the history of European monetary unions. The first agreement was concluded in 1885 between the Norwegian and Swedish central banks which agreed to permit each other to draw overdrafts on each other's accounts at par. This agreement entered into effect in 1888. Denmark joined in 1905. In practice, this meant that the central banks of the three Member States made funds available to each other without charging interest or commission, clearing of which was to take place in gold after the term of credit had expired. In that way exchange rate stability was guaranteed for 100 per cent as the influence of the gold points was completely dismantled, thus preventing speculative capital movements ensuing from exchange rate differences.

The second stipulation concerned banknotes. Where the use of banknotes as a means of payment is concerned, the Scandinavian countries could pride themselves on a long tradition. The oldest central bank was established in Sweden (1656), which already issued banknotes in 1661. The Bank of Norway was established in 1816, that of Denmark in 1818. One of the most striking differences compared with the LMU was that the objective was not only to bring the coins of the three States into common circulation, but also to introduce the different banknotes at parity in the entire Union. In order to achieve this objective, the Swedish central bank and the Bank of Norway concluded the so-termed 'parity agreement' in 1894, the second supplement to the monetary Treaty. By means of this agreement they committed themselves to accept each other's banknotes as legal tender at par value. In 1901, Norway and Denmark concluded a similar agreement. The result was that in the whole area of the Union not only the coins but also the banknotes of the different Member States were accepted at par value (the exchange rate consequently being 1:1:1). The original Treaty did not contain a liquidation clause. In 1884, the stipulation entered into effect that the Treaty could be terminated each year.

Tensions started in 1905, when the political union between Sweden and Norway came to an end. Sweden cancelled the agreement of 1885, but after laborious negotiations finally agreed to a new agreement according to which credits to be made available to each other by the three central banks — now interest-bearing — were limited so as to stabilize the exchange rate. Although those tensions were attributed mainly to political factors, monetary factors also played an important role. Over the years, Sweden and Norway had come to face a net debt position vis-à-vis the Danish national bank, which meant that an outflow of gold from these two countries to Denmark was expected to take place sooner or later. This development was due to the diverging monetary policies conducted by the three national banks. Unlike Norway and Sweden, Denmark's restrictive policy, which strengthened the domestic purchasing power of the Danish crown, caused the Swedish and Norwegian currencies to find their way to Denmark through trade and capital transactions. From the above, Alfred Lansburgh drew, in 1928, the conclusion that in the long-term, monetary union between countries with the same currency can only be realized if these countries harmonize their monetary policies so as to ensure that the currency circulating within the union has the same purchasing power in each Member State. In other words, a monetary union between countries, even if they are not united in a political union, makes sense provided that the participating central banks conduct a fully harmonized monetary policy.

At the outbreak of the First World War, the monetary union fell into decay. In this connection, it is noteworthy that the rules of the game were often cancelled independently by the three Member States. It started with the suspension of convertibility of banknotes, decided on by Sweden and Denmark on 2 August 1914, followed two days later by Norway. Shortly afterwards, a general gold prohibition was proclaimed: by Denmark on 6 August, by Norway on 18 August and finally by Sweden on 25 November 1914. In the subsequent years, the exchange rate of Norwegian and Danish banknotes increasingly came under pressure due to the deterioration of their balances of payments vis-à-vis Sweden resulting from rising inflation. This development induced Sweden to unilaterally end the parity agreement. On 9 October 1915, the Swedish national bank announced a discount for the Danish crown, followed on 1 December by a discount for the Norwegian currency. Though in early 1916 convertibility of the Scandinavian bank-notes was restored, the exchange rate of the Swedish crown was 17 percent above that of Norway and Denmark at the end of World War I.[11]

During the third year of the war, the countries of the Union were confronted with a huge gold influx. Notably the occupying powers tried to benefit from the higher Swedish exchange rate via gold shipments to Denmark and Norway. The result was that the Union threatened to be dragged down along the international inflationary spiral. In the course of 1916, the Union countries, each at a different time, proclaimed a gold embargo: Sweden on 8 February 1916, Norway on 15 April 1916 and Denmark on 22 February 1917. From this, it follows that the central banks did not act jointly, ultimately causing the embargo to have little effect. Denmark and Norway continued to offer gold coins in Sweden, which, under penalty of dissolution of the monetary Treaty, required that the status of legal tender assigned to each other's currencies be revoked. A compromise was reached in April 1917 in the form of the mutual promise to respect the gold embargo. However, shortly afterwards the token coins were to be at the centre of similar tensions. Large amounts of Danish and Norwegian small coins drained away to Sweden, unstopped by the latter's import prohibitions. In 1924, it was agreed that every Member State would have the authority to mint its own subsidiary coins, which would no longer be legal tender in the partner countries. This meant the de facto end of the monetary union, even though the dissolution of the Treaty was never formally ratified. In 1924, Sweden adopted the gold standard, followed by Denmark in 1926 and Norway in 1928, only to abandon it in 1931. This officially marked the end of the Scandinavian Monetary Union.[12]

In short, it may be concluded that the Scandinavian Monetary Union was successful in the sense that its participants were equal economic partners, who had already put their economies in order before the monetary Treaty was concluded, thus giving their national currencies an equal status. That they nevertheless entered into a monetary union was related primarily to their common interest in following the German example by introducing the gold standard. Political tensions and divergences in economic and monetary policies, of which each of the three countries was guilty, disrupted the smooth functioning of the Union after 1905. Under the pressure of the First World War, its significance crumbled even further, until monetary competences had ultimately returned completely to the Member States.

Notes

1. Around 1850, Austria was the largest European State after Russia. The Habsburg Empire encompassed many nationalities. Its borders enclosed Germans, Italians, Hungarians and Romanians as well as ethnic groups which were to make up part of Poland, Yugoslavia and Czechoslovakia. After Austria had been ousted from the German League on account of its war with Prussia in 1866, it attempted to avoid a weakening of its position by catering to the nationalist tendencies of the Hungarians in particular. This led in 1867 to the so-termed *Ausgleich*, where the Austrian Emperor had himself crowned King of Hungary, which was thus made autonomous.
2. Liechtenstein also took part in the German–Austrian Monetary Union.
3. Helfferich (1894), p. 65.
4. The Governor of *De Nederlandsche Bank* Wim Duisenberg drew attention to the Latin Monetary Union in his opening address at the first Colloquium of the European Association for Banking History, held in Amsterdam in September 1992. Its title was 'From Latin Monetary Union to European Monetary Union'.
5. This refers to the seigniorage effect attending the issuance of silver subsidiary coins. This effect corresponds with the discrepancy between a coin's face value and the value, in gold, of the silver contained in it. As a result of the reduction of the

silver content to 80 per cent in 1860 (in that year the gold/silver ratio was 15.29) 1 Swiss franc contained 4 grammes of silver, whose value in gold corresponded with 90 centimes.

6. The objective of the conference was to study the possibility of an international monetary system. The participating countries were virtually unanimous in opting for the single gold standard. The dissenting country was The Netherlands which announced that serious difficulties could be expected if all European countries were to adopt the same metal as standard. This was in favour of bimetallism, not only because the ratio between the two metals would thus be more stable, but also because that would boost the stability of price of the two metals. Adoption of the bimetallic standard by a large number of countries on the basis of one and the same statutory ratio of gold to silver would, in the Dutch view, be a wholly acceptable solution.

7. On the initiative of the United States, another monetary conference was held in Paris in 1878. The United States was in favour of an international monetary union based on the double standard. The conference was doomed from the outset because Germany did not attend and the United Kingdom had no intention of abandoning the gold standard. Again The Netherlands voiced its opinion that bimetallism, if adopted on a wide scale and stringently adhered to, would make it possible for the statutory ratio of gold to silver to prevail.

8. At this conference, bimetallism turned out to have gained a large number of advocates. Only Belgium, Norway and Switzerland still wished to adhere to the gold standard. Before the negotiations commenced, the Dutch delegation had compiled a questionnaire which was unanimously accepted as the guiding theme. The conference was a failure because Germany and the United Kingdom took the stance that, although they were not against the rehabilitation of silver in other countries The Netherlands, the LMU-countries and the United States), they made no bones about their own wish to continue their adherence to the gold standard.

9. See Chapter 6.2.

10. Egner (1925), pp. 48–49.

11. In 1925, the original exchange rate ratio of 1:1:1 had changed into 1 Swedish crown:1.27 Danish crown:1.49 Norwegian crown.

12. After 1931, these countries pursued the stabilization of their exchange rates vis-à-vis sterling. Within this framework, they joined the Sterling Bloc in 1933 (see Chapter 6.2).

5 THE 19TH-CENTURY MONETARY UNIONS ASSESSED

5.1 Supraregional monetary unions

A comparison of the three supraregional unions discussed in this book leads to the conclusion that once political unity had been achieved, standardization of the coin systems could be realized relatively rapidly. In Germany this was stimulated by the introduction of the single gold standard, in Italy and Switzerland by the adoption of the existing French coin system. Although this meant a de facto restriction of national monetary sovereignty in the two latter countries, the de jure competence to make decisions regarding the monetary system remained the province of the national authorities. Italy was less restricted in its autonomy than Switzerland as, by issuing inconvertible paper money, it shielded itself as it were against the problems of bimetallism which France passed on to its partner countries, to Switzerland in particular.

Where the unity of banknotes and the acceptance of these notes as a full means of payments is concerned, it could be stated that — except in Germany — this has been a long-term process. Generally this may be explained from the fact that it usually took a long time before the political unity proclaimed on paper sufficiently caught on in the minds of citizens so that they would identify with the political union. Moreover, in many cases century-old traditions and cultural values had to be abandoned, geographical orientations on sometimes rivalling powers were to be turned upside down and diverging economic processes had to be integrated. Such changes were usually attended by tensions, which, in the monetary field, had been reflected in the use of inferior money, for which paper money issued by the state and banks, rather than coins, offered ample opportunity.

Once political unification was achieved in Italy and Germany, the monetary reform initiated there had, from the outset, an integral character, in the sense that both countries envisaged imposing a uniform regulation in one stage for all elements of the monetary system. In Italy, the reform was only successful with regard to the coins. The centralization of banknotes was impeded notably by the regularly recurring recourse to inflationary financing by its government, which was not in the last place due to its half-hearted attitude towards the Bank of Sardinia. This only increased competition between the rapidly growing number of issuing banks. Nevertheless, it was the chaos caused by these factors which — albeit in the longer term — was the driving force behind the evolutionary process towards one central bank. Developments were totally different in Germany, where the law of the newly unified State assigned a privileged position to the already dominant Prussian Bank from the very beginning, thus giving this bank a head start in developing into the national central bank. The reason why the process of monetary integration went relatively smoothly in Germany is sought primarily in the circumstance that the basis for this process had already been laid before the unification in the form of the Zollverein.[1] To an important extent, this customs union reflected economic cooperation between the many small principalities, which ultimately melted into larger political entities. After 1870, this facilitated economic integration between the North and the South, from which monetary integration could benefit. In Switzerland, monetary reform had purposefully been aimed at coin unification. Issuing of banknotes continued to be a regional matter, so that the process of centralization there was seriously hampered by growing competition between the cantonal banks of issue.

German and Italian monetary unification were comparable in the sense that in both countries, one single State (Prussia in Germany and Piedmont in Italy) actively strove for political unification. Once this had been achieved through military victory, both countries attempted to extend the monetary system to the entire union. The most significant difference between Italian and German unification was that the latter was a long-term and gradual process, whereas unification in Italy was sudden and unexpected, with the added problem that, at the time of political unification, 'a patchwork of economically heterogeneous states'[2] had to be united.

5.2   Inter-European monetary unions

A common characteristic of the inter-European monetary unions was that they were established by sovereign states partly hoping to realize other objectives. For Austria, the central issue was to break the Prussian supremacy, France envisaged reinforcing its economic strength via a global monetary system based on the French model, while the Scandinavian countries attempted to protect themselves from the negative effects exerted by the German unification on the price ratio of precious metals. In practice, these underlying objectives caused monetary integration to become nothing but an empty shell, in the sense that only the existing currency situations were legalised in a treaty, without providing for a next step on the way to monetary unification. The Vereinsthaler introduced in the German–Austrian Monetary Union was a copy of the same common currency circulating earlier in the North and South of Germany. The countries participating in the LMU had also already proclaimed the French coinage system as their own before the establishment of this Union, while in the Member States of the Scandinavian Monetary Union exchange rate stability had already been the main monetary objective of the central banks before the Treaty was drawn up.

From the very beginning, the Treaty between Austria and Germany was doomed to fail due to the different political ambitions of the two rivalling Treaty partners. The prevailing unrest resulting from these differences was disastrous for confidence in the envisaged exchange rate stability. Despite the introduction of a parallel currency, this stability was eroded further by the absence of solid economic and monetary integration between the partners. Austria, whose economy had weakened, was repeatedly forced to resort to inconvertible paper money, driving out high-grade silver money to Germany. In addition, differences in payment habits were insufficiently taken into account. Austria had a long-standing tradition with respect to the use of paper money while in Germany the use of coins had taken such firm hold that the risks of a common coin were not recognized for a long time. Furthermore, there was no supranational regulatory body, which might serve as a platform for consultations in times of calamities.

The LMU was not very successful either. An important problem was the permanent tension between the advocates and the opponents of the bimetallic standard underlying the Union, with each country independently drawing the line based on its own interests. In this respect, the contribution of Angela Redish (1993) is interesting. Unlike general views in literature, she regards the LMU as the final step towards the gold standard rather than a conscious step back to bimetallism. She argues that the fall of the gold price around 1850 had resulted in the de facto adoption of the gold standard by Belgium, France and Switzerland before the establishment of the LMU. The fact that France nevertheless formally adhered to bimetallism (which did not have any disadvantages as it was actually based on gold) was a matter of negotiating tactics rather than hard-line philosophy. Redish agrees with Léon Say that the adoption of the gold standard was aimed at teaching the legislator how to deal with issuing token coins, the very raison d'être of the LMU. Whatever the case may be, experiences with the Union show that besides the problems surrounding bimetallism, the real reason why monetary integration failed was that the participants insufficiently observed one of the most important rules of the game — the harmonization of their economies.

Viewed in that light, the Dutch economist Suardo Posthuma (1982) notes that it is not legal stipulations, but economic factors which determined the exchange rate between the currencies of the various countries. Due to the deteriorated economic situation, Greece and Italy were forced to issue inconvertible paper money, as a result of which fixing an exchange rate vis-à-vis the currencies of the other Member States was doomed to fail. In addition, the Treaty itself was too weak to serve as a solid basis for monetary integration. Only the maintenance of the coins' metal content and weight was provided for, but no regulations were laid down regarding the permissible volume of the coin circulation, nor for the issue of banknotes. What was missing was a mechanism for coordination and policy-making in the case of disruptions. This led to conflicts, each time requiring an adjustment of the Treaty stipulations to the new conditions, which undermined credibility and weakened, rather than strengthened, cooperation. In this respect H. Parker Willis (1901) goes even further in stating that 'The Latin Union as an experiment in international monetary action has proved to be a failure. Its history serves merely to throw some light upon difficulties which are likely to be encountered in any international attempt to regulate monetary systems in common. From whatever point of view the Latin Union is studied, it will be seen that it has resulted only in a loss to the countries involved.'[3] This conclusion seems slightly exaggerated. As Theurl (1992) notes, the Member States did benefit from the union under normal circumstances. The French economic policy, which was based on the considerable reserves held by the *Banque de France* and on a well-functioning capital market, absorbed exogenous shocks, such as sudden changes in the price of gold and silver, interest rate fluctuations or massive outflows of certain currencies.

In the Scandinavian countries Nielsen (1927) ascribes monetary integration in part to the Scandinavian Movement. In his opinion monetary unions have never been underlain solely by economic reasons. A certain culture, mostly translated into mutual solidarity, was a permanent background objective. The fact that the Scandinavian Monetary Union initially operated successfully was related in part to the fairly large degree of economic integration and an adequate budgetary policy, in the sense that, if possible, budget deficits were financed in a monetarily neutral manner. Under these circumstances, the Union could function smoothly, at least as long as it was not faced by exogenous shocks. When political tensions put an end to this situation, the Union crumbled, a process which was reinforced by the uncoordinated nature of the actions taken by the sovereign central banks. In addition, tensions arising during the First World War exerted considerable pressure on cooperation between the central banks. This was illustrated by the fact that measures were not taken simultaneously. The suspension of convertibility and the termination of the parity of the banknotes took place at different times in the three countries, as well as the implementation of the gold embargo, with which Denmark and Norway only complied under Swedish pressure. The fact that the national banknotes were allowed to circulate freely within the Union without being subject to regulations laid down by a supranational issuing institution, was bound to cause problems. In the end, the ever-clearer divergence in economic development forced monetary policy — in the form of a gold blockade, the discount rate and issuing policy — to focus more on the own currency area.

One aspect to be taken into account with respect to the LMU and the Scandinavian Monetary Union is the dominance of an economically powerful Member State. In this context, Giulio M. Gallarotti (1993) speaks about two 'economic satellite systems' each of which 'itself formed a small monetary chain gang centred around the monetary and trade hegemony of Germany and France'.[4] With regard to the LMU, Gallarotti notes that around 1860 the dependence between the Member States had grown to such an extent that if France had given up the dual standard for the gold standard, Belgium, Italy and Switzerland would undoubtedly have followed the French example. Under these circumstances, it was clear that in both currency unions the monetary policies of the hegemonic economies were 'compelling'.

5.3   Provisional conclusions for EMU

The history of the nineteenth-century currency unions allows us to draw a number of provisional conclusions which may be relevant for the present-day monetary union, which is aimed for as an element of post-war Western European integration.

(1)   Parallelism between economic and monetary integration was a prerequisite for the success of supraregional currency unions. In Italy and Switzerland, regional economic disparities obstructed monetary unification, which was ultimately achieved only after a laborious process. The fact that the Swiss Government was more aware of this link than the Italian Government is evident from the fact that it only gradually included its paper money in the monetary unification process. Germany distinguished itself in that parallelism between economic and monetary integration had already been achieved there to a large extent before the newly unified State entered into effect. On the other hand, diverging economic and monetary

policies were the main causes underlying the break-up of the inter-European unions. This divergence manifested itself in an inflationary expenditure and monetary policy conducted by Italy in the LMU, by Austria in the German–Austrian Monetary Union and by each of the three countries participating in the Scandinavian Monetary Union. The fact that, within the supraregional unions, economic imbalances and diverging policies had a positive rather than a negative effect on integration must be ascribed to an important extent to the circumstance that, in those cases, political union guaranteed the irreversibility of the currency union.

(2)   The introduction of a parallel currency as an instrument to stimulate integration was only successful in those cases where the purchasing power of the national currencies participating in the union was more or less the same. Under those circumstances the question arises what the use of such a parallel currency is. Even without the political complications, the Vereinsthaler of the German–Austrian Monetary Union would not have had any chance of success as long as Austria was unable to raise its economy to a similar level and to keep pace with its German ally. In Germany, on the other hand, the Vereinsthaler was able to develop into the 'common coin for all purposes'. This was not so much due to its characteristic of parallel currency, but rather to the fact that the Vereinsthaler was put on the same footing with the North German Thaler. In the end, the Thaler would have crowded out the South German Gulden anyway, not because it was introduced as parallel currency but because it was underlain by the economic strength of Prussia.

(3)   The question whether a monetary union consisting of a dominant state and a group of smaller countries will be successful cannot be answered beforehand. In the LMU, the hegemony of France ultimately resulted in a Union which was lulled to sleep, with the smaller countries — more or less against their will — complying with the wishes of France without being actively involved in promoting French interests. By contrast, the German example shows that, in an economic and monetary respect, the dominance of Prussia had a favourable effect on the newly united State, whose stabilization policy propagated by a strong central bank also had a positive effect on the decision of the Scandinavian countries to introduce the gold standard. In both cases, the policy of the dominant Member State had a 'compelling effect' on the partner countries.

(4)   The absence of a supranational central bank, which would act as a coordinating and controlling body, was considered a serious shortcoming, notably in times of tension. Despite Lansburgh's assertion that monetary union, even between countries which are fully independent in a political respect, may evolve into a guardian of sound monetary policy under the condition that the central banks of these states are prepared to harmonize

their policies sufficiently, history shows that in the inter-European unions the sovereign central banks were unable to play such a role. The fact that, within the supraregional unions, the note-issuing authority did succeed in developing into that role may be ascribed to (a) the presence of a dominant issuing authority, generally favoured by the government and legislation before political unity was achieved and (b) the fact that centralization of its monetary competences after the achievement of political unity was attended by centralization of competences in other policy areas.

Notes

1. See Chapter 14.2.
2. De Cecco and Giovannini (1989), p. 8.
3. Willis (1901), p. 267.
4. Gallarotti (1993), p. 39.

Part II

INTEGRATION IN THE 20TH CENTURY

'When European statesmen were faced with the problem of European unification, they espoused the functionalist approach, adopting federalist points of view with hesitation and halfheartedly only when forced by necessity and discarding them when the pressure diminished.'

(Altiero Spinelli, 1957)

6 THE PERIOD 1918–1945: THE AGE OF EUROPEAN DISINTEGRATION

6.1 The illusion of the United States of Europe

In a political respect, the end of the First World War created a favourable climate for the establishment of movements which considered the realization of a united Europe of paramount importance. With the fall of the Habsburg Empire in 1918, the European Continent had become severely fragmented both politically and economically. This consequently increased the need for a new direction, notably in Western Europe, all the more so as the victory of communism in Russia appeared hardly compatible in terms of politics and economics with the new role assumed by the United States of America after World War I: that of the leading power of the liberal Western World.

The ancient idea of the creation of the United States of Europe was revived in July 1922 by the Austrian Count Richard Coudenhove-Kalergi. He had not forgotten the words spoken by Benjamin Franklin in 1787 with regard to the new United States Federal Constitution: 'I do not see why you might not in Europe carry the project ... into execution, by forming a Federal Union and One Grand Republic of all its different States and Kingdoms.'[1] In Vienna, October 1923, Coudenhove-Kalergi established the Pan-European Movement, its objective being to unite all countries of Europe, except the Soviet Union and the United Kingdom, in one federation where each country would retain its national sovereignty and identity. Only the establishment of such a confederacy would be capable of preventing a new world war and an expansion of the Bolshevik revolution. Coudenhove-Kalergi believed that the United Kingdom should be excluded on account of its interests in the Commonwealth. He was absolutely convinced that the creation of the United States of Europe was dependent primarily on Franco-German cooperation. However, he did not have any other clear ideas of this construction, since he did not think it at all objectionable 'to include in such a democratic federation even fascist Italy, where there was no elected parliament and no political freedom'.[2]

In the period 1926–1935, the Pan-European Movement organized various congresses in Basle, Berlin and Vienna where leading statesmen such as Aristide Briand and Gustav Stresemann expressed their interest in these ideas. On 5 September 1929, Briand presented his European plan to the tenth meeting of the League of Nations, which had been founded in 1919. The plan was received without much enthusiasm. The Italian representative avoided taking a clear position, while the English delegate did not react at all. In economic circles, however, the idea of federalism was well received, notably in France and Germany, where commissions were set up to investigate the economic problems facing a future European Union. Nevertheless, it soon became evident that the climate in Europe was not yet ripe for political and economic integration. The memorandum published by Briand on 1 May 1930 only mentioned a European Association to be established with the assistance of the League of Nations and the foundation of a *Comité politique permanent* on which all European countries would hold a seat. However, the document did not discuss any concrete matters. Germany made its participation conditional upon the revision of the Versailles Peace Treaty, while Norway, Sweden and Switzerland shared the view that a new organization operating parallel to the League of Nations would be redundant. The death of Stresemann and the election victory of the national socialists in Germany in 1930 pushed the plan to the background. Instead of a European Federation, a Study Commission for the European Union was established, which led a shadow existence for a number of years, after which it abandoned, like the League of Nations, its efforts to realize the unification of Europe. Europe disintegrated into regional power blocs, such as the Rome–Berlin axis, the Balkan *Entente* (1934) between Turkey, Rumania, Greece and Yugoslavia and the Baltic Entente (1936) between Estonia, Latvia and Lithuania. This breakdown into regional blocs was to pave the way for a new world conflict.

Another attempt to come to a federal Europe was made by the United Kingdom, where the Federal Union Movement had been established in the 1930s. Relevant in this connection is the warning by Spinelli (1957) against the misconception that the United Kingdom had traditionally been opposed to the idea of a European Federation. He distinguished between the so-termed Latin and Anglo-Saxon approach to the question of European integration. According to Spinelli, it is generally assumed that the Latin countries are used to thinking in terms of 'well spelled-out, written constitutions', whereas the political system in the United Kingdom is based on an unwritten constitution, as a result of which the British might be expected to adopt a more empirical approach in the field of international cooperation. However, Spinelli argues that this is absolutely not true: 'The idea that it is possible to bring about a supranational government by means other than conquest, *i.e.* through free consent of states, and that it is possible to divide sovereignty, assigning portions of it to different organs of the government, is a typically Anglo-Saxon conception.'[3] As true as this may be, it may not be ignored — and even Spinelli points this out — that the views of the Federal Union Movement were to group the united Europe around the United Kingdom, which would be the leading power. Initially, the movement considered an alignment of France, the Low Countries and Scandinavia around the United Kingdom, hoping that the countries subject to a fascist regime would join as soon as that regime had been overthrown. Even during the Second World War, in June 1940, the British politician Sir Winston Churchill, supported by the Frenchman Jean Monnet, put forward the proposal to establish a British–French union which was to serve as the basis for the future united Europe. Every French citizen would automatically be granted British citizenship and vice versa. In addition, the two countries were to form a joint government and parliament. The French rejected the plan, apprehensive as they were of the supremacy of the United Kingdom. This refusal marked the turnaround in the British attitude towards the idea of a federation with the rest of Europe: '...there was a complete loss of faith in Europe, and the old sentiment for unification with Europe was replaced by the firm conviction that no confidence could be placed in the European states'.[4]

During the Second World War, the concept of a united Europe was not forgotten. Insofar as Germany was concerned, it was propagated by the national socialist Government. In Belgium, France and Italy it was mainly the resistance movements that were planning a European unity, but these plans did not go much further than a first exploration of how Europe was to go on after the defeat of nazi Germany. During an underground meeting in Geneva, in May 1944, the various resistance movements exchanged views for the first time as to what would ultimately form the basis of the *Union Européenne des Fédéralistes*, established in the Swiss city of Montreux in 1947. In the years to come, it would be the counterpart to the 'functional approach', of which the Rumanian-born David Mitrany was the spiritual father. For the time being, however, the realization of the United States of Europe would remain an illusion.

6.2   The end of the gold standard

With the outbreak of the First World War, the gold standard was abandoned not only by the belligerent states, but also by countries who were not involved. In 1918, part of Europe considered a return to this system a pre-

eminent means to create some order in the war-damaged economies, even
though it would still take some years before the relevant countries imposed
restraints on monetary expansion to such an extent that the central banks
were able to again maintain the rules of the gold standard.

Under the influence of the recommendations made during the international monetary conference held in 1922 at Genua, all European states,
except Spain and the Soviet Union, reintroduced the pre-war monetary
system in the period from 1925 to 1928, albeit that gold retained its
function as a unit of account, but no longer its function as a medium
of exchange. The new medium of exchange was banknotes based on gold
and deposits. The gold was concentrated with the central banks, which
is why the term gold exchange standard was used. In practice, however,
this system hardly differed from that in use before 1914. Each country had
linked its currency to gold, was prepared to exchange its (fiduciary) medium
of exchange for gold at a fixed price and did not impose any restrictions on
imports and exports of gold. The main difference between this system and
the gold coin standard was that exchange rate stability was not completely
automatic, but resulted from the policies adhered to by the issuing bank
with regard to gold issues. Another difference compared with the old system
was that the authorities were no longer held to the gold weight, which
determined the gold price and consequently parity, laid down at that time
in the coin act. Although this meant more freedom for the central banks,
most European nations still restored the old gold parity, despite the fact
that the war had left a drastic mark on their economies. Only in a few
countries, such as Belgium, France and Italy, the governments opted for a
lower parity.

The ensuing problems were the reason for the instability of international
monetary relationships from the very beginning. The French franc was
undervalued, while sterling was overvalued. This situation and the external
deficits which had originated, during the war, in a large number of countries
as a consequence of over-spending, resulted in extensive gold outflows,
notably to the United States (and, to a lesser extent, to France). The
unilateral character of this capital flow was reinforced by ample international lending, which enabled the countries facing extensive gold outflows
to continue their balance-of-payments deficits. After a global economic
depression began to manifest itself in the autumn of 1929, this capital
movement ended abruptly. On account of a lack of confidence, creditor
countries, headed by the United States, liquidated their — mainly short-
term — credits, causing tensions to arise in Europe against which the gold
standard could not hold its own.

Following the financial crash in Austria and Germany in July 1931,
the United Kingdom abandoned the gold standard in September of that

year. When, during the Economic World Conference of 1933 in London, the United States also announced that they would no longer maintain the gold parity of the dollar, Belgium, France, Italy, The Netherlands, Poland and Switzerland formed the so-termed Gold Bloc in an attempt to save the gold standard. As a counterpart, other states, including the Scandinavian countries, joined the Sterling Bloc, which meant that their currencies automatically followed the depreciation of sterling (notably vis-à-vis the dollar). As a result, the gold currencies became increasingly overvalued. However, as the gold currency countries were unable to counterbalance this appreciation by means of a deflationary wage and price policy, the Gold Bloc only survived for a few years. After Belgium, Italy and Poland had left the group, France, Switzerland, and finally The Netherlands, also decided to abandon the link with gold in September 1936. This marked the end of the gold standard, paving the way for a system of floating currencies.

6.3 Idle hope of monetary and economic cooperation

Although the gold standard had been short-lived, its temporary recovery had given in a number of countries a new impulse to the pursuit of monetary cooperation. This was unhindered by the failure of the LMU. On the contrary, its modest success was ascribed in part to the difficulties ensuing from the double standard, even though it had meanwhile become evident that, apart from the existing coinage system, it was the wrong policy conducted in some Member States which caused the depreciation of metal, resulting in a capital outflow to the partner countries. Consequently these countries lost control of an important part of their money creation. This was insufficiently recognized by politicians and economists who held the view that the LMU would not have been able to function as a full monetary union anyway because the Treaty only concerned the coinage system and not paper money. They felt that the modest success of LMU did not mean *a priori* that a monetary union between countries which maintained a single gold standard would fail.

Against this background, attempts were made in various European countries to reinforce existing forms of cooperation or to enter into new monetary unions. An example of the first activity was the attempt, in the 1920s, of the three Scandinavian countries to reactivate their currency union which had virtually died down, even making allowance for a possible accession of Finland, which did not use the Scandinavian crown. As to the second kind of activity, in the early 1930s, a conference was scheduled to be held in the eastern part of Europe in order to come to the establishment of a *Union Monétaire Balkanique*. The underlying objective of this plan was that such a union would not only be logical on account of the geographical position, traditions and habits of the people of the region, but also that economic and monetary cooperation would increase their economic well-being. The Union would consist of Albania, Bulgaria, Greece, Rumania, Yugoslavia and Turkey. The conference would deal with the possibility of introducing a common currency, whose gold content was to be determined at a later stage. This determination was required because of the different gold content of the national currencies. In the end, nothing was to come of these plans due to the abandonment of the gold standard and the ensuing economic and political tensions in Europe.

The only convention signed during the inter-war period was that between the Grand Duchy of Luxembourg and Belgium, contained in the Treaty of 25 July 1921. This union is known as the Belgo–Luxembourg Economic Union (BLEU). It took effect on 1 May 1922 and provided for the establishment of a customs union. In the monetary sphere, too, the two countries realized far-reaching, albeit incomplete, unification. The Treaty stipulated that the Belgian currency would circulate in the Duchy in addition to the Luxembourg franc. The parity between the Belgian and the Luxembourg franc was, however, not laid down by the convention. Neither did it contain a stipulation that the Belgian currency was legal tender in Luxembourg. The latter was only laid down by law of 23 May 1935, implying an amendment of the monetary agreement between the two countries which had become necessary following the devaluation of the Belgian franc in March of that year.

The customs union between Belgium and Luxembourg had a sequel in the plan to establish the European Customs Union. Since the mid-1920s, this had been the subject of a series of congresses led by the inspiring *Comité Français d'Etudes pour l'Union Douanière Européenne*, chaired by none other than Briand. According to this Committee, the Union would have to be established *'par l'aggrégation progressive des divers Etats autour d'un noyau central'*.[5] This nucleus would have to comprise Belgium, France, Germany and Luxembourg. The other European countries would subsequently, their economic development permitting, join this front group. During various economic conferences in Geneva (1927, 1929 and 1930) it became evident that this plan was nothing but idle hope on account of the differences of opinion between the relevant countries as to how economic cooperation was to be realized. Nevertheless, on 22 December, the Oslo Convention was signed, with Belgium, Denmark, Luxembourg, The Netherlands, Norway and Sweden deciding to enter into a customs union. Due to the fact that the Scandinavian signatories of the Treaty opted out shortly afterwards, the Oslo Convention ultimately resulted in the Treaty of Ouchy on 18 July 1932 between Belgium, The Netherlands and Luxembourg. In this Treaty, the three countries agreed to impose preferential import duties on the other participants, while at the same time gradually reducing these duties. The French committee immediately applauded the Treaty as the '*première étape vers l'Union Douanière Européenne*'.[6] As result of opposition on the part of the United Kingdom, the Treaty was not viable. Apart from that, the political tensions of the 1930s caused the idea of the European Customs Union to be shelved permanently.

6.4 Plans for a European central bank

Plans for the introduction of a European currency were put forward during the European Congress of the Pan-European Movement, held in Basle in the spring of 1932. At this congress, the chairman of the German bank *Berliner Handelsgesellschaft* Hans Fürstenberg held a lecture in which he advocated the introduction of a European currency and preparations for the establishment of a European central bank. His plan received a great deal of attention in the German press, with Lansburgh (1932) fiercely criticising it. In his view, the acceptance of a currency as legal tender is restricted necessarily to the political territory of the State issuing that currency. However, the value of that currency does not depend on the government but on its economic performance even though it is also determined in part by government policies affecting the economy. The result, he argued, is that there are no two countries in the world, where a common currency has exactly the same value. Fürstenberg's proposal with regard to the establishment of a European central bank had been propagated earlier by for instance Emile Francqui and Pierre Quesnay, who had been involved in the Dawes Plan (1924) and Young Plan (1929) for the settlement of German war debts. In the spring of 1930, notably the Young Plan resulted in the foundation of the Bank for International Settlements (BIS) in Basle, the first institutionalized form of cooperation between central banks since the First World War.

The BIS was established by the countries involved in this war. Although the primary objective was to secure reparation payments by Germany, the founders had envisaged the institution to play a role as a cooperative body of central banks from the outset. In order to achieve this objective, regular meetings had been held in the 1920s between central bank governors like Montagu Norman of the Bank of England, Hjalmar Schacht of the Deutsche Reichsbank and Emile Moreau of the Banque de France. 'By the end of the 1920s ... the need for a European centre of central bank collaboration had become so widely recognized that, if the Young Plan had not provided an excuse, another would probably have been found.'[7] During the Interbellum, this will to cooperate constituted an important step forward in the pursuit of the recovery of balanced relationships between the economic and financial structure of the various countries. Although the Economic World Conference of 1933 failed — the BIS had been closely involved in the preparations for this conference — this new organization paved the way for the signing of the Tripartite Agreement in 1936 between France, the United Kingdom and the United States,[8] which were later joined by Belgium, The Netherlands and Switzerland. In the following years, however, the BIS was increasingly restricted in the continuation of its activities as a forum for international discussion due to the fact that the political situation had meanwhile deteriorated considerably.

As becomes evident from the above, the Basle organization was not only aimed at Europe, nor was it intended to act as a supranational body. In this respect, Fürstenberg had taken one step further in advocating the establishment of a European central bank, even though he did not express himself clearly about the tasks and competences this bank would have. A clear opinion of such an institution was given by Lansburgh who stated that the establishment of a European central bank would only be successful if it would have the authority to intervene in an authoritarian manner in the economic policies of each individual member.

While ideas about the European central bank had far from crystallized, it was a fact that the abolition of the gold standard had marked a new era for the central banks. With the abolition of the fixed domestic gold price, there were no longer objective norms for monetary and exchange rate policies. Although the individual central banks maintained their authority to buy and sell gold, and thus the possibility to intervene in the foreign exchange market, these interventions no longer ensued from the nature of the monetary system, but were to be based on explicit policy decisions by the monetary authorities. This meant that, within broad limits, monetary policy might be conducted at the national government's own discretion. It goes without saying that in an era where autarchy had long been replaced by gradually increasing economic interwovenness, these broad limits would create the need for mutual policy harmonization and progressing cooperation between the central banks, not only on a global level but also within Europe. However, concrete action would not be taken until after the Second World War.

In short, it may be concluded that, although common monetary interests admittedly drove countries together during the inter-war period, thus breathing life into the notion of the establishment or reinforcement of monetary unions, these interests could not be defended collectively on account of the underlying economic diversity between the relevant countries. The result was that in the light of growing political divergence hardly any or no monetary integration took place in Europe between 1918 and 1945, the Belgo–Luxembourg Economic Union excepted.

Notes

1. Benjamin Franklin to Mr. Grand. See Smyth, 'Writings of Benjamin Franklin' IX, p. 619, cited by Ernst van Raalte (1931), pp. 6–7.
2. Spinelli (1957), p. 38.
3. Spinelli (1957), p. 39.
4. Spinelli (1957), p. 41.
5. Le Trocqeur (1929), p. 179.
6. Le Trocqeur (1932), p. 283.
7. Jacobsson (1979), p. 96.
8. This agreement, also referred to as the Monetary Triangle Accord, was concluded after the fall of the Gold Bloc. France, the United Kingdom and the United States agreed to avoid a depreciation race to the extent possible. However, due to the continuous depreciation of the French franc, the agreement's objective was not fully met.

7 THE PERIOD 1945–1957: PREPARATIONS FOR INTEGRATION

7.1 High priority for economic cooperation

The Second World War had only just ended when, on the debris, the governments of the industrialized countries made collective attempts to call a halt to the process of disintegration which had set in during the 1930s. The difficulties facing Western Europe in 1945 were of both an economic and a political nature. Economically, there was a strong need for reconstruction, for putting an end to bilateralism and protectionism and for lifting the dire dollar shortage. From a political point of view, the decisions taken during the conferences of Yalta and Potsdam resulted in a split-up of the European continent into West and East, with the Soviet Union preparing itself for tightening its grip on Eastern Europe as part of a policy ultimately aimed at the annexation of the rest of Europe.

Unlike after the First World War, the national state as 'the best expression of political life' had fallen into discredit after 1945. It was Churchill who breathed new life into the ideal of the European confederation by advocating 'a kind of United States of Europe' during his famous lecture at the University of Zürich on 19 September 1946. Like Coudenhove-Kalergi, Churchill held the view that only a European Federation could prevent new wars. Again, it was unclear what he exactly meant by such a Federation. Spinelli doubts the sincere intentions of the Churchill Plan, which he called 'clever and cynical'.[1] Fearing Russian imperialism, the United Kingdom did not openly dare to turn against the plans for European integration, even though it opposed these plans for fear it might create a Continental power. By appointing itself the defender of a united Europe, the United Kingdom tried to take the leading role, so as to be able to steer a possible development in such a direction that a real union would never be realized. The Churchill Plan made no mention whatsoever of a Federation, the transfer of national competences or the establishment of supranational bodies. It only mentioned a European framework within which Franco-

German conflicts could be resolved and the threat of the communist Soviet Union kept in check.

In order to promote economic cooperation, a new United Nations body was set up called the Economic Commission for Europe (ECE).[2] The objective of this Commission was to get the European countries to cooperate in reconstructing Europe. Nevertheless, the first joint action was initiated by the United States of America, which, in the European Cooperation Act, concretely voiced its wish to create a single market in Europe. This wish was closely in line with the recommendation of the European Movement, established in the late 1940s, which advocated economic cooperation by abolishing trade quotas and tariffs during the Congress of Westminster in 1949. Such a step had already been decided on during the Second World War by Belgium, Luxembourg and The Netherlands. Pursuant to the Benelux Treaty of 1 January 1948, these countries had formed a customs union as from that date.[3] Nevertheless, the American plan and the objective of the European Movement were more far-reaching than this 'return to normalcy', which would consist of nothing more than the removal of the trade barriers erected during the 1930s and the Second World War. In essence, the objective was to realize an optimal distribution of labour in Europe by creating a common market, which would ultimately resemble a situation of full competition as closely as possible. The Benelux Memorandum, written for the Marshall conference, held in Paris in the summer of 1947, contained three central elements: regulation of European trade on a multilateral basis, broadening of the convertibility of the European currencies by creating a dollar fund and making use of the German economic potential within the framework of a European recovery programme.

The European Recovery Programme, initiated by the US Secretary of State George Marshall was the basis for post-war economic recovery in Europe. Pursuant to the Economic Cooperation Act, signed by US President Harry Truman on 3 April 1948, no fewer than seventeen European countries received annual dollar assistance in the period from 1949 to 1951 for the reconstruction of their economies. The Act made assistance conditional upon the continued cooperation between the relevant countries. In April 1948, this led to the adoption of the Convention for European Economic Cooperation by the same countries. In October of that year, the Paris-based Organization for European Economic Cooperation (OEEC) was established. Although the organization's primary task was to promote mutual cooperation in implementing the European Recovery Programme, it was not inconceivable that it might develop into a centre for permanent cooperation in the field of economics.[4]

7.2   Political integration via economic cooperation

It should be noted that the initiatives to achieve economic cooperation cannot be seen in isolation. The objective was to incorporate this cooperation into a political framework, which would also offer room for closer cooperation in other areas between democratically-elected governments. With that in mind, the Council of Europe was established in 1949, on the initiative of the European Movement.[5] During its second session in the autumn of 1950, its most important body, the Advisory Assembly, indicated the direction for European cooperation: 'The question whether political or economic unification should come first has already been answered long ago: everyone agrees that they should be developed simultaneously and that they are mutually supporting.'[6] The question was how this could be achieved. Ideas put forward on this matter during the war indicated two options. The first option was to immediately take steps towards a full political union by establishing a European legislative body. The other option was 'gradualist' in approach believing primarily in a functional integration without impeding the existing structures of the national governments. The ideas which dominated the European Movement belonged essentially to those who favoured a 'gradualist' approach to European unity.

Meanwhile, however, it had become evident that little constructive cooperation was to be anticipated within the Economic Commission for Europe due to the participation of the Soviet Union and its satellites. Consequently, it was understandable that the OEEC also engaged in the realization of a regulated trade and payment system. Where the latter is concerned, a case in point was the establishment of the European Payments Union in 1950,[7] which focused on a gradual recovery of the convertibility of the European currencies.

The OEEC pursued a kind of European masterplan through combining, adjusting and coordinating the plans formulated by the individual participating nations. However, it soon became clear that this approach would not be very successful. Due to the fact that the OEEC was based on the principle of unanimity, and thus did not represent a supranational authority, it was unable to actually change the national plans, which had already crystallized. This procedure only encouraged in the Member States sentiments of economic sovereignty. Against the background of the ultimate goal of a politically united Europe, it became evident that an organization with broader economic competences was required. However, Western Europe was very strongly divided on this issue. During a conference at The Hague in 1948, the British and Scandinavian wish to first and foremost promote cooperation between the national governments was diametrically opposed to the aim of other countries on the European Continent to achieve political cooperation at a higher, supranational, level by reducing the role of the national governments. This contradiction became manifest again during discussions on a supranational economic organization. The United Kingdom and, to a certain extent, the Nordic countries, were not prepared to accept the frictions attending the transfer to a single market. On account of their strongly dirigistic economic order, they preferred to realize the objectives underlying economic integration within their national borders.

The reluctance of the United Kingdom led the other countries to conclude that further economic integration would have to be restricted to a small inner group of countries. It was Jean Monnet, then head of the French *Commissariat au Plan*, who made an attempt to bring France and Germany closer together. He drew up a plan providing for international control of heavy industry. According to Monnet, this was the only way to prevent future armed conflicts between the two countries. His intention was to ultimately come to a political federation via this functionalist approach. His fellow countryman, the Minister of Foreign Affairs Robert Schuman, presented this approach as the official French plan for economic and political cooperation. During the negotiations the United Kingdom strongly opposed this *fait accompli*, whereas the Benelux countries, Germany and Italy appeared to sympathize with the plan. It was this group of countries, including France, which founded the European Coal and Steel Community (ECSC) on 18 April 1951. Less than two years later, a single market for coal and steel between the six countries would be realized. The ECSC was the first European community, comprising a supranational High Authority, a Council of Ministers and two supervisory bodies: the Common Assembly (Parliament) and the Court of Justice.

Considerations of a political nature played an important role in the ECSC Treaty. As Schuman stated, the newly formed community would lay the basis for a European federation which would be essential for maintaining peace. Here was the essence of what has since been known as the 'Community method', namely the development towards a political union by means of step-by-step integration of economic sectors. This type of institutional structure contained in the ECSC Treaty represented a major element in the 'gradualist' approach towards political unification. In addition, notably the larger Member States had their own political motives for participating. Germany's approval, for instance, cannot be seen independently of its pursuit of emancipation and re-entry as a full member into the community of nations. In France and Italy, a certain lack of confidence in the capacities of the national governments paved the way for participation in supranational governing bodies.

The outbreak of the Korean War in June 1950 gave new impulses to political integration. The United States urged the Federal Republic of

Germany to make a military contribution to the North Atlantic Treaty Organization (NATO), established in 1949.[8] The French authorities were of the opinion that remilitarization of Germany should take place within the framework of a supranational military organization, in a community modelled in accordance with the then proposed ECSC. In May 1952, a treaty, known as the Pleven Plan,[9] was concluded — again on the initiative of Monnet — providing for the establishment of a European Defense Community (EDC), followed shortly afterwards by a proposal from the Common Assembly of the ECSC for the establishment of a European Political Community.[10] During the preparatory meetings, the Dutch delegation stressed repeatedly that the political competences of such a community should be linked to an economic programme. In mid-1953, this position resulted in the Beyen Plan, presenting proposals for horizontal economic integration via a customs union to a common market attended by the establishment of a political community.

The plan, presented by the Dutch Minister of Foreign Affairs Jan Willem Beyen, in February 1953, clearly illustrates the major extent to which the motives for European integration used in the 1950s were underlain by what had generally become known as the Cold War. His plan mentioned a threat to Western European civilisation, both from within 'where fascist or communist powers try to destroy the democratic character of the political structure of Western European countries' and from without where 'the Soviet Union and its satellites try to annex the territories of these countries'. The best line of defence against the first threat was economic and social soundness, achieved by a gradual improvement of prosperity. The second aspect was more complicated. This concerned the 'existence of a common enemy, the awareness of a joint threat by a concrete danger'. That danger had already strengthened the feeling of European unity. Protection of that unity required military integration. This was, however, not considered possible without political integration, which in turn would not make sense without economic integration. The report stressed that only a lively feeling of unity would induce Member States to make sacrifices required for integration. In other words: if the feeling of unity was to be nurtured and strengthened 'economic, military and political integration must be regarded as three aspects of the same problem, the problem of European integration'.[11]

It was evident, however, that sentiments in Europe were not yet ripe for the link between political and economic integration, advocated fiercely by Beyen.[12] Unlike the Schuman Plan, the Pleven Plan also encountered opposition within the Group of Six, not in the least from France, where political parties fiercely opposed the remilitarization of Germany and European control of the French armed forces. When, after lengthy discussions, the Treaty was finally ratified two years later by the parliaments of four countries, the reason originally underlying the Treaty had disappeared with the termination of the Korean conflict. In August 1954, the French Assembly consequently rejected the proposal. This did not only mark the end of the EDC, but also of political union. What remained was a somewhat half-hearted compromise in the form of the Western European Union (WEU),[13] which was established in 1955 on the initiative of the United Kingdom. In this body, control of the armed forces remained the province of the national authorities. For Germany, regulations were included in order to prevent uncontrolled military expansion there.

The rejection of the EDC marked the failure of the attempts made by the European governments to create a new level of sovereignty and to abandon the road of particularism and nationalism. The real reason for this failure was the slowing down of the policy of supranational integration in the six ECSC countries after the death of Soviet leader Stalin. 'From the very beginning it was evident that his successors did not wish to continue the hard policy of the Cold War .... Facing a difficult period of internal readjustments, they inaugurated the policy of distension. And with the lessening of the danger of war, the enthusiasm of many for European unification also diminished.'[14] However, the rejection of the EDC Treaty strengthened the case for the gradualist approach to European unity.

7.3 The conference of Messina

The WEU could have served to bridge the political gap between the United Kingdom and the ECSC countries. However, the negative attitude of British politicians in this respect strengthened the will of the Six to increase economic cooperation. Again Monnet — this time in his capacity as President of a Committee of Action for the United States of Europe — assumed the pioneering role. There was general consensus on the strategy that, on the basis of the existing ECSC Treaty, a step forward towards cooperation should concern the field of sectoral integration. In this respect, Monnet's idea was to lay down supranational regulations on atomic energy, which were to serve as a driving force of general economic cooperation. The main objective of the five other countries was to realize a common market. They did not reject the French sectoral plan, provided that it would concur with the pursuit of this common market. Although the method of sectoral integration was considered preferable to the horizontal method applied within the OEEC, there were certain objections to an expansion to sectors other than coal and steel. One objection was that it would be difficult to neutralize the differences in economic levels between the countries concerned. Furthermore, there was the risk that successive integration would lead to unequal distribution of either the advantages or the disadvantages of integration and that the delimitation of sectors would be arbitrary. The former Italian Minister of Foreign Trade Ugo La Malfa (1957) ascribed the fundamental weakness of functional integration to the fact that there was no assurance that such integration would last, since there would always be a possibility that the agreements reached would be terminated and there would not be any common institutions endowed with sovereign powers to guide and preside over the process of functional integration.

The most difficult problem was the organizational structure of European institutions and regulations regarding the relationship with the various national governments. In general, a European Federation was considered the ultimate objective. In this Federation, certain government tasks would be centralized within the European governing body while the national governments would maintain their autonomy in other areas, coordinating their activities on a European level, where necessary. However, the drawback of the functionalist approach was that, according to prevailing needs, all kinds of individual institutions would be set up for the various sectors of the European economy without any guarantees that they would cover the whole area while, on the other hand, the risk of overlapping and insufficient democratic control was not inconceivable. Therefore, it was required that the complex of bodies would be streamlined so as to ultimately result in a unity. The complexity of such a process became evident when, in the mid-1950s, the plan to accommodate the OEEC and the High Authority of the ECSC under the political wings of the Council of Europe failed, due, among other things, to the different geographical scope of the existing bodies.

Although the establishment of a supranational organization had repeatedly been considered, it became increasingly clear that such a plan had to be abandoned. On the initiative of the Benelux countries, in June 1955, the Ministers of Foreign Affairs of the six ECSC countries convened in Messina, on the island of Sicily. They deemed it recommendable to temporarily abandon the objective of political integration. The avowed aim of these countries was, as they declared in a resolution adopted on 2 June 1955, a wide form of integration through developing common institutions, the progressive fusion of their national economies, the establishment of a common market and the progressive harmonization of their social policies. It was decided to establish a committee which, under chairmanship of the Belgian Foreign Minister Paul-Henri Spaak was to examine a fresh advance towards the building of Europe.[15] The committee opted for closer economic cooperation, without ruling out further sectoral economic integration. The essence was a common market, with the French and German superpowers haggling over conditions. In exchange for a tariff-free market for its extensive range of manufactures, Germany would grant French overseas territories access to the common market through an association agreement. In addition, Germany would support the French plan for a joint agricultural policy, which was primarily aimed at protecting France's domestic agricultural sector.

In Rome, on 25 March 1957, the Ministers of the six ECSC countries signed treaties on the creation of two new communities: the European Atomic Energy Community (Euratom) and the European Economic Community (EEC), the latter envisaging integration of the whole economy and not simply part of it.[16] In his retrospective of European cooperation, at the twenty fifth anniversary in 1982, the then Belgian chairman of the European Council of Ministers Leo Tindemans called these treaties the basis for a 'Europe of economists and technicians'.[17]

Notes

1. Spinelli (1957), p. 53.
2. On 28 March 1947, the Economic and Social Council of the United Nations established the Economic Commission for Europe, in which the European Member States of the United Nations participated as well as the United States, the Soviet Union and its satellites.
3. In London, in September 1944, the Dutch and Belgian Governments in exile signed a Monetary Agreement and a Customs Union Agreement, which signalled the beginning of the Benelux. Luxembourg was represented by the Belgian Government.
4. The Treaty on the Organization for European Economic Cooperation (OEEC) was signed by seventeen countries, all but one receiving aid under the Marshall Plan: Austria, Belgium, Denmark, France, Germany, Greece, Iceland, Ireland, Italy, Luxembourg, The Netherlands, Norway, Portugal, Sweden, Switzerland, Turkey and the United Kingdom. Spain joined in 1959.
5. On 5 May 1949, the Council of Europe was established by means of a Treaty signed in London by the Benelux countries, Denmark, France, Ireland, Italy, Norway, Sweden and the United Kingdom. The Federal Republic of Germany, Greece and Turkey joined the Council in May 1951.
6. Hartog, F. (1951), 'Moeilijkheden op weg naar een economische eenheid van Europa', The Hague: Ministry of Economic Affairs (Pierson Foundation, integration) 325/I '51.
7. On 1 July 1950, the Member States of the OEEC established the European Payments Union as a clearing house for payments and settlements so as to promote multilateral transactions, with credit facilities being provided by the United States. The Union was liquidated in 1958, after countries had effectively restored the convertibility of their currencies. It was replaced by the European Monetary Agreement by sixteen of the previous Member States plus Spain (Fritz Machlup, 1979).
8. On 4 April 1949 in Washington, the NATO Treaties were signed by the following twelve countries: Belgium, Canada, Denmark, France, Iceland, Italy, Luxembourg, The Netherlands, Norway, Portugal, the United Kingdom and the United States. On 9 May 1955, the Federal Republic of Germany joined NATO.

9. Named after the French Prime Minister René Pleven.
10. The United Kingdom was also invited to take part in the negotiations about the EDC but refused.
11. De Nederlandsche Bank/Beyen, J.W. (1953), Grondslagen voor het Nederlandse standpunt met betrekking tot het vraagstuk der Europese integratie.
12. Although a convinced advocate himself of political integration, Beyen found it hard to convince the Dutch Government to follow his policy. At that time, the cabinet deemed only economic integration worth considering (Kersten (1992), pp. 5–6).
13. The WEU Treaty was in fact the *pièce de résistance* of the 1948 Treaty of Brussels between the Benelux countries, France and the United Kingdom, aiming at mutual military assistance and cooperation in an economic, political and cultural respect.
14. Spinelli (1957), p. 61.
15. According to the Spaak Report, the final objective of European integration was that Europe should try to regain some of its past influential position, geographically located as it was between the powerful United States and the communist bloc.
16. Together with the ECSC Treaty, the Acts on the establishment of the two new Communities constitute the European Charter which became effective on 1 January 1958.
17. 'Europese Raad. Herdenking 25 jaar EG' (1982), *Keesings Historisch Archief*, 23 April, p. 265.

8 THE PERIOD 1957–1969: THE COMMON MARKET

8.1 Economic cooperation

The Treaty of Rome of 1957 may be regarded as the constitution of the EEC. The history of its origins explains both the economic and political character of this Community. Article 2 of the Treaty formulates its objective as follows: 'It shall be the aim of the Community, by establishing a Common Market and progressively approximating the economic policies of the Member States, to promote throughout the Community a harmonious development of economic activities, a continuous and balanced expansion, an increased stability, an accelerated raising of the standard of living and closer relations between its Member States'. The last addition expresses the political character of the EEC Treaty.

By contrast with the OEEC, the supranational element was, in principle, incorporated in the Treaty. In this respect, there was even some consistency in the development from the ECSC to the EEC. In addition to a similar institutional structure (Council, Commission, Assembly and Court), the Treaty held out the prospect of decision-making on the basis of a majority of votes and of binding stipulations and competences. On the other hand, the principle of supranationality had been weakened considerably. For instance, in its relationship with the Council of Ministers, the European Commission had less far-reaching decision-making competences than the High Authority of the ECSC.[1] This weakening was also reflected in the fact that a large number of matters remained unregulated, leaving decision-making to the Council of Ministers. In fact, this development reflected the struggle during the negotiations between The Netherlands and the other Member States. This concerned the Dutch preference for a prominent role for the Commission versus the French dislike of too much emphasis on the supranational element.

The Treaty provided for the establishment of a common market, to be realized during a transitional period of twelve years, divided into stages of four years each. The core of that common market was the customs union which meant that all Member States would gradually reduce their mutual tariffs to nil after 1 January 1959. In addition, the movement of services, persons and capital would also be liberated, albeit that the Treaty only discussed this in vague terms. This objective was to be stimulated in an active and positive manner by means of 'a policy ensuring the optimal satisfaction of needs within the Community'. Although, in principle, the latter did not rule out interference by the Community in the internal economic policies of its Member States, the Treaty did not include provisions which would have eroded national sovereignty in respect of economic, fiscal, monetary or social policy. This was illustrated by the vague stipulation that the Member States were to consider cyclical policy 'a matter of common interest'. In the monetary field, this autonomy was retained as reflected in the article on exchange rate policy. This was also considered 'a matter of common interest', even though coordination of this policy was provided for by the establishment of the Monetary Committee, which was assigned an advisory role.

Although the principle of national sovereignty was maintained unimpaired in the Treaty, the statement of David Coombes (1970) may be fully endorsed that '. . . there was a strong feeling among the founders of the Community that economic union would be only the first step towards other kinds of integration. Although not particularly articulate in this respect, the Treaty is clearly about much more than the removal of restrictions to trade and the evolution of common economic policies and is intended to lead eventually to a political union. This arises mainly from the dynamic nature of the Community. Not only does its constitution contain a number of inarticulate premises which invite interpretation and development, but the whole idea of having common economic policies implies transferring a substantial power of discretion to new centres of decision-making at a Community level.'[2]

The realization of the customs union went off well. In this connection, a positive effect was exerted by the Benelux Treaty, signed in 1958 and effective as from 1 November 1960, which safeguarded the customs union between Belgium, The Netherlands and Luxembourg by means of a decision to maintain a common exchange rate vis-à-vis third countries.[3] Other, no less important, stimulating factors included the generally-felt vigorous post-war economic recovery, as well as the support of the United States for the new Community. Consequently, internal trade tariffs could quickly be reduced, so that the customs union had already been realized on 1 July 1968, marking the start for a common agricultural policy. On 31 December 1969, the transitional period formally ended, fully in conformity with the time schedule mentioned in the Treaty.

After the signing of the EEC Treaty, the division in terms of trade policy between the countries of Western Europe gained a formal character. Opposing to the Group of Six, a Group of Seven was formed, which under British leadership set up the European Free Trade Association (EFTA)[4] in early 1960. The EFTA was established after attempts had failed to create a larger free-trade zone, in which not only the EEC Member States could participate, but also the United Kingdom and other OEEC countries.[5]

Meanwhile, further steps had been taken in an organizational respect to provide a more solid basis for economic and monetary cooperation. After the establishment of the Monetary Committee in March 1958,[6] the Committee of Central Bank Governors was founded in 1964. Its objective was to improve coordination of monetary policy among the Member States. The Committee should hold 'consultations concerning the general principles and the broad lines of policy of the central banks' and 'exchange information at regular intervals about the most important measures that fall within the competence of the central banks, and examine those measures'.[7] On this occasion, the Council of Ministers also decided that future adjustments of exchange rate parities would only be implemented after mutual consultations. The Monetary Committee laid down a procedure for preliminary discussions and examined how the various national monetary policy instruments might be better harmonized.

8.2   The notion of political union

The most important obstacles to further integration were of a political nature. Due to its position within the Commonwealth, the United Kingdom was unwilling to participate in political integration with the countries on the European Continent. France, on the other hand, was starting to regard the EEC as a means to exercise political leadership in Europe against the background of Germany's weak international political position. With that in mind, France, under President Charles de Gaulle, launched a new plan — known as the Fouchet Plan[8] — in the early 1960s for political union. It would take the form of intergovernmental institutions enabling a joint defence and foreign policy. This plan met with strong opposition from The Netherlands, which, for fear that it would be hedged in by France and Germany, demanded that the United Kingdom would also participate in the negotiations. France obstinately refused this, even after the United Kingdom officially announced in 1961 — one year after the start of the EFTA — that it was willing to open negotiations on accession to the EEC.[9] At that time, Germany, under leadership of Chancellor Konrad Adenauer sided with France, but came later into conflict with France on account of the fact that it supported the North Atlantic Treaty.

The idea of a political union ultimately stranded during a conference of the Member States held in Luxembourg in September 1966, where notably France stated that, from now on, it would reserve the right of veto in matters of 'vital national importance'. This was the origin of the (unwritten) rule that decisions deemed of 'vital importance' by a country required a unanimous vote in the Council of Ministers.[10] Due to this veto, not only the Fouchet Plan was off, but also the Commission's proposal to combine the realization of the customs union with a strengthening of the budgetary competences of the European Parliament. This so-called Compromise of Luxembourg of 1966 seriously hampered the pursuit of European economic and political integration. Its exercise of the right of veto placed France in an increasingly isolated position, from which it did not break free until De Gaulle's resignation in April 1969, after he had failed to obtain a majority in a referendum on proposals for political reform.

Notes

1. In the case of Euratom and the EEC, the main powers of decision are shared between the independent Commission and the Council of Ministers representing the Governments of the Member States. The formal powers of the ECSC were entrusted largely to a single independent High Authority.
2. Coombes (1970), pp. 54–55.
3. In view of the fact that the ambitions of the Benelux countries did not go beyond the objectives formulated in the EEC Treaty no separate institutional provisions were required in the Treaty.
4. The European Free Trade Association was founded by Austria, Denmark, Norway, Portugal, Sweden, Switzerland and the United Kingdom by the Convention of Stockholm of 1960, providing for the gradual reduction and possibly abolition of quotas and tariffs on imports from Member States but leaving their tariffs on imports from other countries unaffected.
5. In 1961, the OEEC was incorporated into a new organization: the Organization for Economic Cooperation and Development (OECD), including the United States and Canada. In the following years, Australia, Japan and New Zealand joined this organization. The European countries declined the Soviet Union's offer to collaborate with the new organization for fear of a duplication of the United Nations.
6. On 18 March 1958, the Monetary Committee was established consisting of representatives of the Ministries of Finance and the central banks of the EEC members whose task it was to coordinate their monetary policies.
7. Bainbridge with Teasdale (1995), p. 34.
8. Named after Christian Fouchet, a French diplomat and minister under De Gaulle.
9. This request was followed by Denmark and Ireland, while countries such as Austria, Sweden and Switzerland argued for an arrangement providing for the possibility of association with the EEC.
10. According to the Treaty, qualified majority voting should become the rule for most issues, even those of political importance, after the end of the transitional period. During the first eight years of the Community, unanimity was still required for a large number of decisions, but after July 1966, majority voting became applicable in a larger number of cases.

9 THE PERIOD 1969–1979: A DIFFICULT ROAD TO EMU

9.1 Promising agreements in The Hague

The year 1969 promised to mark a turning point in the process of European integration. This turnaround was heralded by a memorandum of the Commission,[1] urging for a reinforcement of economic and monetary policy coordination and an examination into the possibility of abolishing the mutual fluctuation margins of the currencies participating in the European Community (EC).[2] In order to achieve this objective, not only the Commission, but also countries such as Belgium, Germany and Luxembourg submitted plans for the realization of Economic and Monetary Union (EMU). Already in October 1962, the Commission, then chaired by Walter Hallstein had proposed to achieve monetary union in three stages before the end of 1971. However, this proposal never met with response.

Characteristic for the new plans was that neither the proposal of the Commission, nor the plans proposed by Belgium and Luxembourg explicitly admitted that the pursuit of full EMU would have implications for the Treaty of Rome. Only the German Minister of Economic Affairs Karl Schiller recognized that monetary union was a 'prelude' to political integration. The Dutch Minister of Finance Hendrikus Johannes Witteveen (1970) carried Schiller's reasoning a step further by noting, in May 1970, that political integration is a precondition for a real monetary union. Apart from that, both Germany and The Netherlands continuously stressed the need for parallelism between monetary and economic integration.

On 1 and 2 December 1969, the plans had a sequel in The Hague, where on the initiative of the newly elected French Head of State Georges Pompidou a Summit between the six Government Leaders was held. They agreed to give European integration a new impulse by pursuing a simultaneous enlargement and deepening of the Community. As for the first aspect, negotiations would be opened, not only with those countries which had applied for membership earlier but also with the other EFTA Member States. In this connection, the Foreign Ministers were given the assignment to study the best way of achieving progress in the matter of political unification within the context of enlargement. Where the element of deepening was concerned, EMU was formulated as the final objective of the Community, which should be realized in stages, to be completed in 1980. It was agreed that, in the course of 1970, a commission chaired by the Prime Minister of Luxembourg Pierre Werner would draw up a plan (Werner Report) for the realization of EMU in stages.

The notion of economic and monetary unification was clearly more far-reaching than agreed in the Treaties of Rome. The Werner Report, published in October 1970, provided for a realization in stages of EMU within a period of ten years. In the first stage, exchange rate fluctuations would have to be restricted. Furthermore, the national governments were to make a start with the coordination of monetary and fiscal policies. In the course of stage two, exchange rate fluctuations and divergences in price movements would have to be reduced further. The third stage provided for irrevocably fixed exchange rates, the abolition of national foreign exchange restrictions and the establishment of a community-wide system of central banks after the example of the American Federal Reserve System. The size of the EC budget could then be raised drastically, while the task of coordinating national fiscal and expenditure programmes would be assigned to the Community.

The Dutch Prime Minister Piet de Jong voiced his Government's willingness to take far-reaching measures to achieve economic integration, as this was considered a decisive step towards political unification. This exactly reflected the views of Werner, who described EMU in his report as 'un ferment pour le développement de l'union politique dont elle ne pourra, á la longue, se passer'.[3] This view was closely in line with that of the German authorities. In an interview, Werner admitted in so many words that '... in the last analysis, the development which has started, aims at political unification of Europe. It is true that we need not achieve a European confederation or federation tomorrow. But to arrive at this ultimate goal, we must first take the step of creating an economic and a currency union'.[4] Doubts regarding this 'ultimate goal' later resulted in less far-reaching demands in reports on economic and monetary union in respect of the transfer of competences in the field of budgetary policy.

According to the Werner Report, the objective of EMU was to 'guarantee the growth and stability within the Community, to strengthen the Community's contribution to global economic and monetary equilibrium and to turn the Community into a stable bloc'. In order to achieve this, important policy decisions should be taken on a Community level. This required competences to be transferred to the Community, with democratic control on decision-making being exercised by the European Parliament, whose competences would be expanded. Stage one was to commence on 1 January 1971 and last three years. During that period, one of the main tasks would be to strengthen the coordination of the Member States' economic policies. Another objective was to complete the preparations for adjusting and supplementing the EEC Treaty. The aim was to convene an intergovernmental conference in accordance with the provisions of the EEC Treaty, well before the first stage expired. The Report did not consider it possible to draw up a fixed schedule for the entire project. Some flexibility was required so that the time frame could be adjusted on the basis of experiences gained during stage one. Decisions about later stages would have to be taken at the end of stage one. Consequently the proposals contained no more than general policy recommendations for the achievement of the 'ultimate goal'.

The Werner Report was based in fact on a compromise between Germany and France. Germany had consistently stressed that the establishment of EMU would have no chance of success without the simultaneous creation of a political union. Consequently, the first stage would be used for drawing up a new treaty laying down the ultimate stage and the intermediary stages. The French seriously questioned whether matters should be taken this far. The French Minister of Finance Valérie Giscard d'Estaing preferred to concentrate on measures aimed at realizing the first stage. As there was little controversy on this matter, he anticipated that this would have the most concrete results. As to the ultimate objective, he foresaw complex problems, which could not be solved at that time. Therefore, a very broad definition of the ultimate stage would have to be drawn up, free from dogmatism. The compromise reached was that a recommendation was included in the Report to prepare an amendment of the Treaty during stage one.

In October 1970, the Commission submitted proposals to the Council which were rather different from those made in the Werner Report. The proposal to round off the preparations for the required amendments of the Treaty during stage one had been cancelled. Before 1 May 1973, the Commission itself would, at its own discretion, put forward proposals for the measures to be taken after the completion of stage one. Moreover, the objective of the amendments — the completion of EMU — was not mentioned. With regard to the transfer of national powers in the final stage, the Commission continued to express itself in vague terms. The Werner Report explicitly mentioned a community-wide system of central banks and a centre for decision-making on economic policy, politically answerable to the European Parliament. The Commission stated that, by implementing the stages of the plan, the Community might have the required competences in the economic and monetary field, 'democratically controlled on a Community level'. However, the European Parliament was no longer mentioned. It was furthermore striking that the proposals with regard to the coordination of budgetary policy hardly received any attention. On the other hand, in the monetary field the Commission went so far as to propose that consultations between central banks regarding monetary policy should be underlain by a decision of the Council.

During the discussions on the objectives of EMU, notably The Netherlands was of the opinion that the ultimate objective was to be defined clearly before discussing the stages to realize this objective. The Governor of De Nederlandsche Bank Jelle Zijlstra warned the Dutch Minister of Finance Witteveen against the dangerous misconception that in the monetary area progress would be stronger because political problems in this area would be less complicated than elsewhere. In order to achieve progress on monetary integration he considered it essential that economic integration would be reinforced and that the political and institutional structure of the Community would be strengthened.[5] In this respect, the Dutch views on the integration process were in line with those held in Germany.

The Council of Ministers agreed to the recommendations of the Commission, provided that the project would enjoy the permanent political support of the governments. However, it became evident that political support did not mean the same in the various countries. According to Germany (supported by The Netherlands), the Community was to obtain more competences for an effective coordination of national economic policies. France, on the other hand, focused on increased coordination of monetary policies in advance and was not willing to take any steps beyond those required for stage one.

The Council Resolution of 22 March 1971 referred to the political willingness of the Member States to 'achieve an economic and monetary union within the next decade according to the plan effective as from 1 January 1971'.[6] According to this Resolution, the essential elements of such a union were:

(a) the total and irrevocable convertibility of the participating currencies, abolition of the fluctuation margins of the exchange rates and the permanent fixing of exchange rate relationships, in short all prerequisites for the introduction of a single currency;

(b) a system of central banks, which would later incorporate the announced European Monetary Cooperation Fund (EMCF);

(c) taking the 'required decisions' on economic policy on a Community level with Community institutions being granted the required competences;

(d) subjecting the single policy conducted within the framework of economic and monetary union to consultations with, and decision-making and supervision of, the European Parliament.

Due to pressure, notably exerted by France, the Council of Ministers ultimately left the final date of EMU open, restricting itself to stage one, which would cover the period from 1 January 1971 to the end of December 1973. A plan of action was set up for this period, laying down, among other things, that the Member States would aim at narrowing the fluctuation margins of their exchange rates.[7] Furthermore, agreement was reached on the implementation of a short-term credit facility — the short-term monetary assistance — which should be used between the central banks for the settlement of debts resulting from interventions on the foreign exchange market. In this respect the EMCF would initially be restricted to clearing of foreign exchange interventions ensuing from the narrowing of the margins and management of short-term monetary assistance.

In the political field, a commission had been established shortly after the Summit at The Hague, which, under the chairmanship of the Belgian diplomat Viscount Etienne Davignon would put forward proposals for cooperation. However, its recommendations went considerably less far than those made in the Fouchet Plan. The result was that, from then on, the Foreign Ministers of the Member States would meet twice a year.

9.2 Grave monetary tensions

The decisions mentioned above were taken in a climate of rising international monetary tension. The sustained capital outflow from the United States to Germany resulted on 10 May 1971 in the decision by the German authorities to no longer observe the parity of the *Deutsche* mark vis-à-vis the dollar, a decision which was followed by The Netherlands. France reacted with irritation and informed the other Member States that it would not participate in the meetings of the Committee of Central Bank Governors and the Monetary Committee as long as the fixed parity of the two currencies had not been restored. Meanwhile, in August 1971, the United States had suspended the dollar's gold convertibility. Following elaborate international consultations and the temporary floating of the dollar, in December 1971, the so-termed Smithsonian Agreement was concluded. The dollar was devalued by 7.89 per cent. In addition, the countries participating in the IMF again fixed their exchange rates vis-à-vis the dollar, this time, however, at a fluctuation margin of 2.25 per cent instead of the formerly agreed maximum margin of 1 per cent above or below parity.

For the EC currencies, the new IMF agreement implied a widening of their mutual bandwidth to 4.5 per cent, as a result of which fluctuations of the EC currencies vis-à-vis each other might even rise to 9 per cent in time. In the midst of this tumultuous situation, the Benelux countries decided to restrict the fluctuation margin between their currencies to 1.5 per cent on both sides of parity.

The solution of the European currency problems was fully in the hands of France and Germany. Meanwhile, regular two-day consultations were held between the two countries. At the end of 1971, they came to the conclusion that a rapid return to realistic exchange rates with fixed parities was required. It was stressed that priority would be assigned to Franco–German cooperation — the soul of the European edifice. After this stage had been completed, rapid action could be taken. On 21 March 1972, a new exchange rate agreement was reached with the mutual bandwidth between the EC currencies being narrowed to 2.25 per cent, effective as from 24 April of that year.[8] This marked the birth of what was called the 'Snake in the Tunnel'. In addition to the six EC countries, other participants in this arrangement were Denmark, Ireland and the United Kingdom, which, together with Norway, had signed the Treaty for accession to the Community in January 1972. In view of the fact that the Benelux countries decided to continue their obligation to restrict the bandwidth to 1.5 per cent, a 'Worm' crawled within the 'Snake'.

The agreement on the narrowing of the margins implied that the former system of interventions in one central currency (the dollar) had been abandoned. The fact that from then on interventions could be made in any EC currency forced the system to increase coordination between the central banks. In addition to the narrowing of the margins, it had therefore also been decided to lay down general binding directives for such coordination. This was why the French Minister of Finance and future successor of Pompidou, Giscard d'Estaing, called it the most important step forward since The Hague. His opinion was shared by Werner who stated that the decisions of 21 March 1972 marked the start of stage one of EMU. He had hardly spoken these words when the next currency crisis manifested itself. In June 1972, Denmark and the United Kingdom left the 'Snake', while Germany attempted to put up a defence against the sustained capital inflow by means of imposing more stringent foreign exchange restrictions.[9] In the following months, the only ray of hope came from Denmark, which re-entered the 'Snake' in October 1972, as a result of the positive outcome of the referendum on accession to the EC held there.

On 1 January 1973, Denmark, Ireland and the United Kingdom officially joined the European Community. France's insistence not to let sterling float too long left a bitter taste due to a new currency crisis in February. This ensued from the decision of the United States, taken in February 1973, on a new devaluation of the dollar, this time by 10 percent,[10] followed shortly afterwards by the decision to let the dollar float vis-à-vis the most important other currencies. This dealt the deathblow to the Smithsonian Agreement. By contrast, the 'Snake', though slightly leaner, stayed alive. After Italy had left the arrangement in February 1973, the Council of Ministers declared the other currencies in the 'Snake' to uphold their exchange rate agreements vis-à-vis each other's currencies. As a result, the 'Snake' no longer writhed within the 'Tunnel', but was able to move freely. 1 June 1973 marked the start of the EMCF, which offered financial support when interventions were required in defence of the exchange rate of a certain currency in the 'Snake'.

9.3 Insufficient coordination of monetary policy

Ultimately, the objective of the Werner Report came to nothing. In the course of 1973, the European Commission concluded that economic and monetary policy coordination during stage one had been insufficient. Notably the way in which Europe had reacted to the oil crisis had accelerated the monetary growth rate in various Member States, causing inflation to rise to a very alarming rate. According to the Commission, the reduction of inflationary tendencies should, even more than before, be the primary objective of future economic policy, with a stricter monetary policy only becoming redundant if expenditure could be slowed down via budgetary policy.[11] In view of the above, the Commission put forward proposals for stage two of EMU, which would take three years. One of these proposals comprised a directive for stimulating growth, price stability and employment, designed as a start for harmonization of economic and political instruments. Another proposal concerned the transfer in stages of reserves held by the Member States, starting with 20 per cent on 1 January 1974. Within the Council, France and The Netherlands opposed the Commission's ideas. The Netherlands, which regarded the democratization of the organizational structure as a prerequisite for the next steps towards integration, advocated an interim period during which a number of matters which had received insufficient attention in stage one could be settled.

During the conference of the Heads of State and Government Leaders in Paris in October 1972, the progress in respect of EMU was an important item on the agenda. According to the participants, decisions were to be taken in the course of the following year to enable the transition to stage two of the unification process on 1 January 1974. Emphasis was placed on parallelism of economic and monetary integration. Another aspect concerned the reformulation of the objective of the Community: the realization of the European Union (EU) no later than at the end of 1980. In this connection the EMCF was characterized as the forerunner of a federal system of central banks to be realized in the final stage of EMU. With regard to political coordination, the *communiqué* only contained the recommendation that, in the future, the Ministers of Foreign Affairs should meet four times a year instead of two. It was further agreed that they were to indicate in a report how they intended to improve political cooperation.

At the end of 1973, the Council decided to implement 'a' second stage instead of 'the' second stage effective as from 1 January 1974. This meant that the turning point in the process of European monetary integration had proved to be an illusion. The attempt made by Werner to deepen the Community by means of supranationalization of the Treaty of Rome had foundered on the Member States' lack of willingness in practice even though they had declared the opposite on theory. In the same year, a new Community body was established, although this was not included in the articles of the Treaties of Rome. At the request of France, it was decided that the Heads of State and Government Leaders of the EC countries would convene regularly, in principle twice a year, in the future. The intention of this European Council was to lift decisions on the principles of EMU to the highest level, with these decisions subsequently being elaborated by the Council of Ministers and the Commission. Such meetings were deemed so important that it was decided one year later, in Paris, that the European Council would convene at least three times a year, and more often if necessary, both with the Council of Ministers and the European Commission so as to reinforce political convergence.

In the years to come, inadequate policy coordination would again lead to new currency tensions. Characteristic in this connection was that in January 1974, domestic considerations forced France to leave the 'Snake' while in November Italy, for the same reasons, had to have recourse to the mechanism for medium-term financial assistance created by the Governments of the EC Member States in March 1971. Again, two-day consultations were repeatedly held between France and Germany, this time often behind closed doors between Giscard d'Estaing and Schmidt, who had been well-disposed towards each other from the start. On 10 July 1975, France returned within the 'Snake' at its old parity. The same year, a report was published by a working group, set up by the Commission and chaired by the Frenchman Robert Marjolin, whose task it was to breathe new life into EMU. He noted that the efforts undertaken since 1969 added up to a failure: 'Europe is no nearer to EMU than in 1969. In fact, if there has been any movement, it has been backward: national economic and monetary policies have never in 25 years been more discordant, more divergent than they are today.'[12]

Diverging policies were also to blame for other plans coming to little or nothing. The vaguely formulated European Union in the Report published by the Belgian Prime Minister Tindemans in early 1976, remained just as unattainable as the more concrete approach of the Spierenburg Commission, named after the then Head of the permanent Dutch Delegation at the European Communities. However, the exact meaning of the notion European Union remained unclear. The Dutch Minister of Foreign Affairs Max van der Stoel stated that it was unrealistic to include the objective of a federal Europe in the structure of the European Union: 'How much some Europeans, or probably many of them, regret it, the concrete and harsh reality forces us to recognize that we are far from achieving a federal or supranational Europe and that it is uncertain whether developments will turn in that direction.'[13] An alternative was presented in the *All Saints' Day Manifesto*, in which a group of nine international monetary experts advocated the introduction of a parallel currency, which would serve as the pulling force of monetary union.[14] None of these plans presented a tailor-made solution to the problem of integration as long as the Member States were unwilling to accept the attending political and institutional consequences. In March 1976, the Member States had to face this painful truth, when France was again forced to leave the 'Snake'. In October of that same year, the Deutsche mark appreciated against the currencies of the Benelux and the Scandinavian countries.[15] On that occasion, the Benelux countries abandoned their mutual exchange rate agreement causing the 'Worm' in the 'Snake' to disappear. It was the then director of the *Dresdner Bank* Jürgen Ponto who stated, in June 1977, that Europe lacked the courage to face the fact that inadequacy of economic convergence was at the heart of the monetary tensions.[16] According to Ponto, this was reflected in wage increases in the past three years, totalling 90 per cent in Italy, 66 per cent in France and 28 per cent in the Federal Republic of Germany.

9.4　The road to the European Monetary System

Finally, European policy-makers achieved a breakthrough in the deadlock by means of a reinforcement of the 'Snake' arrangement so as to pave the way for EMU. The solution was found in the Tindemans Report mentioned earlier, which advocated a differentiated approach, with the 'Snake' — being the key to foreign exchange stability — constituting the basis. As a response, it was stressed during the European Council Meeting in The Hague at the end of November 1976, that EMU was to be achieved in stages, with the existing treaties forming the basis for a new policy. It was indeed Tindemans who first suggested a Europe of two speeds, even though he deliberately did not use this phrase. According to his Report, the Member States complying with the criteria would join together via a common plan of action, while the other countries which, for valid reasons, could not participate would remain entitled to join at a later stage.

In early 1978, the discussion flared up again[17] due to a statement of the then President of the European Commission Roy Jenkins who declared before the European Parliament that he envisaged an important role for EMU in the creation of more stable relationships within the international monetary system. A plan of action, presented during an interim meeting by Vice President François-Xavier Ortoli had been received hesitantly by the Council of Ministers, as notably Germany saw it as a clever manoeuvre of the weaker Member States to obtain more credits from the German Government without having to make any concessions to tighter economic and monetary integration. During the European Council meeting in Copenhagen in April 1978, future monetary policy was the main item on the agenda. A commission was set up, consisting of high officials from France, Germany and the United Kingdom, who were to examine how monetary stability could be increased. Meanwhile, discussions were taking place within the Council of Ministers and the Monetary Committee on alternative forms of monetary cooperation. It was, however, again the combined Franco–German efforts which would lead to concrete results.

On 23 June 1978, the German Chancellor Schmidt and the French President Giscard d'Estaing exchanged views on what was to happen with regard to European integration. Both statesmen had taken this decision,[18] because the Commission appointed at Copenhagen had met five times without having achieved any results, notably on account of the rather sceptical attitude of the United Kingdom. What Schmidt and Giscard envisaged became clear during the European Council meeting in the North German town of Bremen in July 1978 where they put forward a proposal for a new monetary system which was to lead to a 'zone of monetary stability' in Europe. Once again, it became evident how quickly and smoothly plans, which in the context of the Community were generally attended by lengthy, intensive and very laborious discussions, could be put to action as soon as the two superpowers, France and Germany, had the political will to act.

So far, Germany, supported by The Netherlands, had always regarded monetary union as the crown on economic convergence, by contrast with France which — together with the United Kingdom and the European Commission — mainly considered monetary unification as the driving force of economic convergence. That Germany took sides with France this time was mainly related to its wish to stabilize the Deutsche mark vis-à-vis the currencies of its European trading partners on account of growing uncertainty about the effectiveness of US economic policy. The changed attitude of Germany prompted discussions on the exchange rate system dominated by a fundamental difference of opinion as to the question how 'symmetrical' such a system should be. France, Italy and the United Kingdom shared the view that the surplus countries (in this case mainly Germany) should bear a higher adjustment burden than they had in the 'Snake' arrangement. France proposed to achieve this objective by means of a system of unilateral interventions vis-à-vis a third currency instead of the 'Snake' system of simultaneous intervention. France wanted to name this currency after an old French coin, the *écu*. Germany rejected this proposal, but ultimately agreed to the Belgian compromise of combining the two systems.

Pursuant to the resolution of 5 December 1978, the European Council decided to introduce the European Monetary System (EMS) as from 1 January 1979, in which all Member States would participate, including the United Kingdom which announced to join the exchange rate mechanism of the EMS at a later date. The regulations to be implemented would be valid for the duration of the transitional period of two years. Within that period, the regulations would be consolidated into one final system. Due to the problems caused by France in the field of the common agricultural policy several weeks later, the EMS entered into force with a lag on 13 March 1979.[19]

Notes

1. This memorandum is known as the Barre Plan, named after the then Vice President of the European Commission Raymond Barre.

2. Pursuant to the Merger Treaty of 18 April 1965, the three Communities merged as from 1 July 1967. This was reflected in the establishment of one Council of Ministers and one European Commission. The amalgamation of the European Coal and Steel Community, the European Atomic Energy Community and the European Economic Community was reflected in the new name: European Community (EC).

3. Werner Report (1970), 'Report to the Council and the Commission on the Realization by Stages of Economic and Monetary Union in the Community', *Bulletin of the European Communities*, Supplement II, October, Luxembourg.

4. Werner (1971), p. 15.

5. This had been formulated even more drastically by Zijlstra's predecessor Marius W. Holtrop (1949). With reference to the discussion on tighter cooperation in the context of the Benelux, Holtrop remarked that 'a common currency and a common central bank were only possible within a political union and not within an economic union' (on Holtrop, see Wim Vanthoor, 1991).

6. Council-Commission of the European Communities, Resolution of the Council and of the Representatives of the Governments of the Member States of 22 March 1971, regarding the realization in stages of Economic and Monetary Union in the Community, Section I, *Official Journal of the European Communities*, C. 28, 27 March 1971.

7. The Werner Report suggested narrowing the fluctuation margin of the currencies of the Member States of the EC as from 1972 to ± 0.5 per cent instead of the

actual margin of ± 0.75 per cent against the dollar. By way of a trial, the central banks had been invited to already narrow the margin to ± 0.6 per cent at the start of stage one of EMU.

8. The 'Snake' arrangement implied that the maximum fluctuation between the EC currencies remained restricted to 4.5 per cent in time.

9. Partly under pressure of the Governor of the *Deutsche Bundesbank* Karl Klasen the more stringent foreign exchange restrictions (the so-termed *Bardepot*) resulted in the resignation of the German Minister of Finance Schiller. He was succeeded by Helmut Schmidt.

10. Due to the devaluations of 1971 and 1973, the official dollar price per ounce fine gold had risen from $ 35 in 1946 to $ 42.2 in February 1973.

11. As a guideline for monetary policy, the Commission had urged a reduction of monetary growth which should equal the increase in gross national product plus a 'normative price rise' to be determined within the framework of economic policy.

12. Marjolin Study Group (1975), On Economic and Monetary Union 1980, Commission of the EC, II/675/3/74, Brussels, March, p. 6.

13. Van der Stoel (1976), p. 45.

14. Published in *The Economist*, 1 November 1975, London.

15. On 18 October 1976, the Benelux currencies were devalued by 2 per cent, the Danish crown by 6 per cent and the Norwegian and Swedish crowns, which had meanwhile joined the 'Snake', by 3 per cent, all vis-à-vis the Deutsche mark.

16. On 28 August 1977, Sweden left the 'Snake'. A realignment took place, with the Norwegian and Danish crowns being devalued by 5 per cent against the other currencies in the 'Snake'.

17. On 13 February 1978, the Norwegian crown was devalued by 8 per cent, after which Norway left the 'Snake' on 12 December of that year.

18. In Germany, Chancellor Willy Brandt was succeeded by the Minister of Economic Affairs and Finance Helmut Schmidt on 16 May 1974.

19. At the end of 1978, France urged the abolition of the system of Monetary Compensatory Amounts (MCAs), a system of subsidies and levies ensuring that prices for agricultural products are virtually the same in all Member States. In March 1979, the Ministers of Agriculture complied with France's wish by deciding that the system of the MCAs would gradually be abolished.

10 THE PERIOD 1979–1989: THE EUROPEAN MONETARY SYSTEM

10.1 The regulations of the EMS

The core of the EMS is the Exchange Rate Mechanism (ERM). Within this mechanism, a central role is played by the European Currency Unit (ECU), whose value and composition would, at the start, be the same as that of the European Unit of Account which had been used so far.[1] The ECU would be used (1) as the *numéraire* in the ERM, (2) as the basis of a deviation indicator, (3) as unit of account in the intervention and credit mechanism and (4) as a mutual means of settlement. For every EC currency, a central rate vis-à-vis the ECU was calculated. These central rates were used to determine a grid of bilateral central rates. The fluctuation margin was set at 2.25 per cent on either side of the central rate with the proviso that currencies which had been floating before 1979 could opt for a margin of 6 per cent on either side. In order to make settlement of intervention balances possible, the Member States created an initial stock of ECUs by means of transfers of 20 per cent of their national gold and dollar reserves to the EMCF in the form of revolving swaps. The existing credit mechanisms[2] available within the Community were expanded and would only be consolidated into one single fund during the ultimate stage of EMU. Within two years of the start at the latest, the agreements and institutions were to be consolidated in a European Monetary Fund (EMF).

The EMS, as launched in Bremen, did not go beyond the transitional stage which would end on 19 March 1981. Although mention was made of the ultimate stage, no final date was laid down. Nevertheless, the suggestion that every two year 20 per cent of the national reserves would be pooled presumed the achievement of the ultimate stage of the EMS within a period of ten years, or in other words in March 1989.

10.2 Stage one

The EMS was no more than a technical construction, in which, on account of the Belgian formula,[3] the ECU in practice did not play the central role envisaged at the time the system was established. As such, the EMS was only a weak reflection of the objectives envisaged in the Werner Report. Parallelism between monetary and economic integration was not mentioned, let alone the need to transfer national competences to the Community or the possibilities of a political union. Under the new system, the Member States were allowed to adjust their exchange rates in the case of serious balance-of-payments disturbances owing to divergent policies. Furthermore, a large number of restrictions continued to be applicable to capital transactions. They provided these countries with a certain room for manoeuvre to conduct divergent policies to such an extent as not to give rise immediately to speculative capital movements in anticipation of exchange rate adjustments.

The functioning of the EMS did not detract from the condition that the underlying objective of a 'zone of monetary stability' only had a chance of success if the economies of the Member States would be better harmonized as well as the policies to be conducted to achieve this. However, that time had not come yet. When — fully in line with the agreement — the functioning of the EMS was assessed in September 1979, the existing exchange rate ratios proved not strong enough to counter the currency speculation provoked by this examination. In the same month, the central rate of the Danish crown was devalued by 5 per cent and that of the other EMS currencies by 2 per cent vis-à-vis the Deutsche mark. Two months later, interventions were again required in the form of a second devaluation of the Danish crown by 5 per cent. The renewed tensions were again due to diverging policies. The small Member States, as well as Italy, showed excessive budget deficits, the result being that the Community did not succeed in narrowing the mutual inflationary differentials.

Of a more fundamental nature was the divergence between France and Germany which was slowly becoming apparent. In February 1981, the Deutsche mark, strengthened by the policy of interest rate rises conducted by the Bundesbank, took over the top position from the French franc within the EMS. The French currency had to abandon this position under the influence of the election outcomes in favour of the socialist President François Mitterand. On 5 October of that year, a general realignment weakened the position of the French franc. Vis-à-vis the Deutsche mark and the Dutch guilder, the central rates of the Belgian franc, the Danish crown and the Irish pound were devalued by 5.5 per cent, while the French franc was devalued by 8.5 per cent. The same was true for the Italian

lira which had already been devalued in March by 6 per cent. Against
this background, the European Council concluded that the transition to
a consolidated system, which was to take place after two years, had to
be postponed for an indefinite period of time. After three years of EMS,
monetary stability was as far off as ever. Between late 1978 and late 1981,
the average inflation rate within the Community had risen from 7.8 per
cent to no less than 11.8 per cent. The accumulated price increase varied
from 14 per cent in Germany to 54 per cent in Italy while France, at 36
per cent, took the middle position. Although the rising rate of inflation
also reflected the effects of the second oil crisis, the Council referred to the
situation as a serious structural crisis.

The realignment of 1983, which meant a devaluation of the French
franc and the Dutch guilder vis-à-vis the Deutsche mark[4] may be considered the turning point in the history of the EMS. It caused France to
change course drastically to an economic policy aimed primarily at price
stability, the objective being to stabilize the relationship between the franc
and the Deutsche mark. The French authorities thus hoped to eliminate
the inflationary differential with Germany, which was regarded as one of
the essential goals of the process of financial and economic restructuring
and deregulation initiated by the Government of Prime Minister Jacques
Chirac. The positive effect of his new policy on the EMS was given an
additional impulse in September 1987, when the EC Ministers of Finance
and the Central Bank Governors reached an agreement in the Danish
town of Nyborg on regulations for monetary policy adjustments in times
of exchange rate tensions. It was agreed to create adequate interest rate
differentials on time and to fully use the maximum bandwidth under certain
circumstances so as to reduce speculative capital movements. The objective
of these agreements was to discourage speculation within the EMS by
turning it into a costly, risky and consequently not very profitable business.[5]
After that, the EMS sailed into calmer waters, at least until the autumn
of 1992.

10.3   A new European élan

In the Council Resolution establishing the EMS, EMU was no longer mentioned as the ultimate objective. The term was re-introduced by the German Foreign Minister Hans-Dietrich Genscher who, in early 1981, unfolded
a plan to bring Europe nearer to its citizens. This objective was to be
realized through the establishment of a European Union, in which economic
integration was to run more parallel with political cooperation. The so-
called Genscher Plan was intended as a European Act, in which cooperation

in the field of foreign policy and security would be mentioned explicitly as a matter to be dealt with by a Council of Foreign Ministers to be set up. The Act itself would assign new competences to the European Parliament and explicitly include cooperation in the areas of politics and security. In addition, the decision-making procedures within the Community would be adjusted as the Council of Ministers would only accept the veto right of Member States in exceptional cases. The latter clashed with the wishes of Denmark, France and the United Kingdom, which did not want to give up this right. A deadlock was created as The Netherlands refused to sign a document in which the veto right — regarded as a violation against the original EEC Treaty — would be laid down formally.

As a result of the realignment of October 1981, the French Minister of Finance Jacques Delors stated in Luxembourg that he considered the transition to EMU unrealistic. Instead, he advocated a reinforcement of the ECU and of monetary cooperation, referring to the periodic monetary consultations between France and Germany. During the European Council meeting in London shortly afterwards, Germany, this time supported by Italy's minister of Foreign Finance Emilio Colombo, presented a proposal (the Genscher–Colombo Plan) to draw up a European Act to convert the relationships between the countries of the Community — now totalling ten[6] — into a European Union, in which economic and monetary integration were to run parallel with political cooperation.

The discussion stranded amidst various exchange rate adjustments which took place in 1982.[7] Typical in this connection were the proposals put forward by the Commission in March 1982, which implied no more than a technical expansion of the EMS. These plans were rejected by Germany, whose Minister of Finance Gerhard Stoltenberg stated that although Germany wished to preserve the EMS, a further expansion of the system was not deemed desirable at that time. During the European Council meeting of June 1983 the European Act disintegrated, under British pressure, into the so-termed Solemn Declaration on European Union. Although this document hardly changed the actual situation, the matter regarding the decision-making procedure ultimately served as a stone thrown in the water whose ripples would soon change into waves on which a new European élan would float to the surface.

The first step in that direction was taken at Fontainebleau, where a committee was set up in mid-1984 on the initiative of the European Council (the Dooge Committee). This Committee consisting of personal representatives of the Heads of State and Government Leaders was given the assignment to draw up proposals for improving cooperation, both in the area of economic and political cooperation. In its Report, the Committee concluded that an Intergovernmental Conference was to be held in order to decide whether a new EC Treaty should be drawn up or whether the existing Treaty should be amended. Further, it was to become a general rule that the decisions of the Council of Ministers would be taken by a majority of votes. Unanimity would have to be reserved for decisions regarding completely new policies. Totally unexpectedly, the Committee received back-up from France and Germany, which, in June 1985, one day before the European Council Meeting at Milan, presented a draft treaty for the European Union focusing notably on political cooperation. During the European Summit of mid-1985,[8] a majority of six countries (the old Six) voted in favour of the Intergovernmental Conference, while the other four shared the view that such reforms could also be achieved by means of a stricter application of the existing Treaty.

Shortly afterwards, the newly appointed President of the Commission Delors made a subtle attempt to include the EMS in the EC Treaty. This entailed the risk that the competence of the EC institutions in respect of Community issues would thus be ratified, and the Commission would be entitled to take initiatives with regard to the future development of monetary cooperation within the Community. It goes without saying that this proposal received very little support from the other EMS partners, Germany, The Netherlands and the United Kingdom in particular. The British Chancellor of the Exchequer Nigel Lawson called the proposal wholly unacceptable. According to him, the inclusion of any kind of monetary dimension in the EC Treaty would mean a legal change which would have political consequences.

During the European Council meeting held in early December 1985 in Luxembourg, agreement was reached on a limited revision of the EC Treaty and a draft treaty on European political cooperation. On this occasion, the Council expressed agreement with the proposal in the Commission's White Paper published in June 1985 to complete the Single Market within the Community before the end of 1992. The Intergovernmental Conference on the amendment of the Treaty — also attended by Spain and Portugal which would join the EC on 1 January 1986 — convened five times and was rounded off in December 1985 with a final agreement which was only slightly different from the agreements in principle reached at Luxembourg, on the understanding that the revision would be laid down in a 'Single European Act'.

In legal terms, the issue boiled down to an amendment of the Treaties in respect of the ECSC, the EEC and Euratom. The main revision concerned the EEC Treaty, where — in accordance with the Commission's White Paper — the completion of the internal market before the end of 1992 was laid down as the official economic target. The consequent strengthening of the Community's decision-making powers was achieved by including an amended decision-making procedure in the Act. In respect of various Treaty articles, decisions would be made with a 'qualified majority of votes' instead of by the 'unanimity of votes' previously required. For the rest, only modest revisions were made. The European Parliament was admittedly given a greater influence, but the Council of Ministers continued to have the final say. As to monetary matters, the Act contained a reference to EMU in the preamble, although an article (102a) added to the EEC Treaty provided that 'insofar as further development in the field of economic and monetary policy necessitates institutional changes', the Treaty will have to be amended. This meant renewed ratification by the national parliaments. The Act also referred to the EMS, even though it was not provided for by European law. Finally, in its 'common provisions' the European Council was institutionalized while European political cooperation was made official as part of the Act. After the Act had been signed by nine out of twelve Member States in February 1987, the other three, Denmark, Greece and Italy soon followed, so that the Act could enter into force on 1 July 1987.

The significance of the Single European Act was not to be overestimated, as evidenced by the comment of the then Dutch Minister of Foreign Affairs Hans van den Broek who called the Act nothing more than an instrument of the political will to introduce the Single Market. According to the Vice President of the European Parliament Siegbert Alber, some matters were described in such a way that there was room for serious misinterpretation. This democratic shortcoming had not been overcome by the signing of the Act. He formulated this problem as follows: 'A principal obstacle is the European dimension of the national governments, which is either totally lacking or only present in a very rough form. Nobody is against Europe in its defence of national interests. But many of these so-called national interests are in practice no more than provincial egoism. Everybody is in favour of Europe as long as it is to his benefit and as long as it does not cost anything.'[9] Like Van den Broek, he stressed the importance of the goodwill of those who are responsible for the process of European integration.

In addition to the common market for goods already achieved, completion of the Single Market entailed that efforts would be made to realize the complete freedom of intra-Community movements of services and capital transactions. In addition to the political will, the 'zone of monetary stability' intended to be created through the EMS was seen as a major prerequisite for the Single Market which would be seriously jeopardized if diverging policies pursued by the Member States were to undermine price and exchange rate stability. That this prerequisite had not been fulfilled as yet became evident when, in April and August 1986 as well as in January 1987, new realignments of the exchange rates participating in the EMS took place.[10]

The next step was taken by Delors, who had meanwhile been appointed Chairman of the Commission. In February 1987, he presented a plan to the European Parliament on the reorganization of the Community. Since 1973, six new Member States had joined the Community, all with their own economic and political set-up, while the basis of cooperation within the community had not been changed accordingly. In the view of Delors, the decision on the Single European Act was to have a sequel in the adjustment of the financial structure of the Community, with expenditure on agriculture being reduced from 70 per cent to slightly over 50 per cent of the EC budget. That this was a tricky matter became evident when the European Council meeting of the end of 1987 at Copenhagen had to be adjourned on account of the lack of political will to take decisions on this matter. Nevertheless, in February 1988, agreement was reached regarding the reduction of expenditure on agriculture. When the Council of Ministers issued a directive to generally liberalize capital movements on 24 June of that year — full liberalization would enter into force on 1 July 1990 — Delors considered this an excellent opportunity for closer monetary cooperation in Europe, because the Ministers also agreed to the inter-institutional accord on budgetary discipline he had advocated. Until 1992, the own funds of the Community would be expanded slightly, while ceilings would be implemented annually with regard to Community expenditure.

Within the EMS, not only France, but also other EC countries had meanwhile realized that the regulations as applied by the countries with hard currencies, Germany and The Netherlands, were essential for a successful anti-inflationary policy. However, this also became a serious dilemma. On the one hand, they recognized the role of the Deutsche mark as the stability anchor, while on the other hand they held the view that a one-sided orientation towards German policy was no longer required now that inflation rates had dropped so dramatically.[11] This was the reason why France attempted to lift European integration above the existing institutional framework of the EMS. The objective was to set up a system in which decisions would no longer be made by the central bank of one specific country, but by all central banks together. To that end, the French authorities proposed, since the autumn of 1987, to discuss the possibility of further monetary integration. In Germany, Minister Genscher, relying mainly on political considerations, welcomed the French suggestion, unlike the Bundesbank, which opposed this idea.

The Franco-German plan was one step further on the road to EMU. The next step was taken in June 1988 when the European Council decided in Hanover to set up a Committee of Experts for the management of Economic and Monetary Union. This Committee largely consisted of the

Central Bank Governors of the twelve Member States, chaired by Delors. It was laid down that this Committee would submit concrete proposals to the European Council, which would convene in Madrid in 1989. On this occasion the United Kingdom declared that neither a European Central Bank nor a European currency were required for the establisment of EMU. By contrast Germany would regard proposals in that direction as the crown on progressing monetary cooperation. Apart from that, the Council of Ministers approved, in June 1988, a new mechanism for financial support of the balance of payments, in which the medium-term credit mechanism and the instrument of the community loans were combined. The new mechanism would be financed from loans raised in the capital market by the Community. By way of exception, recourse could also be had to the EC Member States. The use of the new mechanism is subject to conditions regarding the economic policy conducted by the relevant Member States.

Notes

1. The European Unit of Account (EUA) was introduced by way of Council Regulation of 23 October 1962 within the framework of the common agricultural policy. The value of this EUA was identical to 0.88867088 gramme fine gold. In 1971, the EUA was no longer used in the agricultural sector as a result of the introduction of the monetary compensatory amounts. However, the EUA was used for conversion of transactions effected by the European Fund for Monetary Cooperation established in 1973. With the signing of the Treaty of Lomé (cooperation between the EC and 64 developing countries in Africa, the Caribbean and the Pacific) on 28 February 1975, the EUA was defined for this purpose as a basket of the currencies of the EC Member States: Deutsche mark: 0.828, sterling: 0.0885, French franc: 1.15, Italian lira: 109, Dutch guilder: 0.286, Belgian franc: 3.66, Luxembourg franc: 0.14, Danish crown 0.217, Irish pound 0.00759. As from 1 January 1978, the budget of the Community was denominated in EUA. The ECU, which was introduced in 1979 was made up of the same currencies.

2. In addition to the (unrestricted) very short-term credit facility related to currency interventions within the framework of the common exchange rate mechanism, the credit mechanism of the Community consisted at that time of (a) the short-term credit facility (three months with a possibility of extension) and (b) monetary assistance in the medium-term (two to five years). The short-term credit facility ensued from the agreement between the central banks of 9 February 1970 and was later adjusted repeatedly as a result of the accession of new Member States and the raising of the credit facility. Monetary assistance in the medium-term concerned an agreement between the governments of the EC Member States of 22 March 1971.

3. According to the Belgian compromise, the ECU is used within the EMS as the basis for the so-termed divergence indicator. As before in the 'Snake' arrangement, the intervention obligation only applies if the intervention limits vis-à-vis the other currencies in the ERM have been reached.

4. On 21 March 1983, the central rate of the Deutsche mark revalued by 2 per cent vis-à-vis the Dutch guilder. Furthermore, the Irish pound devalued by 7 per cent, the French franc and the Italian lira by 6 per cent, the Belgian franc by 2 per cent and the Danish crown by 1 per cent vis-à-vis the Dutch guilder.

5. One aspect of this so-called Basle/Nyborg agreement was the expansion of the financing possibilities within the EMS. The duration of financing of interventions in EMS currencies against their intervention rates was extended by one month to at most three and a half months. Furthermore, the ceiling for the amount which may be extended automatically, was doubled. In addition, the principle was adopted that intramarginal interventions are eligible for financing to a considerable amount, provided that this is not in conflict with the domestic monetary policy of the creditor country. Finally, the central banks stated that they were willing to accept ECUs for the settlement of interventions in excess of the existing limit of 50 per cent as long as this would not lead to an unbalanced composition of the national reserves.

6. On 1 January 1981, Greece had joined the EC.

7. On 22 February 1982, the Danish crown was devalued by 3 per cent and the Belgian franc by 8.5 per cent vis-à-vis the other currencies participating in the ERM. On 14 June, the French franc was subsequently devalued by 10 per cent, the Italian lira by 7 per cent and the other EMS currencies by 4.5 per cent vis-à-vis the Deutsche mark and the Dutch guilder.

8. On 1 July 1985, Greece joined the EMS, though it did not take part in the ERM. On 22 July of the same year, the Italian lira was devalued by 8 per cent and the Greek drachme by 15 per cent vis-à-vis the other EMS currencies.

9. 'Verklaring van de heer Siegbert Alber, vice voorzitter van het Europese Parlement', *Bulletin van de Europese Gemeenschappen* (1986), 2, p. 9.

10. On 7 April 1986, all other EMS currencies were devalued against the Deutsche mark and the Dutch guilder: the French franc by some 6 per cent, the Belgian franc and the Danish crown by some 2 per cent, the Italian lira and the Irish pound by some 3 per cent. On 8 August 1986, the Irish pound was devalued by another 8 per cent against the other EMS currencies. On 12 January 1987, the Belgian franc was devalued by 1 per cent, the French franc, the Italian lira, the Danish crown and the Irish pound by 3 per cent against the Deutsche mark and the Dutch guilder.

11. In the whole OECD area, in 1986, the average price rise was limited to 2 per cent, the lowest rate since 1961 (*Annual Report*, De Nederlandsche Bank 1986, Chapter 6, p. 133).

11   THE PERIOD 1989–1995: THE WAY TO 'MAASTRICHT' AND ITS REPERCUSSIONS

11.1   The elaboration of proposals in the Delors Report

In April 1989, Delors presented his Report[1] containing concrete proposals for the realization of Economic and Monetary Union to the Ministers of Finance. The core of that Union was fixed, invariable exchange rates. According to the Report, this implied a single monetary policy, to be conducted by a European System of Central Banks (ESCB) whose task would be to ensure the maintenance of domestic price stability. In order to be able to perform this task, the system would operate independently of national governments. Furthermore, it underlined parallelism between economic and monetary integration. Within this framework, binding regulations had been formulated with regard to the size and financing of national budget deficits. The way to EMU would be realized in three stages, for which, however, no deadline was set. During the first stage, coordination of economic and monetary policies should be strengthened within the existing institutional framework. In addition, preparations were to be made for an amendment of the EEC Treaty. This amendment would be required in respect of the envisaged transfer of sovereignty in the monetary and budgetary policy sphere at a later stage, which could only be decided on by unanimous vote. Stage two would start with the entry into force of the new Treaty. During this stage, the ESCB would be established although the transfer of monetary competences should not take place before the third and final stage which would mark the start of EMU with irrevocably fixed currencies.

Like Werner, Delors held the view that EMU could be realized within a period of ten years. He also advocated a gradual approach in three stages, with focus being placed on the harmonization of budgetary policy. The difference between Werner and Delors was that the latter went less far in transferring national competences in this area to the Community. Delors recommended that the Community would oversee the overall economic situation, assess the consistency of developments with regard to common objectives and formulate guidelines for policy. This related to the implementation of limits on national budget deficits and the prohibition against monetary financing of these deficits by central banks. In other words, the Delors Report provided for a partial centralization of budgetary policies and for full centralization of monetary competences by the establishment of a whole new institution — the ESCB — which was to conduct a common monetary policy for the whole Community. In view of the fact that the latter aspect would corrode national monetary sovereignty, this proposal implied an amendment of the EEC Treaty.

From the very beginning, the United Kingdom was the most fervent opponent among the EC Member States of the proposals presented by Delors. The British government did not want to hear of an amendment of the Treaty of Rome and, through Prime Minister Margaret Thatcher, expressed its view that neither a European central bank nor a European currency were required for the realization of EMU. The Prime Minister opposed the stipulation in the Report that acceptance of stage one of EMU, in which, incidentally, the United Kingdom was willing to participate, automatically implied acceptance of the next two stages. The option created by Delors to transfer national competences to a supranational institution were interpreted by the British Chancellor of the Exchequer Lawson as the formulation of the ultimate objective of EMU: a political union, some sort of United States of Europe. In his opinion, this structure was not in line with Britain's views on the EC.[2]

During the Summit held in Madrid in June 1989, the Council managed to reach a compromise. It was decided that stage one of EMU would start on 1 July 1990, the date of the entry into force of the directive on the general liberalization of capital transactions in Europe, and that negotiations for stages two and three would start as soon as possible. In addition, 'competent bodies' would make preparations for an Intergovernmental Conference which was to decide on the amendments of the EEC Treaty. In December of the same year, it was agreed in Strasbourg that this conference would be held before the end of 1990. Attention was paid separately to the political aspect of the pursuit of integration in a proposal launched by France and Germany in April 1990. The proposal suggested that democratic control be increased, thus giving political unification its legal basis, as from 1 January 1993. In a letter to their colleagues, the German Chancellor Helmut Kohl and the French President François Mitterand suggested that a conference be held on European Political Union (EPU) concurrent with the discussions on EMU. In Dublin, Ireland, the twelve Member States formally agreed to hold parallel Intergovernmental Conferences to amend the EEC Treaty in order to pave the way for the introduction of a political, economic and monetary union.

11.2   Stage one of EMU and new proposals for EPU

In anticipation of the European conferences, stage one of EMU started on 1 July 1990. At that time, much progress had been made with regard to the liberalization of capital movements. France had already abolished all restrictions, while countries such as Italy and Spain had eased their regulations. In the spring of 1990, the segregation between the free and regulated exchange market was abolished in Belgium and Luxembourg, marking the end of the double market system in both countries.

With the start of stage one of EMU, the discussion on the future of EMU flared up again. According to the European Commission, stage two was to enter into effect on 1 January 1993 and would last as briefly as possible. During the meeting at Rome, the EC ministers nevertheless failed to reach agreement on the speed of integration. Spain suggested that stage two should start on 1 January 1994, the transition to stage three lasting some five to six years. In September 1990, the Deutsche Bundesbank also became involved in this discussion, imposing the absolute demand that EMU be based on economic and financial harmonization between the Member States. The Bundesbank referred to anti-inflationary policy and a contractually imposed budgetary discipline. In the final stage, which, according to its Governor Karl-Otto Pöhl could be achieved through a lengthy transitional process, the independence of the ESCB had to be guaranteed, so as to enable it to impose sanctions on governments not observing budgetary discipline. During a special conference of the European Council in Rome, in October 1990, virtually all Member States expressed their approval of the Spanish proposal for the start of stage two. The only exception was the United Kingdom, which held on to the proposal made earlier for a gradual transition to EMU by means of the introduction of a so-termed 'hard' ECU, which would circulate concurrently with the existing twelve national currencies and whose creation and regulation would be the province of a European Monetary Fund.

A week before the start of the Intergovernmental Conference, the German Chancellor and the French President put forward new proposals for the way in which political unity could be realized. Mention was made of a common foreign and security policy which would culminate in a common defence policy. Furthermore, they held the view that a clear organizational relationship with the WEU should be established, as the WEU would ultimately form part of the new political union. Their proposal was criticized among other countries, notably by The Netherlands, which feared a disturbance of the balance between the existing Community bodies.

11.3   The Intergovernmental Conferences

On 15 December 1990, the European Council opened the two Intergovernmental Conferences in Rome. It was confirmed that, in the year to come, the two conferences would perform their activities concurrently, the objective being to round off both meetings before the end of 1993. During the discussions on EMU it soon became evident that there was no support for the proposal of the United Kingdom on a parallel currency. France and Spain advocated the hardening of the existing ECU as the forerunner of the ultimate European currency. Spain regarded the European Monetary Institute (EMI) to be established during stage two, as the clear forerunner of the ESCB. In line with this view, Germany expressed its preference for a politically-independent institution which would lay down its commitment to conduct an anti-inflationary policy in its Statute. Contrary to this view was the French proposal which emphasized the need for full democratic control of the future central bank, to be assigned to the existing EC Council of Ministers. In March 1991, Luxembourg, which held the chairmanship of the EC in the first half of 1991, came up with a compromise. The EC governments would lay down general directives for exchange rate policy, to be implemented after consensus was reached with the ESCB, while maintaining the objective of price stability.

On 19 March 1991, within the European Parliament, Governor Pöhl of the Deutsche Bundesbank again warned against a premature introduction of the European currency. He referred to the Deutsche mark which was introduced in former East Germany in mid-1990. This had been effected 'without any preparations or any possibility of adjustment, and thus at the wrong exchange rate'. He called the result 'a disaster as the new currency had fully destroyed the competitive position of the area'.[3] That same month, the German Foreign Minister Genscher visited his French colleague Roland Dumas to discuss the timetable for the various stages of EMU. In a joint statement, they suggested that the ESCB be set up at the beginning of stage two. During stage three, the new independent central bank would bear sole responsibility for the implementation of monetary policy and the stability of the currency. In general, this proposal was in line with the agreements which had been reached between the majority of the Member States during the extraordinary meeting of the European Council in Rome in October 1990. In general, the draft Statute of the ESCB, which had meanwhile been drawn up by the Committee of Central

Bank Governors, was consequently adopted. The system would consist of the ESCB, whose primary task would be the conduct of monetary policy aimed at price stability. The ESCB would be composed of the ECB and the central banks of the participating Member States, which would only have an implementing task. The ESCB will have an independent position and is not allowed to follow instructions by national governments or community bodies. During the meeting of the EC Council of Ministers in April 1991, Germany, supported by The Netherlands, made the reservation that stage two would only enter into effect in 1994 if the national economies had been harmonized sufficiently, notably where control on inflation and balance-of-payments deficits were concerned. With regard to the further development of EMU, the European Council agreed in June 1991 to postpone final decisions on this matter until the Summit at Maastricht scheduled for the end of 1991.

The Intergovernmental Conference on EPU started with the proposals of Genscher/Dumas. The bottom line of their plan was that the Heads of State and Government Leaders of the Community would decide by unanimous vote which aspects of foreign policy would form part of the common policy. Subsequently, a decision would be taken by the Council of Ministers, with a majority of votes. With regard to the WEU,[4] the two Ministers suggested that it might initially serve as a link between the EC and NATO, but would be incorporated into the Community before 1998 at the latest (when the 50-year old Treaty of Brussels expires). These proposals were rejected by non-WEU members, as well as by The Netherlands and the United Kingdom which feared that their ties with the United States would be disrupted. In February 1991, the matter was discussed by the ministers, who reached a provisional accord, with the WEU acting as intermediary between the European Union and NATO. In March, The Netherlands presented a proposal in which the European role in the field of security and defence was linked to the North-American political and military obligation in respect of the security in Europe.

Again it was Luxembourg which tried to reach a compromise on political cooperation. In a draft treaty it indicated which national competences could be amalgamated in a foreign and security policy. Unanimity had to be the rule, though decisions on joint action would be taken by a majority of votes. Proposals regarding the role of the European Parliament and the Council of Ministers incorporated in the draft treaty gave rise to warnings by the Chairman of the Commission, Delors, for the real danger that the Commission would degenerate into nothing more than a secretariat for the Council of Ministers. In June 1991, the ministers of Foreign Affairs and Defence of the WEU Member States convened. It was stressed that the objective of the WEU was to contribute to solidarity within the Atlantic Treaty. However, it was also accepted that a European political unity implies a clear identity in the field of security and defence. Shortly afterwards, the Luxembourg government presented a new draft treaty, containing the reference to a 'federal objective' of the EPU, to a Commission slimmed down from seventeen to twelve members and to a European Parliament which would have a say in the Council of Ministers. The new draft treaty assumed that decisions regarding areas falling within a common security policy would be taken on the basis of consensus in the European Council. After that, decisions on these matters would be taken by a weighted majority in the Council of Ministers. The decisions made by the EPU on defence matters could be taken wholly or partly by the WEU, but this issue is to be re-examined in 1996 when the treaty as a whole will be subject to scrutiny.[5] In line with the proposals put forward by Luxembourg, The Netherlands also presented a draft treaty, maintaining the federal objective and advocating the transfer of more competences to the Commission and the European Parliament. This Parliament should be entitled to veto bills proposed by the Council of Ministers with a majority of votes. This draft treaty triggered fierce criticism from the other Member States, of which some (including the United Kingdom) considered it too radical, while others (including France) considered it insufficiently far-reaching. Ultimately, the Ministers rejected the proposal. As for EMU, the European Council decided to postpone final decisions on controversial issues until the European Council meeting at Maastricht to be held in late 1991.

11.4 The Maastricht Treaty on European Union

The European Council meeting held on 9 and 10 December 1991 at Maastricht marked the formal end of the two Intergovernmental Conferences. Agreement was reached on a framework for a Treaty on the European Union. This Treaty, better known as the Maastricht Treaty, comprises the agreements on political, economic and monetary union.[6] Prior to this, on 2 May 1992, a treaty was signed in Oporto, Portugal, establishing the European Economic Area (EEA), a free trade area between the fifteen Member States of the EU and Iceland, Liechtenstein and Norway. Switzerland signed the Treaty, but rejected it by referendum at the end of 1992. Furthermore, on 1 January 1993, the Single Market was virtually completed between the EU countries which meant that the majority of the 300 legislative proposals to remove the physical, technical and fiscal barriers to the free movement of goods and services had been adopted and incorporated into Member States' legislation at an accelerated pace.

In addition, the free movement of capital had also been realized very rapidly. As the EEA Treaty entered into force on 1 January 1993, most Single Market legislation applies throughout the European Economic Area. However, it should be borne in mind that the completion of both the European Economic Area and the Single Market was not tantamount to economic union. The decisive move towards such a union will have to be brought about through the convergence of economic, and especially, budgetary policy to be conducted by the Member States.

The amended EC Treaty regards EMU as one single process, which implies that the Member States accept this Union as the final objective. Meanwhile, on 1 January 1994, stage two of EMU entered into effect, which is regarded as a period of increasing convergence, particularly with regard to price stability and sound public finance. As from the same date, the Frankfurt-based European Monetary Institute was started. The EU Treaty further stipulates that the Commission and the Council of Ministers will inform the European Council of the progress achieved by the Member States on the way to EMU. In order to assess such progress, a number of convergence criteria has been laid down regarding inflation, long-term interest rates, the financial deficit and the national debt ratio.[7] Before 31 December 1996, the European Council will decide whether the economies of a majority of the Member States meet these criteria. This means, among other things, that the Member States aim at preventing excessive budget deficits in stage two, with a procedure being included in the Treaty applicable if a Member State does not meet that criterion. However, the consequent sanctions do not yet apply in stage two. If the majority of the Member States meet the convergence criteria at the end of 1996, the European Council may decide with a qualified majority to start stage three. If no date has been set for stage three by the end of 1997, the ESCB shall be established around 1 July 1998, with stage three entering into force on 1 January 1999 at the latest for the countries complying with the criteria at that particular point in time. The ESCB will be a politically independent supranational institution, whose primary objective will be to achieve price stability. In view of the above, it has been determined that, with regard to exchange rate policy, the EC Council of Ministers may give general directives to the ESCB which may not be in conflict with the objective of price stability and are not binding upon the ESCB.

In the agreement on European Political Union the term 'federal' has disappeared. On the other hand, emphasis is placed on the so-termed principle of 'subsidiarity', with decisions being taken at the lowest possible level. Although the Treaty introduces new areas falling within the scope of the competences of the Community, the common policy in the areas of foreign affairs, defence and justice will constitute separate 'pillars' beyond the scope of the Community's normal decision-making mechanisms. According to the Treaty the EU is to show its identity in the international field 'by implementing a common foreign and security policy of which the possible introduction of a common defence policy will form part'. On this basis, the Council of Ministers will decide when a matter is the subject of possible Community action.

Once such a decision is made, the size, objective and duration of the action must be described accurately. The Council must subsequently take decisions on any matters occurring during the course of the action by a qualified majority of votes. Common action is binding upon the Member States. Furthermore, the WEU, which is called 'an integral component of the development of the Union' is requested to elaborate on and implement decisions by the Union which have much ground in common with defence policy. Finally, the possibility has been left open to revise the stipulations laid down in the Union Treaty, insofar as they relate to the WEU. This may be effected on the basis of a report to be drawn up by the Ministers on behalf of the European Council in 1996, assessing the progress made, and experiences gained, with respect to the integration of the WEU into the Union.

The stipulations regarding the political union are clearly less far-reaching than those on EMU. No detailed time schedule has been laid down, the position of the WEU remains vague, the competences of Community institutions have not been delineated, the issue of unanimity remains unchanged whereas no more than informal recommendations have been made on the reinforcement of the roles of the European Parliament and the European Commission. It was the Bundesbank which immediately denounced this shortcoming. With reference to the signing of the Treaty on 7 February 1992 by the Heads of State and Government Leaders of the twelve Member States, the Bundesbank urged the national governments to work out the structure of the envisaged political union in greater detail as it considered political unification a prerequisite for a successful EMU. Before ratifying the Treaty, Germany caused some commotion when, in the summer of 1993, some Members of Parliament brought a case before the German Constitutional Court in Karlsruhe in order to force a decision on whether the transfer of national competences to a supranational institution is in conflict with the democratic principle embedded in the national constitution. In early October 1993, the Court ruled that this was not the case, thus paving the way for the entry into effect of the Maastricht Treaty.

The ruling of the German Court put the meaning of the Treaty in perspective in the sense that the Court reserved the right to hold the Treaty against the constitution in case of a conflict between European legislation and the German Constitution. According to the initial explanation of

German legal experts, the German Court in its capacity as guardian of
the constitution would, under those circumstances, overrule the European
Court, a unique fact in EC history. Moreover, the Court considers the
Treaty terminable if it is not sufficiently guaranteed that the EMU criteria
agreed on are complied with. This entails the risk that the envisaged
European Monetary Union and the European Political Union do not pave
the way for a European federal state but simply for a European league of
nations.

Following a difficult ratification process, the Treaty took effect on 1
November 1993. Under pressure of the United Kingdom, the social chapter
was excluded from the Union Treaty. In addition, a special protocol was
adopted allowing Denmark and the United Kingdom to opt out of stage
three of monetary union ('opting out' clause).

11.5   Repercussions for the 'zone of stability'

Since the Basle/Nyborg agreement of 1987, exchange rate realignments
within the EMS had not taken place for a number of years. In addition
to a more flexible intervention policy, the central banks had managed to
cushion exchange rate tensions by conducting a more active interest rate
policy. This affected the opinion on the functioning of the EMS in a positive
manner, as becomes evident from a remark made by the Dutch Central
Bank Governor Duisenberg: 'On balance ... the EMS has proved successful
and has contributed in a large measure to eight years of uninterrupted
economic progress in Europe'.[8] Optimism with regard to the sustainability
of stable exchange rates only increased when the Spanish peseta acceded to
the ERM in June 1989, while the Italian lira returned to the narrow band
in January 1990. Sterling found its way back to the ERM in October of
that year.[9] In the same month, Norway linked the crown to the ECU, while
Belgium announced that it would follow the Deutsche mark more strictly
in the future. In April 1992, the Portuguese escudo also joined the ERM
with a fluctuation margin of 6 per cent on both sides of its central rate.

Tensions arose after Denmark's rejection of the Union Treaty in a referendum on 2 June 1992 and the announcement by the French President the
next day that in his country a decision on the Treaty would also be taken
by means of a referendum (announced for September 1992). In the run-
up to the referendum, the EC Ministers of Finance attempted to dispel
nervous sentiments in the foreign exchange market by issuing all sorts
of reassuring statements, while unsuccessfully exerting heavy pressure on
Germany behind the scenes to relieve tensions by means of interest rate
reductions. On 13 September 1992, the lira was devalued by 7 per cent vis-

à-vis the other EMS currencies. This was attended by a modest German interest rate reduction, which did not, however, restore calm. A few days later, following extensive interventions, Italy and the United Kingdom withdrew their currencies from the ERM while the Spanish peseta was devalued by 5 per cent. The Italian Government envisaged a rapid return to the ERM, but has not yet been able to realize this objective. Its request for ECU 8 billion financial assistance within the framework of the EC mechanism for medium-term financial assistance in support of the balance of payments was granted in early 1993 by the Council of Ministers. Despite the positive outcome of the French referendum held on 20 September 1992, in which a small majority said 'yes' to ratification of the Treaty, the French franc became subject to downward pressure. This could be warded off by a common statement by the French and German monetary authorities that the parity between the two currencies was in accordance with the 'fundamentals' of the two countries, after which calm was restored on the foreign exchange markets. This was followed by action in the form of a French interest rate increase and intervention support by the Bundesbank. Shortly afterwards, in November 1992, the Spanish peseta again came under pressure which resulted in a devaluation of this currency and of the Portuguese escudo, by 6 per cent.[10]

The Danish 'no' to the Maastricht Treaty was lifted in October 1992, when seven out of eight parliamentary parties reached a national compromise, on the basis of which they promised to approve an announced second referendum. By doing this, they reached out to the European Council, which arrived at a compromise on the Danish problem at the end of 1992 in Edinburgh.[11] Despite this agreement, the foreign exchange markets remained unstable. In May 1993 — a few days before the second Danish referendum — new exchange rate adjustments were required, with the Spanish peseta and the Portuguese escudo being devalued by 8 per cent and 6.5 per cent, respectively. After Denmark had ultimately voted in favour of the Treaty, tensions did not ebb. This was due to disagreement on the interest rate policy to be conducted, a matter gradually concentrating on France and Germany. In June, this culminated in a direct conflict after France had decided, unilaterally, to lower its interest rates, followed by a number of other Member States. Despite extensive interventions by the central banks,[12] the ensuing tensions resulted in the dramatic decision of 2 August 1993 to widen the fluctuation margin of the EMS currencies from 2.25 per cent to 15 per cent above or below their central rates, except between the Deutsche mark and the Dutch guilder, for which, pursuant to a separate agreement, the mutual bandwidth of 4.5 per cent was maintained.

It should be noted that the currency crisis of September 1992 cannot be compared to that of August 1993. According to Duisenberg (1993), the exchange rates were clearly overvalued in mid-1992: due to the diverging budgetary deficits and inflationary differentials, shifts had taken place in the national competitive positions without resulting in a corresponding adjustment of exchange rates. However, in the summer of 1993, exchange rates were not overvalued. According to the Dutch Governor, the prevailing tensions had to be ascribed to the lower credibility of the system since September 1991, the ongoing deterioration of economic activity and serious doubts in the exchange market regarding the determination of the monetary authorities to keep inflation in check by means of adequate interest rate increases.

Following a period of relative calm on the foreign exchange front — the permissible wider fluctuation margins were not used in 1994 — tensions within the EMS rose again in the spring of 1995. In addition to political instability, uncertainties in the financial markets were fuelled again by a lack of confidence in the policies conducted by the monetary authorities in various EMS countries. This notably concerned doubts regarding their willingness to make the necessary interventions and to use monetary instruments, notably the interest rate instrument, to achieve exchange rate stability. On 6 March 1995, the Spanish peseta was devalued again, now by 7 per cent and the Portuguese escudo by 3.5 per cent. Characteristic in this respect was furthermore the situation of the Italian lira, which, since its withdrawal from the ERM in September 1992, had lost around a quarter of its value as at the end of March 1995. The French franc came under pressure in the run-up to the presidential elections, despite the willingness of the French authorities to increase the short-term interest rate differential vis-à-vis Germany.

Apart from the above tensions within the EMS, positive results could be reached in 1995 with regard to other aspects of the Maastricht Treaty. In France, a far-reaching revision of the central bank act was implemented, providing for more autonomy of the Banque de France as from 1 January 1994. In conformity with the Maastricht Treaty, the pursuit of price stability is included in this Act as an explicit objective of monetary policy. In Belgium, the central bank act was amended too as well as in Spain, where the central bank was given full responsibility for the formulation and implementation of monetary policy aimed at price stability in the new bank act adopted in 1994.

Another favourable aspect was the progress made on the expansion of the Community. On 1 January 1995, Austria, Finland and Sweden joined the European Union following the outcome of the referendums held in 1994. Of the original Member States of the European Free Trade Association applying for membership of the EU, only the Norwegians voted against accession. As from 1 January 1995 all new Member States acceded to the EMS. Only Austria also joined the ERM on 9 January 1995, a move which does not undermine this country's exchange rate policy aimed at maintaining a close link between the Austrian schilling and the Deutsche mark.

Finally, at the Summit held in Madrid in December 1995, it was agreed that the future single currency will be called 'Euro' and that the next Intergovernmental Conference will be held at the end of March 1996 in Turin. On the basis of hard figures, the EU leaders will decide, 'as early as possible' in 1998, which Member States fulfil the conditions for joining. During the conference in Madrid, the Heads of State and Government Leaders re-affirmed that there would be no dilution of the convergence criteria agreed at Maastricht. On 1 January 1999 EMU will begin with the irrevocable locking of exchange rates and the transfer of interest rate and foreign exchange policy to the European Central Bank.

Notes

1. The Delors Report was the product of the Central Bank Governors of the twelve Member States of the EC, two members of the European Commission and three independent experts.
2. In his address to the House of Commons, Lawson put it as follows: 'I would be perfectly happy with a sort of quasi monetary union of the kind that we had in the world at the time of the gold standard; it is interesting that with the gold standard there was no control of national fiscal policy or budgetary policy, no world-wide regional policy, none of that nonsense, and yet the gold standard worked. It was a form of monetary union but it was one from which any member country could depart whenever it wished' (cited by Szász, 1989, pp. 33–34).
3. Statements of Governor Pöhl are cited in *Keesings Historisch Archief*, June 1991, p. 366.
4. All EU countries are members of the Western European Union except Austria, Denmark, Ireland and Sweden which are observer members.
5. In the new draft treaty, the competences of the Community requiring a majority of votes were expanded to areas such as energy, education, communication, health, culture, industry and tourism.
6. The EU Treaty consists of

   (1) stipulations regarding amendments to the Treaties on EEC (becomes EC Treaty in which EMU is included), on Euratom and ECSC,
   (2) stipulations regarding common foreign and security policies and
   (3) stipulations concerning cooperation in the field of justice and internal policy.

7. In order to be allowed to participate in the final stage of EMU, the Member States must meet the following criteria:

   (1) Inflation, measured by the consumption price rise may not be more than 1.5 per cent in excess of the average of the three lowest-inflation rate countries.
   (2) Long-term interest rate cannot deviate more than 2 per cent from the interest rate in the three lowest-inflation rate countries.
   (3) The budget deficit of the public sector should not exceed 3 per cent of gross domestic product (GDP).
   (4) Public debt may not be in excess of the limit of 60 per cent of GDP.

Finally, the exchange rate of the relevant currency must have been in the 'normal' band of the exchange rate mechanism for the past two years.

8. Duisenberg,W.F. (1989), pp. 16–17.
9. The return of the Italian lira to the narrow band, in January 1990, was attended by a devaluation by 3.68 per cent. Like the Spanish peseta, which had joined the ERM in June 1989, sterling had a fluctuation margin of 6 per cent on either side of the central rate vis-à-vis the other ERM currencies. At that time, the Greek drachme and the Portuguese escudo were the only EMS currencies not included in the ERM.
10. Sweden decided to let the crown float, preceded in September 1992 by Finland and followed in December 1992 by Norway.
11. In October 1992, the Danish Government presented a White Paper, stating that it wanted certain clauses to be included in the Union Treaty allowing Denmark to opt out of the monetary union and the common defence stipulations. The European Council added a decision to the Treaty as well as three statements 'exclusively applicable to Denmark and not to other current or future Member States'.
12. The July crisis resulted in interventions to the amount of some $ 70 billion (two-thirds of the interventions during the September crisis of 1992), of which some $ 58.5 billion were in support of the French franc and $ 7.5 billion in support of the Danish crown.

12 ASSESSMENT: PERIOD 1918–1995

12.1 Lack of parallelism between economic and political integration

When reviewing the European development after 1918, it may be concluded that monetary cooperation only began to take shape after the Second World War. Although countries were admittedly forced to form monetary blocs due to the abolition of the gold standard between the two world wars, their attitude towards monetary integration was underlain primarily by defensive considerations. At that time, there was no constructive will in Europe to cooperate in the economic and monetary sphere. Moreover, such a will could not flourish in a climate in which nationalist movements became more and more powerful, putting the proponents of European unification to silence.

This changed after 1945. The Second World War had seriously discredited the political significance of the national state. Cooperation in Europe became the new device. However, the idea of a United States of Europe revived by Churchill in 1946 had to be abandoned shortly afterwards due to the lack of constructive cooperation by the communist power bloc. This was notably why the integration plans were restricted to Western Europe, where economic cooperation initiated in the Marshall Plan primarily had a political and defensive character. The reason was that a new conflict between France and Germany had to be prevented, while the threat of the Soviet Union had to be kept in check. However, political integration started off slowly hindered as it was by a fundamental difference of opinion between the United Kingdom and the Scandinavian countries on the one hand and the other Western European countries on the other with regard to the question as to what extent the final consequence of integration — the transfer of national competences to a supranational authority — had to be accepted. This question badly affected the pursuit of political unification from the start. Although the government leaders and their representatives never lost sight of the concept of political union after 1945, once propagated, its contours remained too vague for actual decision-making. Moreover, the construction suggested was more often than not inspired by expediency. The most far-reaching proposal was the French Pleven Plan of the early 1950s, which was rejected by France itself after the direct threat had disappeared with the termination of the Korean conflict.

With the establishment of the European Economic Community in 1957, Europe definitely opted for the primacy of economic integration. For some Member States this form of cooperation was the lever which would ultimately have to lead to political unification. Of these States, Germany was the most important advocate. Here, the consideration applied that economic cooperation was the only way to regain respect, which, for the time being, had to be considered impossible through foreign policy. Other Member States regarded economic integration as an instrument to protect the position of their own country to the highest possible extent. Prominent representatives of this group were France and, at a later stage, the United Kingdom. The position of the latter was fairly comfortable in the sense that it regarded its traditionally close relationships with the United States and the Commonwealth as a preferable alternative to economic association with Europe.

Post-war history shows that, on the European continent, clear impulses were given to the pursuit of economic integration each time France and Germany reached agreement, which, incidentally, did not always mean that they pursued common objectives. Fears of German supremacy, irrespective of the side it would come from, was usually the motive underlying French plans and proposals to come to greater European political cooperation. This motive was reinforced by the ever-suppressed desire of France to play the leading role in Europe. For Germany, the overtures in the economic field continued to be the most appropriate means to meet its no less suppressed desire to control at least a few strings, if not to play the first fiddle in the political orchestra. On the other hand, the same history shows that each attempt at integration threatened to get bogged down or even failed completely, as soon as both countries came into conflict, either explicitly or implicitly, or held diverging views on essential elements of the integration process.

During the end of 1969 Summit at The Hague, there still seemed to be unanimity on the future strategy according to which economic integration would at least keep pace with tighter monetary cooperation, a desire also shared by The Netherlands, one of the smaller Member States, which repeatedly voiced its view that this strategy was a prerequisite for the success of EMU. This changed after the introduction of the EMS. The French/German initiators abandoned the principle of parallelism to some extent by attempting to revive economic and, ultimately, political cooperation through monetary integration. However, even in this changed constellation, France was pursuing an aim of its own. After the transition to the EMS, it stood at the side of the economically weaker Member States, at least until 1983. These States regularly proposed for an adjustment of the System by means of an extension of the existing credit facilities enabling them to continue their economic policies, which were hardly aimed at stability. Only after France had expressed its willingness, in 1983, to give price stability the highest priority in its monetary policy, was calm restored in the EMS for a number of years. By taking this step, France apparently recognized the position of Germany as the anchor country in the EMS, which also implied that it accepted the System's asymmetry, which although not envisaged on paper, was enforced in practice by the German policy. To what extent France will maintain this policy attitude remains to be seen. Nevertheless, the French interest rate policy during the currency crisis in March 1995 and the primacy of the objective of price stability, recognized by the newly independent French central bank, raise hope.

However, on the whole, there cannot be any other conclusion than that, in the past fifty years, Western Europe has not succeeded in simultaneously setting in motion economic, monetary and political integration. The Maastricht Treaty does not undermine this conclusion as it does not remove the problems indicated above. The question arises to what extent this Treaty embodies the post-war objectives of policy-makers with regard to European integration. To answer this question, it seems useful to repeat the quote, cited in Chapter 7.2, of the Advisory Assembly of the Council in Europe in 1950: 'The question whether political or economic unification should come first has already been answered long ago: everyone agrees that they should be developed simultaneously and that they are mutually supporting'.

What was considered economic unification in 1950 has been realized to a large extent in the establishment of the Single Market and the European Economic Area. However, the liberalization of capital flows forming part of these processes has drastically reinforced the need for a deepening of unification, in the sense of increased economic convergence and intensified policy coordination within the European Community. In these areas, achievements have been and still are insufficient. The Treaty of Rome gave little hold for such achievements. The Werner Report did, but missed the political back-up. What was left was an attempt to use monetary integration to enforce economic integration. However, the tensions erupting within the EMS since the autumn of 1992 once again make it clear that without deepening of the integration process, the pursuit of the Maastricht Treaty is doomed to fail. These tensions illustrate that the requirement of tight economic convergence can only prosper if Member States no longer base their decisions on national interests for political considerations.

12.2   Weak response to the convergence criteria

So far, this requirement has not been fulfilled as can be seen from Table 12.1 which shows to what extent the recent economic and monetary development of the Member States have met the convergence criteria formulated in the Treaty of Maastricht. For reasons of clarity, it is indicated in Table 12.2 how many criteria are met by each individual country in the period considered.

From these two tables, it becomes evident that in 1995 only Luxembourg met all convergence requirements. It is furthermore noteworthy that the anchor country Germany, after having met the four criteria in 1994, could not fulfil this requirement in 1995 due to the unfavourable results with regard to the public deficit. Therefore, Germany and Denmark rank second

Table 12.1   Assessment of compliance with EMU criteria 1994–1995

Area or country	Inflation rate		Long-term interest rate		Public deficit		Public debt	
	1994	1995	1994	1995	1994	1995	1994	1995
EMU (reference values)	3.1	2.9	10.0	9.9	−3	−3	60	60
Belgium	2.4	1.5	7.7	7.5	−5.3	−4.5	135	134
Denmark	2.0	2.1	7.8	8.3	−3.8	−2.0	76	74
France	1.7	1.8	7.2	7.5	−6.0	−5.0	48	52
Germany	2.6	1.8	6.8	6.8	−2.6	−3.6	50	59
Greece	10.9	9.3	20.8	17.3	−11.4	−9.3	113	114
Ireland	3.0	2.7	7.9	8.2	−2.1	−2.7	91	86
Italy	4.0	5.3	10.5	12.2	−9.0	−7.4	125	125
Luxembourg	2.3	2.0	6.4	6.0	2.2	0.4	6	6
Netherlands	2.7	1.9	6.9	6.9	−3.2	−3.7	78	78
Portugal	5.2	4.2	10.5	11.4	−5.8	−5.4	69	71
Spain	4.7	4.7	10.0	11.3	−6.6	−5.9	63	65
UK	2.4	2.8	8.0	8.2	−6.8	−5.1	50	53
Austria	3.0	2.3	7.0	7.1	−4.4	−5.5	65	68
Finland	1.1	1.0	9.1	8.8	−5.8	−5.4	60	63
Sweden	2.2	2.6	9.6	10.3	−10.4	−7.0	80	81

Explanatory notes: the figures with regard to inflation and long-term interest rates represent the annual percentage increases. The public deficit and public debt are expressed as percentages of Gross Domestic Product (GDP). Figures in grey indicate that the convergence criterion is met.

Source: De Nederlandsche Bank, *SIR-Weekbulletin,* 26 January 1996.

Table 12.2   Number of EMU criteria met

Area or	Convergence criteria		Devaluation more
country	1994	1995	than 2 years ago*)
EMU reference value	4	4	
Belgium	2	2	12 January 1987
Denmark	2	3	12 January 1987
France	3	3	12 January 1987
Germany	4	3	
Greece	0	0	not in ERM
Ireland	3	3	1 January 1993
Italy	0	0	not in ERM
Luxembourg	4	4	12 January 1987
Netherlands	2	2	21 March 1983
Portugal	0	0	6 March 1995
Spain	1	0	6 March 1995
UK	3	3	not in ERM
Austria	2	2	
Finland	3	2	not in ERM
Sweden	2	1	not in ERM

*) Devaluation against other EMS currencies. The currency of each Member State has to stay within the 'normal' bandwith of the EMS for at least two years without any adjustment of its rate on its own initiative.

together with France, Ireland and the United Kingdom. This group is followed by The Netherlands, where the weak points are the public deficit and public debt, as well as by the new Member States Austria, Finland and Sweden. The economically weaker Member States, such as Greece, Italy, Portugal and Spain have met the access criteria for stage three to an insufficient extent, if at all.

Looking at the degree of economic convergence since 1991, the year in which, in Maastricht, the European Council reached agreement on the European Union, the results presented in Table 12.3 are not hopeful.

Between 1991 and 1995 the average inflation was reduced considerably although in both years the actual rate remained above the convergence criterion. Looking at the criteria for public finances the outcome deteriorated in that actual public deficit hardly changed while the average public debt as a percentage of GDP has increased to more than 75 per cent, which is far above the targeted EMU rate of 60 percent.

Table 12.3   EMU reference values compared with the averages of the actual results in the EU Member States in 1991 and 1995

Averages	1991	EMU reference value	1995	EMU reference value
Inflation	6.3	4.4	3.1	2.9
Long-term interest rate	11.0	11.4	9.2	9.9
Public deficit	-4.9	-3.0	-4.4	-3.0
Public debt	67.5	60.0	75.3	60.0

Source: De Nederlandsche Bank, *Annual Report* 1991 and *SIR-Weekbulletin*, 26 January 1996.

The fact that only one out of fifteen Member States currently meets all the required convergence criteria indicates that there is a long way to go yet. This also applies to the supranational stipulations laid down in the Maastricht Treaty with regard to the ESCB. As good as they may sound on paper, they will remain nothing more than empty words without the political will and willingness of the Member States to achieve permanent convergence of their policies and economies. The broadening of the Community, in the sense of an expansion of the number of Member States evident since the fall of the Berlin Wall in 1989, which as such is in line with the ideas of the founders of the Community, threatens to complicate rather than facilitate this process.

12.3   Insufficient guarantees for EMU

The conclusion voiced in 1950 that economic and political unification are mutually supporting, has ultimately turned out to be no more than idle hope. It is true that since the Treaties on ECSC and EEC a multitude of plans have passed in review in order to translate the foothold for political union offered in these Treaties into action. So far, however, this has not (yet) led to concrete results in the sense of Schuman's European federation which he considered essential for maintaining peace. The Maastricht Treaty also provides little hope that EMU, as Werner put it in 1969, will be the ferment of the development towards a political union. Consequently, the present structure of the EU insufficiently guarantees the irreversibility of the process. The explanation must be sought in the remark made by Max van der Stoel (1976), that the sovereign state has ultimately turned out to be a more obstinate phenomenon than it was generally considered to be in the 1950s. This obstinacy is the real problem underlying one hundred and fifty years of European integration. He added that the European Union should have the character of an intermediate stage. The plans put forward occasionally by various groups to proceed with a core group of countries seem to go in that direction. Under these circumstances, 'Maastricht' may be considered a compromise in the sense that it is a return to the small inner group of countries, already advocated in 1950, which presently consists of the old Six minus Italy. The proponents of this strategy hope that this group may give concrete substance to the post-war pursuit of integration.

Ultimately, the obstinacy observed by Van der Stoel is also at the heart of the problem which the Dutch journalist Bart Tromp (1994) has described as the two opposite scenarios affecting the process of European integration: political unification versus the preservation of the national state. The author rightly points out that this difference in objectives could be bridged as long as the integration process was aimed at the establishment of a Single Market. This objective created the possibility to conceal the different scenarios by statements on closer cooperation in the future, while, at the same time, ample opportunities were at hand to adorn the community institutions without formally corroding the essential aspects of national sovereignty — defence and foreign policy. However, the closer the realization of the Single Market, the harder it became to conceal the differences between the two scenarios. It is this problem which was at the basis of the complex and sometimes non-transparent decisions made during the Maastricht Summit.

Part III

ON THE EVE OF THE 21ST CENTURY

'So there is a good chance to make the whole story a success if the rules of the game are followed and if the negotiations planned for 1996 clarify the horizon for real political union.'

(Hans Tietmeyer, November 1993)

13 LESSONS FROM THE PAST

13.1 Differences and similarities

It goes without saying that the steps taken in the twentieth century to realize an intensification of monetary cooperation differ in more than one respect from monetary integration in the previous century. Above all, this concerns the monetary system itself. When the gold standard was abandoned in the 1930s, the metallic system was replaced once and for all by the paper standard. Consequently, the position of the issuing banks changed fundamentally everywhere. The leading ones evolved from a circulation bank to a central bank, functioning ultimately as a bankers' bank and lender of last resort. During the gold standard, the central bank's most important task was to maintain a stable gold price. Nowadays it is responsible primarily, through monetary policy, for the stability of the currency. For this purpose, the modern central bank has a whole range of more or less detailed monetary policy instruments at its disposal, by means of which price stability and consequently stable exchange rates may be archieved. Despite these different circumstances, it would definitely go too far to come to the conclusion that a comparison between European monetary integration in the nineteenth and twentieth centuries considered here would be neither useful nor educational.

The EMS, which is at the heart of EMU in the Maastricht Treaty, is a form of cooperation between sovereign states. In this respect, the System may be compared with inter-European monetary unions of the nineteenth century. This comparison will show that there are differences and similarities. One of the striking differences with past unions is that after the Second World War monetary cooperation was not controlled by political rivalry as witnessed between Austria and Prussia, nor did it lead such a sleeping life as the LMU. Moreover, it was not disrupted by exogenous calamities, the ruin of the Scandinavian Monetary Union. Although the EC has not been free from external shocks, such as the two oil crises and the collapse of the Bretton Woods System, these shocks have stimulated rather than weakened post-war economic and monetary cooperation. Apart from the constructive

attitude of some European policy-makers, this is also presumably related
to the fact that, unlike in past unions, post-war economic cooperation
started more or less from scratch. In other words: there was no question of
economic dominance of one single state, as a result of which the aspect of
rivalry was hardly relevant initially. Only after Germany had conducted a
successful policy aimed at monetary stability for a large number of years,
did it evolve into the anchor country of the Community. However, before
it was recognized as such, its supremacy in this field was no longer an issue
of political controversy, all the more so because most other Member States
of the Community had meanwhile also picked the fruits of this policy.

Nevertheless, this development masks also an element of weakness which
can be seen as one of the similarities with past inter-European unions.
A qualitative step forward in the sense of a deepening of the European
integration process is still to be taken in the European Union. That
this did not happen in the nineteenth century was mainly related to the
circumstance that there was no form of political integration whatsoever.
As a result, the inter-European unions were in fact nothing more than an
institutionalization of the existing situation, having no political basis at
all. On the contrary, during the post-war integration process, economists
and politicians were constantly aware of the relation between monetary and
political integration, although this awareness has barely led to any concrete
results. The aim to achieve supranational unity via sectoral economic integration, initiated in the ECSC Treaty, was abandoned with the adoption of
the EEC Treaty, which envisaged integral, rather than sectoral, unification
of the national economies. The possibility of supranationality, which was
also incorporated in this Treaty could not, however, be put into action
due to the mutually opposed interests of the Member States. As a result,
economic and monetary integration still finds itself in a situation where
policy-making continues to be the province of national governments and
national central banks. Where monetary integration is concerned, a step
forward is taken by the Maastricht Treaty, envisaging the establishment of
the ECB as a supranational institution. On the way towards irrevocably
fixed exchange rates, this plan is indeed a preferable alternative than the
proposal made earlier to use the ECU as parallel currency. Experiences
from the nineteenth century indicate that Gresham's Law would be applicable here too, for as long as the ECU would not be as 'hard' as the
Deutsche mark as the anchor currency — between 1979 and 1995, its ECU
central rate decreased from 2.51 to 1.91 — the common currency would
soon be qualified as 'bad money'.

In the field of economic integration, the policy continues to be intergovernmental, with the national governments having to comply with the
convergence criteria stipulated. The degree to which this is achieved, is

determined by the voluntary cooperation of the Member States and cannot be enforced. Consequently, the road to stage three might well be long. The question, therefore, arises whether the time schedule set in Maastricht has been a useful step or whether the duration of stage two has been miscalculated. One of the positive aspects of the pressure exerted on the Member States is that the time schedule for realizing more convergence is relatively short. On the other hand there is a risk of undermining the credibility of Member States should they not be able to comply with the requirements within the time frame set. These concerns are fuelled by earlier attempts, described in part II, which have failed. But even if stage three could start on time, either by a small group of core countries (two-speed Europe) or by the whole group together, this step will still not be irreversible as long as economic and budgetary policies continue to be implemented on a decentralized level. However, centralization in these areas would inevitably mean a transfer of sovereignty.

In some respects, the way in which the EMS currently functions is similar to that of the nineteenth-century supraregional unions. Some of these unions were characterized by a dominant circulation bank (Bank of Sardinia, Prussian Bank). The same is true for stage two of EMU, in which the Deutsche Bundesbank holds a dominant position. The Statute of the ECB has even been based on its model. Nevertheless, there is a difference between the EMS and the supraregional unions. It may not be expected that uncoordinated action by the national banks of the other Member States would pave the way for monetary union, as was the case in Italy and Switzerland in the nineteenth century where competition between the issuing banks ultimately reinforced the need for central regulation. Experiences gained since the establishment of the EMS in 1979 show that non-compliance with the rules lead to unsustainable tensions within the ERM which only slow down monetary unification. This means that the way to the ECB is only passable through better harmonization with the stabilizing policy of the leading central bank — in this case the Bundesbank. Should there be any opposition to its primacy, it should be borne in mind that this may be overcome less simply than in the supraregional unions of the nineteenth century, due to the absence of a political framework.

13.2 Conclusions

When reviewing the process of European integration over the past fifty years, it seems that most of the provisional conclusions drawn in Chapter 5.3 on the basis of the experiences with the nineteenth-century monetary unions are still applicable today.

(1)   In the nineteenth century, the divergences in economic and monetary policies led to disintegration of the currency unions, insofar as these consisted of politically independent states. By contrast, post-war divergencies in the same policies, also conducted by independent states, reinforced rather than weakened the monetary integration process in Europe. Nevertheless, the lack of coordination between their monetary policies and the insufficient degree of parallelism between economic and monetary integration turned out to be an important — if not the essential — cause underlying tensions which have erupted repeatedly in the EMS.

(2)   Under those circumstances, the introduction of a parallel currency, proposed by some Member States, as an instrument to promote integration was rightly rejected by European policy-makers. As long as this currency is not as 'hard' as that of the economically most prosperous Member State, it would rapidly be qualified as 'bad money', which would be driven out by 'good money'.

(3)   In the nineteenth century, the stabilization policy, propagated by a strong central bank, had a 'compelling' effect on the other members of the unions. After 1945, Germany, starting from scratch, gradually developed into the leading Member of the European Community. The stabilization policy of the Bundesbank has had a 'compelling' effect on the response of the other Member States of the EMS to control inflation.

(4)   The establishment of the ESCB will only partly meet the conditions which turned the supraregional monetary unions of the nineteenth century into a success. The second condition, notably centralization of competences in other areas, is not met.

When following this line of thinking to the present plan for EMU, the conclusion is justified that, even if a supranational central bank is considered one of the essential characteristics of EMU, the success of the Union entails that competences in the other policy areas must also become the province of a supranational body. This requires a political union or at least a growing degree of parallelism between economic, monetary and political integration as long as EMU has not reached its final stage. The strategy of parallelism shall then be the only way to make EMU not only sustainable but also irreversible. In this respect the stability pact recently proposed by the German Finance Minister Theo Waigel may be regarded even more important than the Treaty of Maastricht. It provides the EU with automatic sanctions on countries which have excessive budget deficits. The acceptance of these sanctions by the Member States would guarantee a supranational element not only in monetary but also in fiscal decisions.

14 EPU AS THE ULTIMATE OBJECTIVE OF EMU?

14.1 EMU as optimum currency area?

The essential question with regard to post-war European integration concerns the ultimate objective of EMU. Already in 1969, Werner answered this question very clearly by saying that EMU is the most appropriate means to achieve the 'ultimate goal' of political union. However, within Europe, there is a certain dualism regarding this matter. Although the idea of political union has never been completely abandoned and is still propagated strongly by Germany (supported by The Netherlands), political union has never been formulated as the final objective in any of the agreements, reports and treaties drawn up since 1969, including the Maastricht Treaty. This is also why the transfer of budgetary competences advocated pithily by Werner, has either not been mentioned at all or has only been referred to in very vague terms ever since.

Due to the lack of clarity about the political union, it seems as if EMU has become an objective in itself. This impression was only reinforced by the Maastricht Treaty. If this is indeed the case, the question arises whether the pursuit of economic and monetary union is underlain by an economic motive. In recent economic literature, European Union is sometimes considered an optimum currency area. Theory of optimum currency areas suggests that the benefits of monetary union, consisting of lower transaction costs, should be balanced against the costs related to the loss of monetary independence and of exchange rates as an adjustment instrument for restoring economic equilibrium.

According to Barry Eichengreen (1993) 'neither theory nor empirical work provides clear evidence on the balance of these costs and benefits'.[1] As to the benefits, empirical evidence shows, for the EC as a whole, no significant effects of exchange rate variability on trade and investments, whereas the expected reduction of currency conversion costs as a result of monetary union seems to be disappointing as well. On the other hand, the low level of factor mobility together with the limited wage flexibility imply that the loss of monetary autonomy will not be without costs. 'Only if it can be argued that a single currency is a concomitant of the Single Market, the benefits of which are likely to be substantial, can the case for a European currency be made with confidence.'[2] In the view of Eichengreen, market integration can proceed under floating exchange rates as well as under a common currency. In the first case national industries might be confronted — under the pressure of the disappearance of trade barriers — with a serious deterioration of their competitive position because of 'capricious' swings in exchange rates. Therefore, it is for reasons of political economy, and not for economic efficiency, that monetary unification is a logical corollary of economic integration. Although economic union could in principle be accompanied by either floating rates or a single currency, the one alternative that is not viable is that of fixed exchange rates. No matter how seriously public authorities promise not to meddle with exchange rates, an escape clause will always exist as the possibility can never be ruled out that other governments and circumstances still require a change of policy, and hence a realignment. From his point of view, Eichengreen considers the transitional period currently opted for a problem.

Some remarks can be made to these arguments. The author expects the benefits of the Single Market to be substantial. At the same time he presumes that it does not matter if this Market proceeds under floating rates or a single currency. That presumption seems at least doubtful because in the first case it would mean that the danger of protectionism can be ruled out. Apart from that, it is difficult to see why floating rates would hardly have any effect on trade and investment if national industries fear loss of competition from fluctuation in exchange rates. That Eichengreen sees this differently is presumably related to the fact that the United States assesses the relationship between the single currency and a single market differently than Continental Europe. Goodhart (1995) ascribes this to an 'associated disagreement over the determinants and merits of having the exchange rate determined by market forces'.[3] The Americans have more confidence in the fundamental market forces and consequently regard flexible exchange rates as the most appropriate instrument to maintain the economic balance between the various economies. By contrast, Europeans pay more attention to the hidden element of speculation, which may cause serious disruptions, long enough to be significant in an economic and political respect.

The above gives rise to the view that the theory of the optimum currency areas probably offers few possibilities for the future united Europe. According to Goodhart (1995), it is clear that, in essence, monetary union serves political cohesion, of which centralization of budgetary policy is one of the crucial components. However, if that would mean coordination of budgetary policy, Eichengreen refers to empirical evidence which shows that 'the cross border macroeconomic effects of fiscal policy are small'.[4] On the one hand, an increase in government expenditures will have, through the absorption of foreign as well as domestic goods, a positive transmission effect. On the other hand, the expected rise in domestic interest rates spill over into higher rates abroad which is a source of negative international transmission. In practice these two effects largely cancel out. Consequently, it is in the view of Eichengreen, the 'regional coinsurance effect' alone that is said to be a necessary concomitant of monetary union. This effect is brought about by an increase of net transfers from the federal government to a member state if it enters a recession not experienced by the rest of the federation.

As true as this may be, Eichengreen is not clear about the relationship between the monetary union and political cohesion. He pays little attention to the risks to which the EU will be exposed if the budgetary instruments remain the province of the national states. That this risk cannot be neglected becomes evident from his concern that 'fixed' exchange rates never rule out the possibility of a change in government leading to a change in policy. The cause for this concern can be no other than the lack of enforcement powers which creates the opportunity for Member States to use the budgetary instrument as an escape clause for letting national objectives prevail over the common priority aims of EMU.

14.2 Political union through EMU?

If the pursuit of a monetary union is indeed based on political considerations, the question arises whether it is possible to achieve political union through EMU. The German politician Klaus Kinkel calls EMU a means to keep peace in Europe. In this respect, lessons should be drawn from the past. History has shown that political unification has rarely, if ever, been accomplished through economic and monetary integration. This conclusion is supported by Tromp who summarizes the developments which took place in the previous century as follows: 'Economic unification in France was enforced by the central government in Paris. The driving force of Italian unification was not economic integration but nationalistic resistance against foreign occupants .... What about the German unification? Was not this unification preceded by the *Zollverein*? Was there not an economic basis, or at least a commercial basis, on which Von Bismarck could built? Apparently yes, but without the political and military manoeuvres of 1848 and 1870, the customs union would have remained what it was, a system of agreements which did not function too well nor was it of particular economic importance. In this case, economics did not precede politics.'[5] With this statement, Tromp more or less agrees with the views of the German Bundesbank and the Swiss National Bank, whose Governor Marcus Lusser, in 1992, noted the following with regard to past inter-European unions: 'Probably, those historical monetary unions could have survived if there had been available a financial compensation (*Finanzausgleich*) to the participating countries. This compensation requires, indeed, a high degree of political solidarity which can only be reached within a political union.'[6]

If EMU is to function as a means of carrying EPU, it must be guaranteed that the decisions of Maastricht are embedded in a political structure rising above the level realized after the entry into effect of the EU Treaty. In order to achieve this, parallel progress of EMU and political integration seems to be a prerequisite. Meeting this condition is all the more pressing, now that the risk is not inconceivable that the process of integration in a Europe without eastern borders will concern an expansion rather than a deepening. EMU is the most appropriate instrument to shape this deepening as it has the potential to develop its own dynamism from which the need for a political union will grow. This dynamism should be attended by the pursuit of a stronger role for the European Commission as a politically independent body and an expansion of the competences of the European Parliament, as a result of which the principle of supranationality included in the original Treaty of Rome may become more concrete. Nevertheless, today's politicians realize perfectly well that political integration will never go beyond the minimum requirements for economic integration. What it ultimately boils down to is to find a European identity beyond this minimum of shared national interests.

The importance of a reinforcement of this European identity for the future development of EMU obtains an additional dimension when the effects are examined of the crumbling of political unities on monetary union. History has seen marked examples of such disintegration, notably in the twentieth century. The termination of the First World War in 1918 also marked the end of the Habsburg Empire, consisting of the Empire of Austria and the Kingdom of Hungary.[7] After its establishment in August 1867, the two areas constituted a supraregional union with completely liberalized trade, a centralized monetary policy and two separate central government budgets, each of which contributed to the financing of joint expenditure and public debt. After the political split-up in 1918–1919, the Austrian currency continued to be in circulation in the whole area for some time. The problem arose how this was to be reconciled with the acquired political and fiscal autonomy of the new states. By way of provisional solution, Austria first concluded a treaty with Czechoslovakia, according to which representatives of this State would be included in the management of the Austrian–Hungarian Bank. This Bank would not be involved in public financing. The intention failed due to the fact that the new State provided the Austrian crowns held by Czechoslovakian residents with its own stamp which meant the creation of monetary autonomy for Czechoslovakia. This act was immediately followed by the new Kingdom of Serbs, Croats and Slovenes. In 1920, all other newly formed nations had their own currency.

That monetary union without political union is not necessarily doomed to fail is, on the other hand, evidenced by the BLEU. As described in Chapter 6.3, this union was attended by a far-reaching albeit incomplete monetary unification. The result was a monetary association which is still the cornerstone of the BLEU. Nevertheless, the continued circulation of the two currencies reflects Luxembourg's wish to maintain its identity. Although the BLEU has other characteristics of a monetary union — the national reserves of the two countries are pooled and a single monetary policy is conducting for the whole area — this does not alter the special nature of the monetary relationship between the two nations. For instance, Luxembourg's financial institutions may, in practice, easily by-pass the restrictive monetary policy of the Belgian authorities on account of their financial structure, which is why they hardly ever, if at all, need to have recourse to the rediscounting facilities of the National Bank of Belgium. Furthermore, the position of Belgium as the dominating partner is a characteristic of this relationship which cannot be ignored. The population of Belgium is twenty eight times that of Luxembourg, while its national income exceeds that of Luxembourg by almost the same order of magnitude. According to the Belgian economists Herman Verwilst and Marc Quintyn (1982), this characteristic alone accounts for the exceptional position of the BLEU compared with the textbook versions of economic and monetary union.[8]

Finally, the importance of political integration for the success of the EMU plans appears to be underlined by the more recent developments in Europe. Cases in point are the events taking place in the countries of former Eastern Europe since the crumbling of the communist system. Here too, monetary union could not, or only with the greatest effort, withstand the termination of supranational unions as is shown in the disintegration of the Soviet Union, Czechoslovakia and Yugoslavia.[9] By contrast, the German reunification in 1990 indicates that the success of a monetary union between east and west can be ascribed exclusively to political reunification, which made it possible to enforce social consensus for huge financial support to the new German States, probably for years on end. The Governor of the Swiss National Bank Lusser wondered if such a financial compensation would haven been thinkable if the former German Democratic Republic, on the one hand, would have accepted the Deutsche mark while keeping, on the other hand, its own national identity?[10]

It goes without saying that EMU is not comparable to the German monetary union, in which two totally different economic systems were united. Nevertheless, the German example shows that in a monetary union between economically unequal partners, the bottleneck is what Lusser called a financial compensation which is only acceptable within a political union. It is for this reason why the Bundesbank seizes every opportunity to stress political union as a prerequisite for making EMU sustainable. In that case the question has to be answered if the strategy to be followed with regard to the convergence criteria is the right way.

14.3   EMU criteria as an instrument of credibility?

The Bundesbank attaches to strict compliance with the convergence criteria agreed in Maastricht. Nevertheless, additional stipulations seem required if the Maastricht Treaty is to provide sufficient guarantees for the participants in EMU to meet their obligations, even after having entered stage three. Views on this matter differ widely. The Belgian economist Paul de Grauwe (1995) wonders whether these criteria are the most appropriate instruments to actually enforce convergence between the Member States of the European Union. He holds the view that countries currently pursuing these standards may well do so for opportunist reasons. Once they have gained membership of the union 'they will reveal their true preferences'.[11] But even if the candidate Member States take the criteria seriously and submit purposefully to the process of deflation, this still does not guarantee — here De Grauwe agrees with Eichengreen — that their future national representatives in the ECB will abide by the same discipline. De Grauwe warns of a paradox in which the danger of a dichotomy is inherent, as a result of which a two-speed Europe would be a step backward rather than forward in the current process of integration. This paradox is found in the circumstance that, from the viewpoint of credibility, countries with a high rate of inflation and high public debt will succeed more easily in getting their economies in order once they have become a member of EMU than when they have to meet the criteria before they join. Therefore, 'the transition to EMU should put less emphasis on convergence requirements and more on strengthening the future monetary institutions of the union'.[12] Doubts about the usefulness of the convergence criteria are also expressed by the German economist Jürgen von Hagen (1995) who pretends that numeral restrictions are no effective means to reduce public debt. He refers to the history of the United States where governments of individual states conducting a stringent budgetary policy create opportunities for off-budget activities. Formal restrictions induce granting of subsidies whose financing is not included in the budget. Fiscal disipline was only brought about by the absence of any obligation of the Federal Government to support an individual state in the case of a financial crisis.

De Grauwe's fears of a division within the Community are not unfounded. Although the core group may be meant to serve as the driving force for other Member States, the fact remains that credibility would be seriously undermined if these countries failed to put their house in order shortly after the start of EMU. The question arises whether the alternative advocated by him is really preferable to the requirement that the convergence criteria must be met before access may be gained to EMU. Much will depend on the political will of countries outside the core group to actually pursue the objective of EMU. What really matters is the political will to conduct a policy aimed at stabilization. For this to be reached, reduction of public debt is a prerequisite whose fulfilment does not depend on membership of EU. If this willingness is absent, 'credibility' will remain an empty word. In that case the alternatives suggested by De Grauwe would not be a solution for the coordination problem which will then make the criticism uttered by Von Hagen with regard to the convergence criteria indisputable.

From the foregoing, one can maintain that credibility is not only a matter of concern for the stragglers but also for the future Member States of the core group.[13] For the time being, the countries of this group are confronted with three problems.

(1)   In 1995, only one country of the core group met the criterion for public debt. In 1996, public debt in Belgium, Ireland and The Netherlands will far exceed the permissible level of 60 per cent. It is hardly likely that these countries will meet this criterion before 1998. If the 'credibility' of the core group is not to be endangered, budgetary measures should be taken by these countries, notably in the short-term, in order to ensure that the pace at which public debt decreases become 'satisfactory'.

(2)   As advocated earlier, the start of EMU only makes sense if France and Germany jointly support the project. This means that the two countries should show greater unanimity in the political sphere. Already since the early 1950s, their views on the integration process have not run parallel. Although both admittedly pursue a simultaneous expansion and deepening of EU, this pursuit still masks diverging national interests. In the past, Germany has consistently stressed that it regards political union as an essential complement to EMU. The fall of the Berlin Wall has reinforced Germany in its opinions, as it wishes to integrate the Central European neighbouring countries into the post-war Western European system so as

to prevent the creation of a political vacuum. Viewed in this context, Germany regards the inner group as the driving force behind the other Member States. By contrast, France has always regarded European integration primarily as an instrument to consolidate, and possibly increase, its influence in Europe. It still holds this view. Instead of a core group of countries forming the nucleus of a federal Europe, France advocates an intergovernmental Europe, consisting of various groups, in which both France and Germany would invariably participate.

(3) In Germany, EMU threatens to become the plaything of the political struggle to win the electorate's favour. Due to the public's growing opposition to the replacement of the hard Deutsche mark by a new single currency, it is not inconceivable that Germany has an interest in postponing the process, favouring an expansion rather than a deepening of the European Union.

These complications will have to be discussed during the next Intergovernmental Conference of 1996. In its November 1995 report EMI explicitly states that '...The Treaty's insistence on the irreversibility of the move to Stage Three and the European currency area further underscores the importance of carrying through in an integrated manner all the elements required to bring the ambitious project to fruition.'[14] This shows that in the short run much has to be done to avoid that the sequel to 'Maastricht' will follow years later.

Notes

1. Eichengreen (1993), p. 1322.
2. Eichengreen (1993), p. 1353.
3. Goodhart (1995), p. 7.
4. Eichengreen (1993), p. 1340.
5. Tromp (1994), p. 63.
6. 'Währungsunion erfordert viel Solidarität', in *Die Welt*, 5 December 1992.
7. That this Treaty was not free from tensions becomes evident from the following quote of Van Walré de Bordes: 'With the disruption of the Monarchy, the barriers of all the long-standing national, political and economic jealousies had been broken. The Czechs, the Yugoslavs, the Poles and the Hungarians hastened to seal up the issues of their new frontiers .... Vienna was regarded as a gigantic parasite, the city of lotus-eating idlers' (Van Walré de Bordes (1924), p. 7 cited in Dornbusch (1992), p. 397).
8. With regard to the relationship of the BLEU with The Netherlands coordination of economic policy is mentioned as an explicit objective in the Benelux Union Treaty. Nevertheless, Duisenberg (1992c) holds the view that clear successes with regard to policy coordination have only been achieved in respect of mutual exchange rates. As a result of the financial and economic problems of the 1970s and early 1980s, coordination in the other policy areas has not been developed further. However, this does not mean that no activities have been developed to achieve further economic integration of the Benelux economies, reflected in e.g. trade.

9. In this respect, the Baltic States are good examples. Shortly after they gained independence, they introduced their own currencies: the Estonian *crown*, the Latvian *rouble* and the Lithuanian *talon*. Moreover, the former rouble zone is also disintegrating: Kazakhstan has introduced the *tenge*, Uzbekistan the *som*, Ukraine the *karbonavets*, while Moldova, Azerbaijan and Armenia have replaced the rouble by the *leu*, the *manat* and the *dram*, respectively.
10. See note 6.
11. De Grauwe (1995), p. 4.
12. De Grauwe (1995), p. 9.
13. Recently, Austria and Ireland have expressed their desire to join this group.
14. European Monetary Institute (1995), p. 4.

15 SUMMARY AND CONCLUSIONS

This book focuses on the question whether, in the light of the experiences gained in the nineteenth century, a united Europe as formulated on the eve of the twenty-first century in the Maastricht Treaty will have a chance of success.

In response to this question, Part I presented a description of nineteenth-century monetary unions. A distinction was made between two types of unions: those ensuing from the process of political unification (supra-regional unions) and those entered into between politically sovereign states (inter-European unions). In the first category, a currency union was rapidly achieved although it sometimes took many decades before full unity was reached. This can be ascribed to differences in trade, culture, traditions and social and political developments. Within the political state these divergences had to be changed into a common denominator. This resulted in tensions, which, with regard to payments, were reflected primarily in the diverging use of inconvertible paper money, as a result of which the success of efforts to centralize this means of payment was conditional upon the success of the reorganization process. In the second category, the same types of divergences and tensions usually led to the termination, sooner or later, of cooperation. The will to adjust was limited or non-existent, due to the fact that there was no political structure enforcing such a will.

From that point of view, monetary integration as realized in Western Europe in the twentieth century was discussed in Part II. The conclusion is that in the past fifty years European policy-makers did not succeed in bringing about economic, monetary and political integration simultaneously. With the establishment of the European Economic Community, a 'Europe of technicians and economists' was opted for. There were constantly plans for political integration, but these plans were stranded due to the superpowers' conflicting interests. The establishment of the EMS did not change this materially, albeit that monetary union has since functioned as the driving force of economic, and possibly, political integration. The EMS also forms the core of EMU, envisaged in the Maastricht Treaty.

In Part III, lessons were drawn from the past. The most important lesson was that monetary union is only sustainable and irreversible if it is embedded in a political union, in which competences beyond the monetary sphere are also transferred to a supranational body. In this respect, the Maastricht Treaty provides insufficient guarantees, as budgetary policy as well as other kinds of policy (price and wage policy and social policy) remain the province of the national governments. Consequently, there is a risk that EMU is regarded as a goal in itself. Although in some economic literature this may be justified on the basis of the theory of optimal currency areas, the conclusion was that this theory seems to be not very appropriate and that the major justification for realizing EMU is underlain by political motives. EMU is the most suitable instrument to deepen European integration, as it may potentially develop its own dynamics from which the need for political union may arise. History has shown that a currency without a state will not survive. Therefore, EPU must remain the final objective of EMU. This is not only in line with the concept of unification as described in the Werner Report but also in accordance with the intentions of the founding fathers of the EEC.

Until then, all EU Member States face the task of successfully completing stage two. Only such a success might warm the political climate to further unification. This means a huge challenge for Europe because — as this study has shown — economic and monetary unification has hardly ever, if at all, preceded political unification. Against this background, the conclusion can only be that the 'question' mentioned by the Council of Europe in 1950 regarding political and economic unification still needs to be answered nearly fifty years later. Such an answer may only be found if none of the Member States have any doubts that 'both should be developed simultaneously and are mutually supporting'.

This conclusion implies that, in the near future, the Community will face its most crucial challenge on the political side of its development, for one of the main lessons of the history of European integration in the past one hundred and fifty years may well be that unification will not proceed without some kind of incentive of a political nature.

Appendix 1   Overview of measures taken in the 19th-century European monetary unions

SWITZERLAND 1848–1931

7-5-1850   The first federal Act stipulates that the franc, made up of five grammes of silver with a metal content of 90 per cent fine silver, is to be the Swiss unit of account.

16-1-1852   Decision by the Federal Council providing that Belgian, French and Italian coins are wholly equated with Swiss coins.

31-1-1860   A federal Act provides for the official ratio of French gold coins of one hundred, fifty, forty, twenty, ten and five francs. At the same time the metal content of the silver coins, other than the five-franc coin, is reduced to 80 per cent fine silver so that they gain the character of subsidiary coins.

26-12-1865 Switzerland is a signatory to the Treaty on the LMU.

5-3-1866   Switzerland ratifies its participation in the LMU.

22-12-1870 The Federal Council is authorized by law to mint gold coins, for account of the Confederation or private persons, in conformity with the provisions of the LMU. This means that gold coins can be minted of one hundred, fifty, ten and five francs with a content of 90 per cent fine gold on the basis of 0.32258 gramme per unit of account.

15-1-1873   The implementation rule takes effect specifying the conditions under which private persons are permitted to mint gold coins for their own account.

8-7-1876   An agreement (Konkordat) is reached between the major banks of issue to accept each other's banknotes. This agreement takes effect as from 1 September 1876.

1-7-1882   An act comes into force (Banknotengesetz) enabling the Confederation to make arrangements for the insurance and redemption of banknotes.

7-9-1889   The minting of gold ten-franc coins is abandoned by law.

6-11-1895   Switzerland signs the amended monetary agreement of the LMU.

6-10-1905   Establishment of the Swiss National Bank. By law, the Bank is given the monopoly to issue banknotes for which it is obliged to maintain a metal cover of 40 per cent of the circulating notes.

5-1-1909   The Federal Council decides to permit the minting of ten-franc coins again.

30-7-1914   The Government gives forced currency to the banknotes issued by the National Bank.

3-8-1914   The gold standard is abandoned by the Swiss Government.

4-10-1920   Switzerland prohibits the import of silver five-franc coins from the other LMU countries.

28-12-1920 The Government withdraws foreign silver five-franc coins.

31-3-1921   Under the Decree of 28 December 1920, the silver five-franc coins of the other LMU countries cease to be legal tender in Switzerland.

1-1-1927   Switzerland considers the LMU disbanded.

8-2-1927   All foreign coins of the LMU are withdrawn from circulation in Switzerland. Private persons can exchange them without a loss for Swiss currency until end-March.

28-3-1930   The Swiss Government decides to abolish the forced currency of the banknotes as from 1 April 1930.

3-6-1931   A new Coinage Act provides for the single gold standard. The unit of account is to be the Swiss franc with a value equalling 0.29032 gramme fine gold. The Act provides for the minting of gold coins of one hundred, twenty and ten francs, which are legal tender in Switzerland to unspecified amounts, while the silver five-franc coin becomes a subsidiary coin.

ITALY 1861–1927

24-8-1862 The Act on the unity of the Italian monetary system takes effect. The lira is officially recognized as the unit of account throughout the unified area. Authorization is granted for the unrestricted minting of gold coins of one hundred, fifty, twenty, ten and five lira as well as the minting, solely for private account, of silver coins of five lira. The metal content of the gold lira coin is 90 per cent fine gold and its weight is 0.290322 gramme fine gold. The silver lira coin contains 90 per cent fine silver and has a weight of 5 grammes.

24-12-1865 Italy is a signatory to the Treaty on the LMU.

1-5-1866 The Decree takes effect granting the Banca Nazionale nel Regno d'Italia (BNR) the privilege to issue banknotes (with forced currency). The forced currency of the notes of the other issuing banks is acknowledged by which it becomes possible to exchange them for BNR notes or for metal.

3-9-1868 The Coinage Act of 1862 is extended to the provinces of Venice and Mantua, following their liberation from Austria.

30-4-1874 The Bank Act of that date is the first attempt to unify the issuance of banknotes. The right to issue is granted to no more than six institutions. The amount of notes to be issued by each of the issuing banks is subject to restrictions. The BNR has the largest quota (350 million lira). Violation of the quota ceiling is subject to a penalty. From 1885 onwards, the quota may be exceeded as long as the entire excess is covered by metal.
Another act comes into effect providing for the creation of a consortium of issuing banks which is authorized to issue 1 billion lira worth of notes with forced currency.

26-4-1876 The free minting of silver is suspended. The silver five-lira coins issued remain in circulation.

1-4-1880 The BNR's ceiling for issuing banknotes is raised to 450 million lira.

27-4-1881 The forced currency of banknotes is, in principle, abolished. It is up to the Government to stipulate by decree when the convertibility of the banknotes is to be restored. The consortium of issuing banks is disbanded as from 30 June. Its banknotes retain their forced currency until 31 December 1883. This period is extended to 1 June 1893.

12-4-1883   The convertibility of the banknotes is restored under the Decree of 1 March 1883.

10-8-1893   The new Bank Act becomes effective after the banking crisis of 1891 has led to the merger of the two Tuscan issuing banks (Banca Toscana di Credito and the Banca Nazionale Toscana) with the BNR to form the Banca d'Italia. The Act grants the right to issue banknotes to the Banca d'Italia, as well as to the Banco di Napoli and the Banco di Sicilia, for a period of twenty years. Metal cover is put at 40 per cent. The Act also assigns the status of legal tender to banknotes in provinces where these issuing banks have an establishment, a branch or a representative office.

21-2-1894   The convertibility of the banknotes is again revoked.

31-12-1907 The issuing ceiling for banknotes which need not be covered entirely by metal is raised to 908 million lira, of which 600 million lira is accounted for by the Banca d'Italia. The Act also stipulates that the silver subsidiary coins may represent no more than 2 per cent of the metal reserves of the issuing banks.

4-8-1914   The ceiling for the banknote circulation is raised. Further increases are fixed on 13 August and 23 November 1914, so that the ceiling is set at over 1.8 billion lira, of which 1.3 billion lira is accounted for by the Banca d'Italia.

25-6-1926   The monopoly of banknote issuance is provided for by revoking the issuing rights of the Banco di Napoli and the Banco di Sicilia as from 30 June. The gold and foreign exchange reserves of the two banks are transferred to the Banca d'Italia, which thus becomes the only issuing bank for the Kingdom of Italy. The Act also provides for the convertibility of the banknotes of the Banca d'Italia into gold or into foreign currencies.

7-9-1926   The issuing ceiling of the Banca d'Italia is set at 7 billion lira. An extraordinary tax is levied for banknotes issued above this ceiling.

21-12-1927 Italy introduces the gold exchange standard, with the parity of the lira being fixed at 7.919 grammes fine gold per one hundred lira.

GERMANY 1871–1910

4-12-1871   The gold mark becomes the standard coin. The Coinage Act provides for the minting of ten and twenty-mark coins. Individuals are not permitted to mint coins. With the permission of the Government, the Chancellor fixes the minting quotas. Silver is no longer minted. Certain old silver coins in circulation (including the Vereinsthaler) retain their status of legal tender.

9-7-1873   A second Coinage Act provides for the minting of gold five-mark coins. Gold twenty-mark coins may be minted without restriction so long as the minting plants are not engaged exclusively in minting for the Government. The Act provides for the minting of silver coins of five, two and one mark, and of smaller coins as well as copper and nickel subsidiary coins whose number is limited per head.

14-3-1875   Persuant to the Bank Act of this date, the Reichsbank is established as from 1 January 1876. Banknotes are not legal tender and State cashiers are not formally obliged to accept them. The notes can be exchanged for metal as from July 1875. The bank is held to purchase gold at a fixed price of 1392 marks. Other issuing banks are permitted to continue their activities under certain conditions. Under the 1875 Act, denominations of one hundred, two hundred, five hundred, one thousand and a multiple of one thousand marks can be brought into circulation. Each bank's issuance of uncovered banknotes is subject to a ceiling: 250 million marks for the Reichsbank and 385 million marks for all other issuing banks combined.

22-9-1875   The monetary system becomes effective for the entire German territory as from 1 January 1876. After this date, the issuing banks are permitted to issue only banknotes denominated in marks.

7-6-1899   Amendment of the Act establishing the Reichsbank, with the ceiling for the issuance of uncovered banknotes being raised to 450 million marks (the total issue of uncovered banknotes is fixed at 541 million marks).

1-6-1900   The ceiling of the circulation of silver coins is raised from ten to fifteen marks per head.

1-1-1901   The margin within which the private issuing banks may set their discount rates is limited (an earlier limitation was introduced on

7 June 1899). They are not permitted to fall below the official rate of 4 per cent. If the rate is lower, the discount rate may not be more than 0.25 per cent point below that.

20-2-1906   The Reichsbank is authorized to issue banknotes in denominations of fifty and twenty marks.

1-10-1907   The old silver Vereinsthaler loses its status of legal tender to unspecified amounts as from this date.

1-6-1909   A new Coinage Act enters into force, introducing the mark as Reichsgoldwährung with a metal content of 1/2790 kilogramme fine gold. The amended Bank Act of that same date provides for the legal tender status for the banknotes issued by the Reichsbank (hence not for the banknotes issued by the private issuing banks). The ceiling for issuance of uncovered banknotes by the Reichsbank is raised to 550 million marks (the total issue of uncovered banknotes is set at 619 million marks).

1-1-1910   The banknotes issued by the Reichsbank become legal tender. As from this date they can be exchanged for gold coins minted by the Reich.

GERMAN–AUSTRIAN MONETARY UNION, 1857–1867

24-1-1857   A monetary treaty is concluded between the States of the German Zollverein, Austria and Liechtenstein (the Vienna Treaty) with a fixed exchange rate being agreed between the Prussian Thaler, the South German Gulden and the Austrian Gulden. The Treaty turns on the Vereinsthaler, which has a fixed exchange rate vis-à-vis the other three currencies.

1-5-1857   The Vienna Treaty enters into force. It is valid until 31 December 1878. After that date it is to be extended for five-year periods, as long as none of the Member States has withdrawn from the Treaty two years before expiry.

6-9-1858   In Austria, the banknotes become convertible which means that they can be exchanged for high-grade silver coins.

1-11-1858   In Austria, the silver Gulden is introduced as the sole statutory unit of account. The Priviligierte Oesterreichische Nationalbank is permitted to issue only Gulden-denominated banknotes which may be exchanged for high-grade silver coins.

21-4-1859   Austria reverts to inconvertibility of its banknotes.

27-12-1862   The statute of the Nationalbank formally provides for the renewed convertibility of banknotes as from 1867. To that end, the metal reserves are to be raised, the banknote circulation is to be reduced and part of the state debt is to be repaid.

13-6-1867   The *Ausgleich* between Austria and Hungary means the end of the German–Austrian Monetary Union as from this date.

LATIN MONETARY UNION, 1865–1926

23-12-1865 The LMU is concluded between Belgium, France, Italy and Switzerland. The Treaty provides for the unrestricted minting of gold coins and silver five-franc coins, which can be exchanged at par within the LMU. The metal content of the silver subsidiary coins is fixed at 83.5 per cent. These coins are legal tender only to a limited amount which is fixed to six francs per head in each Member State.

1-5-1866 Italy revokes the convertibility of its banknotes. The Union Treaty does not provide for sanctions against this measure.

1-8-1866 The Treaty enters into force, and is valid until 1 January 1880. After that date it is to be extended for fifteen-year periods, unless a Member State has announced, one year in advance of expiry, that it wishes to discontinue its membership.

1-1-1869 Greece becomes a member of the LMU.

14-7-1870 France revokes the convertibility of its banknotes.

31-1-1874 A supplement is added to the Treaty, providing for a quota for each Member State for the year 1874 for the minting of silver five-franc coins.

5-11-1878 A new monetary Treaty is drawn up, prohibiting the minting of silver five-franc coins. Only gold coins may be minted to unlimited amounts though the existing silver five-franc coins continue to be legal tender. At the same time, the Italian subsidiary coins lose their status of legal tender within the LMU, until this country restores the convertibility of its banknotes. The Treaty becomes effective for six years. Under this Treaty, the LMU in fact adopts the gold (limping) standard.

6-11-1885 A new monetary Treaty is drawn up which includes a liquidation clause. This clause obliges each Member State to repurchase, at par value, its own silver five-franc coins which are in circulation in other Member States when the Union is disbanded. Belgium undertakes to adhere by this arrangement only on 12 December 1885. An attempt on the part of France to give the five-franc coins legal tender status throughout the Union fails.

15-11-1893 Amendment of the monetary Treaty of 1885 providing for nationalization of Italian subsidiary coins.

15-11-1895 A supplement to the Treaty of 1885 assigns a non-recurring quota to Switzerland for silver subsidiary coins.

29-10-1897 A supplement to the Treaty of 1885 provides for a general raising of the quota of silver subsidiary coins within the Union from six to eleven francs per head.

4-11-1908 A supplement to the Treaty of 1885 raises the quota for silver subsidiary coins within the Union from eleven to sixteen francs per head.

13-3-1915 The Swiss Government introduces a law which prohibits all trade in silver coins used by the other Union countries.

25-3-1920 A supplement to the Treaty of 1885 provides for the mutual nationalization of French and Swiss silver subsidiary coins. The Swiss quota is raised from eleven to twenty-eight francs per head.

4-10-1920 Switzerland prohibits the import of silver five-franc coins from the other Union countries.

28-12-1920 Switzerland announces that, following a transitional period of three months, it will no longer exchange silver five-franc coins, which have not been minted within its own borders, at a fixed rate. This is contrary to the stipulations of the Union Treaty of 1865.

9-12-1921 A supplement to the Treaty of 1885 provides for formal acknowledgement by the other Member States of the Swiss measure of 1920. Belgium, France, Greece and Italy agree to repurchase, subject to certain conditions, part of the coins minted by them which are in circulation in Switzerland. From then on, Switzerland is linked to the LMU only through its gold coins.

24-12-1925 Announcement of the Belgian Government that Belgium will withdraw from the LMU as from 1 January 1927. Switzerland subsequently announces that it considers its membership of the LMU terminated effective from 1 January 1927. This is the end of the LMU.

SCANDINAVIAN MONETARY UNION, 1873–1931

18-12-1872 Denmark (which then still includes Iceland) and Sweden decide to form a Monetary Union. The Scandinavian crown, with a value of 1/2480 kilogramme fine gold, becomes the common unit of account within the Union. Each Member State mints its own crowns, with its own mint stamp. The crowns of the two States are mutually exchangeable at par. The national subsidiary coins are given legal tender status within the Union.

27-5-1873   The monetary Union Treaty is ratified in Stockholm.

1-1-1877   Norway becomes the third member of the Scandinavian Monetary Union pursuant to the Treaty of 16 October 1875.

1-1-1879   As from that date subsidiary coins are accepted as legal tender within the Union to limited amounts only.

1-8-1888   An agreement concluded in 1885 between Norway and Sweden becomes effective, entailing that the central banks of the two Union countries conclude a clearing agreement under which they undertake to provide each other with unrestricted three-month credits, free of charge, followed by settlement in gold. The objective of the agreement is to equate the exchange rates between the currencies with the gold parity, in other words, the margin between the gold import and export points is eliminated entirely. Denmark joins this agreement in 1905.

1-1-1894   The central banks of Norway and Sweden agree to accept each other's banknotes at par. In 1901, a similar agreement is concluded between the central banks of Norway and Denmark (parity agreement).

30-9-1905   The central bank of Sweden withdraws from the 1885 agreement. A new arrangement is introduced, with the central banks of the Union countries limiting their mutual lending and charging commission.

2-8-1914   Denmark and Sweden abolish the convertibility of their banknotes, followed two days later by Norway. In early 1916 the convertibility of the notes of the three States is restored.

6-8-1914   Denmark prohibits the export of gold.

18-8-1914   Norway prohibits the export of gold.

9-10-1915   The central bank of Sweden annuls the parity agreement, announcing a discount on the Danish crown and, on 1 December 1915, also on the Norwegian crown.

25-11-1915   Sweden prohibits the export of gold.

8-2-1916   Introduction of the gold blockade by Sweden.

15-4-1916   Introduction of the gold blockade by Norway.

22-2-1917   Introduction of the gold blockade by Denmark.

18-3-1920   Sweden abolishes the convertibility of its banknotes.

19-3-1920   Denmark and Norway abolish the convertibility of their banknotes.

1-4-1924   Sweden restores the gold standard, so that the central bank obtains the sole right to import gold. Within the Union, each country is given the right to mint its own subsidiary coins, which are legal tender only within its own borders. This in fact marks the end of the Monetary Union. As from the same date the convertibility of banknotes is restored.

27-12-1926   Denmark restores the gold standard, followed in May 1928 by Norway.

16-4-1928   Norway restores the convertibility of its banknotes.

23-12-1929   Denmark restores the convertibility of its banknotes.

27-9-1931   Norway abandons the gold standard followed by Sweden on 28 September and Denmark on 29 September.

Appendix 2   Chronological overview of economic, monetary and political cooperation in the European Community: period 1945–1995

1946

19/9   In Zürich, the British politician Winston Churchill advocates the establishment of a sort of *United States of Europe* in which France and the defeated Germany are to play the leading roles. Churchill holds the view that the United Kingdom is not to play a role in this united Europe. It has its role to play in the Commonwealth.

1947

28/3   Establishment by the United Nations of the *Economic Commission for Europe*. The participants are the European Member States of the United Nations, the Soviet Union and its Satellites.

1948

1/1   A common customs tariff is introduced between Belgium, Luxembourg and The Netherlands pursuant to the *Benelux Treaty*. This Treaty is based on the monetary agreement of 21 October 1943 between the Belgo–Luxembourg Economic Union and The Netherlands, fixing the official rate of exchange between the Belgian franc and the Dutch guilder, and on the Customs Agreement of 5 September 1944, providing for the common customs tariff between the three countries.

16/4   Convention of the *Organization for European Economic Cooperation (OEEC)*, is signed by seventeen countries with Spain joining in 1959. Its main objective is the furtherance of a balanced expansion of the European economy by promoting economic cooperation among the Member States.

1949

5/5   Establishment of the *Council of Europe* by the Benelux, Denmark, France, Ireland, Italy, Norway, Sweden and the United Kingdom with Germany, Greece and Turkey joining in 1951. The objective of the Council is to realize a closer union between the Member States as well as to stimulate their economic and social progress.

1950

9/5   Official announcement by the French Minister of Foreign Affairs Schuman of the establishment of a *common market for coal and steel.*

1/7   *The European Payments Union* takes effect, the participants being the Member States of the OEEC. The objective of the agreement is to stimulate free intra-European goods and optimum currency areas probably offers system.

1951

18/4   Signing of the Treaty establishing the *European Coal and Steel Community (ECSC)* by the Benelux countries, France, Germany and Italy.

1952

27/5   Signing of a provisional Treaty for a *European Defense Community (EDC)* according to the Pleven Plan. This Plan was rejected by the French Assembly in August 1954.

21/7   The *ECSC* enters into effect.

1953

24/7   A protocol is signed by the Governments of the Benelux countries regarding the *coordination of economic and social policies* among its three Member States.

1954

20/8   The Treaty establishing the *EDC* is rejected by the French National Assembly.

1955

6/5 Establishment of the *Western European Union (WEU)*. The Treaty provides for economic, social and cultural cooperation among the Benelux, France, Germany, Italy and the United Kingdom.

1-2/6 *Conference of Messina*, during which the six ECSC countries decide on a common market and the common development of peaceful use of nuclear energy.

1957

25/3 Signing of the *Treaties of Rome* on the establishment of the European Economic Community (EEC) and the European Atomic Energy Community (Euratom). The EEC Treaty provides for the establishment of a Customs Union within a period of twelve to fifteen years.

1958

1/1 Treaties on the *EEC* and *Euratom* take effect.

3/2 Signing of the Treaty to establish the *Benelux Economic Union*. The Treaty is entered into for a period of fifty years and provides for free movement of goods, services, persons and capital among the three Member States.

18/3 Under the Treaty of Rome the *Monetary Committee* is established whose task it is to coordinate monetary policies conducted in the Member States of the EEC.

29/12 The European Payments Union is replaced by the *European Monetary Agreement (EMA)*, on the basis of which thirteen countries decide to make their currencies convertible.

1959

1/1 First reduction of *intra-Community customs tariffs* for manufactured products by 10 per cent.

1960

4/1 Signing of the Convention of Stockholm establishing the *European Free Trade Association (EFTA)* by Austria, Denmark, Norway, Portugal, Sweden, Switzerland and the United Kingdom. Iceland accedes the Convention in March 1970 followed by Finland, which has been an Associate Member since 1961, in January 1986.

11/5   The EEC Council of Ministers (unless otherwise stated, the Council of Ministers is understood to be the Council of Economic and Finance Ministers (Econfin Council)) adopts the first directive for the implementation of article 67 of the EEC Treaty regarding the *liberalization of capital transactions.*

1961

1/1   Second reduction of *intra-Community customs tariffs* for manufactured products by 10 per cent.

10/2   On the initiative of France, the Fouchet Committee is established to consider possible amendments in the Treaty of Rome. In November the *Fouchet Plan* is presented in which closed cooperation on foreign and security issues is recommended.

31/7   Denmark, Ireland and the United Kingdom request *negotiations about access to the EEC.*

30/9   The OEEC is converted into the *Organization for Economic Co-operation and Development (OECD).* The participants include the European Member States of the OEEC, Canada and the United States. Later, the OECD is expanded with Japan (1964), Finland (1969), Australia (1971) and New Zealand (1973).

29/11   The Fouchet Committee publishes a draft Treaty on *European Political Union (EPU).*

31/12   Extra reduction of *intra-Community customs tariffs* for manufactured products by 10 per cent.

1962

14/1   Start of stage two of the transitional period towards a *Common Market,* after agreement has been reached on a Common Agricultural Policy.
Intra-Community customs tariffs for manufactured products are lowered on 1 January and 1 July, each time by 10 per cent.

5/2   The French President De Gaulle advocates a *European confederation.*

9/2   Spain requests negotiations on closer *cooperation with the EEC.*

17/4   *Negotiations on EPU* are interrupted because Belgium and The Netherlands request a decision on accession by the United Kingdom.

30/4   Norway requests *negotiations on accession to the EEC*.

                                    1963

1/1   *Intra-Community customs tariffs* for manufactured products are
        lowered by 10 per cent. This means a total reduction of these
        tariffs of 60 per cent.

22/1   The German Chancellor Adenauer and the French President De
        Gaulle sign the *Franco–German Cooperation Treaty*, effective as
        from 1 July.

                                    1964

8/5   Decision by the EEC Council of Ministers to establish a *Committee
        of Governors of the Central Banks* of the Member States of the
        EEC.

3-4/7   Franco–German meeting on a possible re-opening of discussions
        regarding *political union* in Europe.

2-3/12 The Council of the OECD decides to extend the *EMA* for one
        year.

                                    1965

1/1   Reduction of *intra-Community customs tariffs* for manufactured
        products by 10 per cent.

18/4   Signing of the *Merger Treaty* of the ECSC, EEC and Euratom. Its
        purpose is to create a common Council of Ministers and a common
        European Commission for the three European communities.

30/6   France withdraws from EEC discussions on account of problems
        concerning the financing of the *Common Agricultural Policy*.

                                    1966

1/1   Entry into effect of the third and last stage of the Customs Union,
        attended by the eighth reduction of *intra-Community customs
        tariffs* for manufactured products by 10 per cent.

28-29/1 *Compromise of Luxembourg*. In deviation from the EEC Treaty,
        the principle of majority voting in the EEC Council of Ministers
        is abandoned.

11/5   Agreement between the Member States of the EEC on the financing of the *Common Agricultural Policy* until the end of the transitional period towards the Common Market.

1967

11/5   Official request from the United Kingdom to join the *EEC*. This is followed by *requests for accession* from Denmark, Ireland and Norway.

1/7   The *Merger Treaty* of 18 April 1965 enters into effect. In addition to one Council of Ministers, the High Authority, EEC Commission and Euratom Commission merge into one European Commission for the European Community (EC).
        Reduction of *intra-Community customs tariffs* for manufactured products, by 10 to 15 per cent depending on the product.

1968

1/7   The EEC reaches the stage of *Customs Union* for manufactured products.

3/10   Belgium suggests closer *cooperation within the WEU* in the field of foreign policy. This suggestion is rejected by France.

1969

17/7   The EC Council of Ministers accepts the *proposal of prior consultation* on all important decisions or measures of a Member State on economic policy.

9/8   *Devaluation* of the French franc by 12.5 per cent vis-à-vis the dollar.

24/10   *Revaluation* of the Deutsche mark by 9.29 per cent vis-à-vis the dollar.

1-2/12 Conference of Heads of State and Government Leaders *(European Council)* at The Hague on the simultaneous expansion and deepening of the Community. The final objective formulated there is *Economic and Monetary Union (EMU)*.

22/12   Agreement in principle between the EC Member States on the future financing of the *Common Agricultural Policy*.

1970

9/2   Decision by the EC central banks to establish the *short term credit facility* to be used for the settlement of debts resulting from interventions in the foreign exchange market.

5/3   The Commission publishes a *plan in stages* for realization of EMU.

6/3   The EC Council of Ministers sets up a working group, headed by the Prime Minister of Luxembourg, Werner, who is to work out the plan in stages in detail. In addition, high officials are charged with the compilation of a report on *European political cooperation* led by the Frenchman Davignon.

22/4   Signing of the agreement to reinforce the *competences of the European Parliament* and the assignment of own resources to the EC.

30/6   Denmark, Ireland, Norway and the United Kingdom start with *negotiations on accession to the EC.*

16/10 *Werner Report* proposes to realize EMU in three stages, the first of which will last until the end of 1973. The process is envisaged to be completed in 1980.

19/11 Meeting of the EC Council of Ministers (of Foreign Affairs) within the framework of political cooperation, in conformity with the *Davignon Report.*

1971

24/1   Two-day consultations between France and Germany. Both countries express their *willingness to create EMU* with the other four EC partners. However, no date is fixed.

9/2   The European Council approves the *plan in stages* for EMU.

22/3   Resolution of the EC Council of Ministers, which uses the *Werner Report* as starting point for the creation of EMU. The political willingness is evident to realize economic and monetary union 'within the next decade according to the plan, taking effect on 1 January 1971'. Under pressure from France, the Council leaves the final date open, restricting itself to stage one, which will enter into effect on 1 January 1971 and will take three years.
Decision of the EC Council of Ministers to implement the *mechanism for medium-term financial assistance* for a period of four years, starting from 1 January 1972.

10/5   Germany and The Netherlands decide to let the exchange rates of the Deutsche mark and the guilder float vis-à-vis the dollar.

15/8   *Suspension of the dollar convertibility* by US President Nixon.

23/8   The *central banks of the Benelux countries* agree to support each other's currencies in order to prevent the exchange rate from deviating more than 1.5 per cent on both sides of parity.

3/12   During their two-day consultations, France and Germany urge Europe to return to *realistic exchange rates* at fixed parities. Franco–German cooperation will be assigned highest priority.

18/12   *Agreement of Washington*, providing for the restructuring of exchange rates. The yen is revalued by 7.66 per cent, the Deutsche mark by 4.61 per cent and the guilder and the Belgian franc by 2.76 per cent. The gold parities of the French franc and sterling remain unchanged, while the Italian lira and the Swedish crown are devalued by 1 per cent and the dollar by 7.89 per cent. Furthermore, agreement is reached on a widening of the margins on both sides of the central rate to 2.25 per cent instead of the permissable margin of ± 1 per cent stipulated by the IMF.

1972

22/1   Signing of the *conditions for accession to the EC* by Denmark, Ireland, Norway and the United Kingdom.

10/2   Two-day consultations between France and Germany. The French President Pompidou urges for a *European Europe*, which is to prove its independence vis-à-vis the United States.

7/3   The EC Council of Ministers and the Committee of Central Bank Governors decide to reduce the *fluctuation margin* between EC currencies to 2.25 per cent on 1 July at the latest.

21/3   In a resolution of the EC Council of Ministers, the *decision of 7 March 1972* is formalized.

24/4   The agreement on the narrowing of the mutual fluctuation margin (*'Snake' in the 'Tunnel'*) takes effect.

1/5   Denmark, Ireland and the United Kingdom join the *EC intervention mechanism*.

18/5   In a statement before the Council of Europe, Werner says that the decisions of 21 March 1972 mean the entry into effect of *stage one of EMU* which will end on 31 December 1973.

23/5   Norway joins the *EC intervention mechanism.*

22/6   The Bank of England stops its *foreign exchange interventions.* As a result, the United Kingdom no longer participates de facto in the intervention system. This step is followed by Denmark and Ireland. Nevertheless, Ireland maintains its fixed rate against sterling.

21/8   The Benelux countries maintain the fluctuation margin of ± 1.5 per cent between their currencies (*'Worm'* within the *'Snake'*).

12/9   In Rome, the EC Council of Ministers decides to establish the *European Monetary Fund* before the end of stage one.

26/9   In Norway, the population votes against *accession to the EC* in a referendum.

10/10   Denmark resumes its participation in the *EC intervention mechanism* after a positive outcome of the referendum on accession to the EC.

19/10   In Paris, the European Council confirms that the decisions with regard to stage two of the unification process as from 1 January 1974 should be made in the course of 1973. It is decided to establish a *European Monetary Cooperation Fund (EMCF)* before 1 April 1975 as the forerunner of a federal system of central banks to be realized in the final stage of EMU.

24/10   The Council of the OECD decides to end the *EMA* as from 31 December 1972.

18/12   The Committee of Central Bank Governors creates provisions to increase the elasticity of the *EC intervention system.* Intra-marginal interventions are allowed, i.e. interventions which will take place before the 'Snake' currencies have dropped to their bottom rate. In addition, the Committee agrees to a more flexible application of the settlement regulation.

1973

1/1   *Accession* of Denmark, Ireland and the United Kingdom to the
           EC.
           The *free-trade agreement* of the EC with Austria, Portugal, Swe-
           den and Switzerland takes effect.

12/2   *Devaluation* of the dollar by 10 per cent (the new official gold price
           is 42.2 dollar per ounce fine gold).
           Italy leaves the '*Snake*'.

19/3   The countries participating in the intervention system — the Be-
           nelux, Denmark, France, Germany and as from that date Norway
           and Sweden — suspend the link between their currencies and
           the dollar. Against each other's currencies they will maintain
           a fluctuation margin of ± 2.25 per cent vis-à-vis the central rate.
           This marks *the end of the Bretton Woods System*.
           Revaluation of the central rate of the Deutsche mark by 3 per cent.

1/6   The *EMCF* takes effect.

22/6   Italy has recourse to *short-term monetary assistance* to an amount
           of 1.8 billion dollar.

28/6   Proposals by the Commission on *pooling of the national foreign
           exchange reserves* and reinforcing short-term monetary assistance.
           The Commission advocates a pooling of the national reserves in
           stages. The first 20 percent should be pooled on 1 January 1974.

29/6   *Revaluation* of the central rate of the Deutsche mark by 5.5 per
           cent.

17/9   *Revaluation* of the central rate of the guilder by 5 per cent. The
           new central rate of the guilder is SDR 0.298056, representing a
           gold content of 0.264874 gramme fine.

9/11   The Commission puts forward new proposals to stimulate the
           process of integration. France and The Netherlands raise objec-
           tions to the transition to stage two. France cannot accept that
           three Member States have floating exchange rates whereas The
           Netherlands object to insufficiently democratic structures.

15/11   *Revaluation* of the central rate of the Norwegian crown by 5 per
           cent.

17/12 Decision of the EC Council of Ministers to start *'a' stage two* which will end on 31 December 1976. The objective of this stage is to achieve essential progress in establishing EMU, so that it may be realized on the agreed date of 1 January 1980. Furthermore, the short-term monetary assistance will be reinforced. The proposed initial deposit — now 10 per cent of the gross reserves as at the end of December 1973 — will be examined.

1974

21/1 France leaves the *'Snake'* for a period of six months. The five remaining Member States (Benelux countries, Denmark and Germany) jointly decide, together with Norway and Sweden, to maintain the mutual fluctuation margin of ± 2.25 per cent.

15/2 Some Members of the Commission warn the European Parliament against economic problems within the Community. At a real growth rate of 2 to 3 per cent, the *inflation rate* is expected to be only marginally below 10 per cent.

18/2 Resolution by the EC Council of Ministers on the realization of a high extent of *convergence of the economic policies* conducted by the Member States (Convergence Decision).

18/3 Italy uses the *short-term monetary assistance facility* agreed in July 1973.

8-9/7 During their two-day consultations France and Germany agree that the *fight against inflation* is a prerequisite for economic and political integration in Europe.

21/10 Resolution by the EC Council of Ministers regarding the creation of *Community loans* (to a maximum of 3 billion dollar) in order to finance balance-of-payments deficits due to oil price rises.

18/11 After two extensions of short-term monetary assistance, each time by three months, the EC Council of Ministers decides to grant a loan within the framework of *medium-term monetary assistance* to Italy, totalling EUA 1.2 billion with an average maturity of three and a half years. The United Kingdom does not participate, but is willing to extend its participation in short-term monetary assistance (EUA 0.4 billion). The loan is effected on 18 December.

9-10/12 In Paris, the European Council decides to meet three times a year with the EC Ministers of Foreign Affairs, or more often as necessary, in its capacity as Council of the Community and on account of *political cooperation.*

1975

20/2   Creation of a *mechanism for raising Community loans in support of the balances of payments* of the EC Member States.

18/3   Establishment of the *European Regional Development Fund* which takes effect on 16 October 1975.

19/3   As a result of the Lomé conference, the *EUA* is defined. It consists of a basket of nine EC currencies (share of Germany 27.3 per cent; of The Netherlands 9 per cent). At a number of European institutions, the EUA is used as from 21 April as the accounting unit.

10/7   France returns to the 'Snake' at the old parity of the franc. The EC Council of Ministers and the Central Bank Governors invite Switzerland to a discussion on a *possible association with the 'Snake' countries.*

20/10   Meeting of the *Benelux Economic Union.*

20/11   The Swiss Parliament decides to postpone a possible association of Switzerland with the *'Snake'.* Objections to such association are expressed by France.

28/11   For the time being, Italy does not return to the *'Snake'* partly because of the large inflation rate differential vis-à-vis Germany.

1-2/12 In Rome, the European Council expresses its view that the economic activities of the Community and those in the field of *political cooperation* should be coordinated.

8-9/12 With reference to the *international monetary conference* held in Rambouillet on 16 and 17 November (attended by France, Germany, Italy, Japan, the United Kingdom and the United States), the Governors of the Central Banks of the 'Snake' countries and the US Federal Reserve Bank decide to consult each other on a daily basis on the situation in the foreign exchange market, the objective being to prevent strong exchange rate fluctuations of the dollar.

22/12   Resolution of the EC Council of Ministers regarding the extension of the *mechanism for medium-term financial assistance* by four years, in connection with the recourse by Italy to this mechanism.

1976

7/1   Publication of the *Tindemans Report* which advocates a differentiated approach, taking the 'Snake' as the core of foreign exchange stability.

16/2   During the meeting of the EC Council of Ministers, the Belgian Minister of Finance De Clercq calls the existing *exchange rates* realistic and correct. According to his French colleague Fourcade, 'Rambouillet' has functioned perfectly.

14/3   The EC Council of Ministers grants *Community loans* to Ireland (300 million dollars) and Italy (1 billion dollars).

15/3   France leaves the 'Snake' again. The *Benelux arrangement* (the 'Worm') is cancelled.

2-3/4 In Luxembourg, the European Council does not succeed in reaching agreement on *directives* to counter the economic and monetary problems.

26/7   The Dutch Minister of Finance Duisenberg suggests that *target zones* be implemented to reduce the exchange rate differentials between 'Snake' currencies and other currencies.

18/10 *Realignment.* Vis-à-vis the Belgian franc and the Dutch guilder the official central rate of the Deutsche mark is raised by 2 per cent while the central rates of the Norwegian and the Swedish crowns are reduced by 3 per cent and that of the Danish crown by 4 per cent. The Commission points out that the consultation procedure in respect of exchange rate realignments agreed on in the resolution of 18 February 1974 has not been complied with.

9/11   The EC Council of Ministers considers the Dutch proposal on *exchange rate target zones* not feasible for the time being. The German proposal to publish reference data about the expansion of the money supply is applauded by the majority of the Council.

22/11 Within the framework of *Community loans*, the EC Council of Ministers decides to place a loan in the capital market for the benefit of Italy because the United Kingdom terminates its credit granted to Italy within the framework of short-term monetary assistance.

29-30/11 At The Hague, the European Council stresses that the European Union will be realized gradually with the existing treaties forming the basis for new kinds of policy. Furthermore, the Council requests the Monetary Committee and the Committee of Central Bank Governors to elaborate on the Dutch proposal on *exchange rate target zones* and to examine under which conditions this proposal may be put into practice.

1977

4/4   *Realignment.* Vis-à-vis the other currencies in the 'Snake' the official central rate of the Swedish crown is devalued by 6 per cent and those of the Norwegian and Danish crowns by 3 per cent.

18/4   The EC Council of Ministers approves a *Community loan* of 500 million dollars to Italy. This means that the maximum volume of this loan is reached (3 billion dollars, including interest).

1/7   End of transitional period towards full abolition of *intra-Community customs rates* for the three new Member States (Denmark, Ireland and the United Kingdom) which joined the EC in 1973.

28/8   Sweden leaves the *'Snake'*. The official central rates of the Norwegian and the Danish crowns are devalued by 5 per cent vis-à-vis the other currencies in the 'Snake'.

31/10   The British authorities decide to no longer oppose further *appreciation of sterling*.

21/11   Decision of the EC Council of Ministers to expand the *EC credit mechanisms*.

5-6/12   In Brussels, the European Council discusses various documents of the Commission on EMU. The Council urges for a reinforcement of *coordination of the economic policies* conducted by the Member States and for the strengthening of monetary solidarity by means of adjustment of the Community credit mechanisms.

19/12   Decision by the European Council of Ministers regarding the adjustment of the *mechanism for medium-term financial assistance*. (The maximum commitments of the Member States are doubled and expressed in EUA. The stipulations regarding the conditions for assistance and control on compliance with these conditions are adjusted.)

1978

13/2   *Devaluation* of the Norwegian crown by 8 per cent vis-à-vis the other currencies in the 'Snake'.

7-8/4   During the meeting of the European Council in Copenhagen a committee is set up consisting of high officials from France, Germany and the United Kingdom to examine how *monetary stability* can be increased.

5/6   The Monetary Committee starts discussions on alternative forms of *monetary cooperation*. Cases in point are pooling of a part of the national foreign exchange reserves, the determination of monetary growth objectives in the individual Member States and the expansion of the role played by the EUA. According to the Belgian Chairman Van Ypersele, new life should be breathed into the EMCF and the EUA should be converted into a European monetary unit.

19/6   The EC Council of Ministers puts forward proposals for an alternative *monetary system*: (1) maintenance of the 'Snake' with the possibility of accession for non-'Snake' countries. (2) A new monetary arrangement with a currency basket. The exchange rate may fluctuate vis-à-vis this basket within a certain margin. (3) The creation of the European Monetary Fund following the example of the IMF.

7-8/7   In Bremen, the European Council discusses proposals which have been elaborated on by the French President Giscard d'Estaing and the German Chancellor Schmidt. It concerns a new *monetary system* which is to lead to a 'zone of monetary stability in Europe'.

24/7   The EC Council of Ministers elaborates on the agreement in principle without laying down any technical details. The system is referred to as *European Monetary System (EMS)*.

16/10   Agreement in principle by the EC Council of Ministers, with the Commission being granted the competence to raise loans in order to stimulate investments in the Community to a maximum amount of EUA 1 billion (*Ortoli lending facility*).

4-5/12 In Brussels, the European Council adopts a resolution pursuant to which the EMS will be introduced as from 1 January 1979. All Member States will participate, including the United Kingdom though its participation in the exchange rate mechanism will follow on a later date. The core of the EMS is the common *Exchange Rate Mechanism (ERM)* providing for stable, though adjustable, exchange rates. The EMS is based on a new *European Currency Unit (ECU)*, whose composition is initially identical to that of the EUA. The arrangements are valid for the starting phase of the EMS and will be consolidated in a final system within two years.

12/12   Norway leaves the *'Snake'*, which from that time only consists of the Benelux, Denmark and Germany.

29/12   Due to problems with France regarding the *Common Agricultural Policy*, the attempt to determine the central rates on 29 December fails, as a result of which the EMS cannot start as from 1 January 1979.

30/12   Decision by the EC Council of Ministers regarding the extension of the *mechanism for medium-term financial assistance* until the end of December 1980.

1979

13/3   The *EMS* becomes effective (ECU central rate of the guilder is set at 2.72077). Initially, the United Kingdom does not participate in the ERM. Italy opts for a margin of ± 6 per cent. The countervalue of the 20 per cent deposit by the participants in the EMS of the national gold and foreign exchange reserves in the form of a three-monthly swap with the EMCF amounts to ECU 24 billion.

14/5   Within the framework of the *Ortoli lending facility*, the Commission is authorized to place a first tranche of EUA 500 million in the capital market.

21-22/6   In Strasbourg, the European Council develops *policy guidelines* for harmonization of economic policies between the Member States, the coordination of their budgetary policies and the fight against inflation and unemployment.

28/6   The Greek Parliament ratifies the *Accession Treaty* of Greece to the EC.

1/7   The United Kingdom participates in the *revolving swaps* in the EMCF. As a result the countervalue of the initial transfer of gold and dollars rises to over ECU 29 billion, of which ECU 18 billion is held in the form of gold.

24/9   *Realignment* within the EMS: the Deutsche mark is revalued by 2 per cent and the Danish crown is devalued by 3 per cent vis-à-vis the central rates of the other EMS currencies (ECU central rate of the guilder: 2.74748).

29-30/11   In Dublin, the European Council recognizes that despite the progress made as a result of the coordinated economic approach decided on during the European Council meeting in Bremen, the objectives pursued, notably continued growth and the *fight against unemployment*, have not fully been realized. A common approach is essential with priority being assigned to the fight against inflation.

30/11   *Realignment* within the EMS: the Danish crown is devalued by 5 per cent vis-à-vis the central rates of the other EMS currencies (ECU central rate of the guilder: 2.74362).

13/12   Proposals of the Commission to *replace the EUA by the ECU* in four areas: the general budget, the whole of Community actions, support measures under the Lomé Convention and the areas falling within the scope of the ECSC Treaty.

1980

29/1   The Commission proposes a second tranche of loans to be contracted to an amount of EUA 500 million in accordance with the *Ortoli lending facility.*

27-28/4   In Luxembourg, the European Council calls the reduction of economic divergence and the strengthening of weak economies important *conditions for the development of the EMS.*

9/5   On the initiative of the European Movement, the *Congress of Europe* is organized in Paris in commemoration of the Schuman Declaration of 9 May 1950.

12-13/6   In Venice, the European Council discusses the international situation, which is dominated by repeated *oil price rises.*

15/7   The EC Council of Ministers decides to authorize the Commission to issue a tranche of EUA 400 million in accordance with the *Ortoli lending facility.*

17/11   The transition of the EMS to a *consolidated system*, which was to take place within two years, is postponed for an indefinite period of time. The agreement on the *pooling of reserves*, applicable for the transitional period, will continue to be effective for two more years after 19 March 1981.

1-2/12   In Luxembourg, the European Council is determined to continue its pursuit of a *strengthening of the EMS* until it enters the institutional stage 'at the right time'.

15/12   Decision by the EC Council of Ministers to extend the *mechanism for medium-term financial assistance* until 31 December 1982, unless the final stage of the EMS will start before that date.

16/12   Decision of the EC Council of Ministers to *replace the EUA* in Community decisions by the ECU as from 1 January 1981.

1981

1/1   Greece becomes the *tenth EC Member State.* It participates in the EMS but not in the ERM.

6/1   In Stuttgart, the German Foreign Minister Genscher launches a proposal on the EU. The plan is intended as a *European Act,* in which the EC Council of Ministers will only accept the veto right of Member States in exceptional cases. Denmark, France and the United Kingdom wish to retain this right. The Netherlands refuses to sign a document formally laying down the right of veto.

23/3   *Realignment* within the EMS: the Italian lira is devalued by 6 per cent vis-à-vis the central rates of the other EMS currencies (ECU central rate of the guilder: 2.81318).

23-24/3   In Maastricht, the European Council considers a strengthening of the dialogue with the US desirable so as to come to *common discussions on monetary policy* and interest rates.

29-30/6   In Luxembourg, the European Council stresses that within the EC the highest priority should be assigned to *coordinated measures* against unemployment and inflation.

5/10   *Realignment* within the EMS: vis-à-vis the central rates of the Deutsche mark and the guilder, the Belgian franc, the Irish pound and the Danish crown are devalued by 5.5 per cent, while the French franc and the Italian lira are devalued by 8.5 per cent (ECU central rate of the guilder: 2.66382).

19/10   The French Finance Minister Delors says in Luxembourg that the transition to *stage two of EMU* is not realistic.

26-27/11 In London, the European Council urges for a better coordination of economic and monetary policies and for the promotion of the use of the ECU for EC loans. Delors declares himself openly in favour of a strengthening of the ECU and monetary cooperation. The so-called Genscher–Colombo plan is also discussed. This plan tries to convert the relationship between the ten Member States into a *European Union (EU)* by means of a European Act. In this Union, economic integration should run parallel to the political development. After the meeting the Vice President of the Commission Ortoli states that it is impossible at this time to start the institutional stage of the EMS.

14/12 Proposal by the Commission for granting it the authority to raise *Community loans* to an amount of ECU 1 billion in order to stimulate investment in the Community.

19/12 The Belgian Central Bank Governor De Strycker urges for the termination of the *transitional stage of the EMS*. In the past thirteen months, the dollar rose by 45 per cent against the ECU.

1982

22/2 *Realignment* within the EMS: devaluation of the Danish crown by 3 per cent and of the Belgian franc by 8.5 per cent against the central rates of the other EMS currencies (ECU central rate of the guilder: 2.67296). Luxembourg was only informed of the Belgian intention at the last minute. This leads Prime Minister Werner of Luxembourg to conclude that the Belgian–Luxembourg monetary agreement, which dates from May 1935, should be adjusted.

15/3 The Commission proposes a *technical elaboration of the EMS* (settlement of intervention debts in ECUs and expansion of intra-marginal interventions). Germany opposes those proposals.

29-30/3 In Brussels, the European Council commemorates that it was twenty five years ago, notably on 25 March 1957, that the Treaties establishing the EEC and Euratom were signed. During consultations on the economic situation, the Council talks about a serious *structural crisis within the EC*.

26/4 The EC Council of Ministers approves the Commission's proposal to raise one single *Community loan* of ECU 1 billion.

14/6 *Realignment* within the EMS: the French franc is devalued by 10 per cent, the Italian lira by 7 per cent and the other EMS currencies by 4.5 per cent vis-à-vis the central rates of the Deutsche mark and the guilder (ECU central rate of the guilder: 2.57971).

28-29/6   In Brussels, the European Council discusses the *accession negotiations* with Spain and Portugal.

5/7   The meeting between Belgium and Luxembourg results in an *agreement to consult* each other more intensively in case of realignments and, if possible, to link up with the strongest currency.

19/10   Proposal by the Commission to authorize *Community loans* of ECU 3 billion.

10/11   Benelux Summit (the first since 20 October 1975) advocates an intensification of cooperation within the *Benelux Economic Union.*

3-4/12   The European Council instructs the EC Council of Ministers to reach a decision on the measures proposed by the Commission to reinforce the *internal market.*

17/12   Decision by the EC Council of Ministers to extend the *mechanism for medium-term financial assistance* by two years, unless the final stage of the EMS enters into effect during this period.

1983

10/1   *Devaluation* of the Greek drachme by 15.5 per cent against the other EMS currencies.

7/2   The EC Council of Ministers agrees to the Commission's proposal to place *Community loans* to an amount of ECU 3 million in the capital market to finance investments which meet the EC objectives.

21/3   *Realignment* within the EMS: against the central rate of the guilder, the Irish pound is devalued by 7 per cent, the French franc and the Italian lira by 6 per cent, the Belgian franc by 2 per cent and the Danish crown by 1 per cent. The central rate of the Deutsche mark vis-à-vis the guilder is raised by 2 per cent (ECU central rate of the guilder: 2.49587).

17/5   Decision of the EC Council of Ministers and the Committee of Central Bank Governors to assign a *fictitious exchange rate to sterling* in the ECU on the basis of the market rate of 17 May (ECU central rate of the guilder: 2.52595).

20/5   The revision of the Convention of 1935 culminates in the establishment of the *Luxembourg Monetary Institute (LMI)* as the central bank of Luxembourg. The LMI has no powers in the field of credit policy, which remains in the hands of the National Bank of Belgium. The LMI will, however, manage the reserves of Luxembourg, centralize the monetary competences and represent Luxembourg at international monetary fora (Luxembourg remains a member of the BLEU).

17-19/6 During the European Council meeting in Stuttgart, the Genscher–Colombo Plan loses momentum. Under pressure from the United Kingdom, the European Act should be changed into a *'Solemn Declaration'* on European Union.

4-6/12 Despite intensive preparations, the European Council in Athens does not achieve any result on even one single important problem facing the Community. Differences of opinion on the reform of the *Common Agricultural Policy* and financing of the Community cannot be bridged, so that every decision-making possibility with regard to a re-launching of the Community and its expansion with Spain and Portugal are blocked.

1984

1/1   Abolition of the last *tariff restraints* and quantitative restrictions for trade in manufactures between the EC and the EFTA. This results in the establishment of the world's largest free trade zone, a market of some 312 million consumers.

17/2   The European Parliament adopts a draft *Treaty on EU* with a majority of votes.

19-20/3 In Brussels, the European Council focuses on the financing of the Community. There is a difference of opinion between the United Kingdom and the nine other Member States on the extent to which the United Kingdom should be compensated for its *contribution to the Community budget* which it considers to be excessive.

25-26/6 In Fontainebleau, the European Council sets up an ad hoc committee (*Dooge Committee*) which will work out the proposals for improving European integration, including political cooperation.

15/9   The EC Council of Ministers decides on a revision of the *composition of the ECU*, in accordance with the EC Council Resolution of 5 December 1978 providing for the establishment of the EMS.

This revision does not result in a change in ECU central rates. The Council honours the request of the Greek Government to include the drachme in the ECU.

3-4/12   In Dublin, the European Council expresses its concerns about the delay in the *integration process*. It urges for a reinforcement of the EMS and a more important role for the ECU.

10/12   The EC Council of Ministers decides to extend the *mechanism for medium-term financial assistance* until 31 December 1986, unless the final stage of the EMS enters into effect before that date.

1985

28-29/3 In Brussels, the European Council discusses the final report of the *Dooge Committee*. This report urges, among other things, for an *Intergovernmental Conference (IGC)* to negotiate a draft Treaty on EU. In order to improve the decision-making process, the Committee suggests that decisions be taken with a qualified majority of votes within the Council of Ministers. Unanimity should become an exception. The Council decides to continue deepening these proposals in bilateral contacts, so that final conclusions may be reached during the meeting in Milan.

14-15/4 In an informal agreement, the EC Council of Ministers approves the agreement of the Committee of Central Bank Governors to raise *interest payments on the ECU*, which has so far been linked to the official discount rates, to the market level. The agreement further comprises the possibility for central banks in countries not being Member States of the EC and international monetary institutions to include official ECUs in their reserves. In addition, the obligation to accept ECUs in settlement of mutual intervention debts will be expanded.

21/5   Italy presents a draft mandate, which proposes that the IGC will negotiate a *Treaty on a gradual establishment of the EU*. The Netherlands suggests that the objective of the conference will be to revise the EEC Treaty in accordance with its article 236 and to draw up a protocol for the consolidation and institutionalization of political cooperation.

8-9/6   Informal meeting of the EC Council of Ministers (of Foreign Affairs) during which the United Kingdom submits a document on the decision-making process (adjustments not requiring an amendment of the EEC Treaty) as well as a *draft agreement on political cooperation.*

14/6   The Commission publishes a *White Paper* on the completion of the internal market. This Paper contains measures to be taken until 1992 in order to remove all physical, technical and fiscal obstructions between the EC Member States.
In *Schengen*, the Benelux countries, France and Germany sign an agreement on the gradual abolition of controls at their frontiers.

28-29/6   In Milan, the European Council discusses the IGC. A French Memorandum is published on the progress reached with regard to the building of Europe as well as a *Franco–German draft Treaty on EU.*

2/7   Luxembourg submits a draft for the *amendment of the EEC Treaty.*

22/7   *Realignment* within the EMS: the Italian lira is devalued by 8 per cent vis-à-vis the other EMS currencies (ECU central rate of the guilder: 2.52208). Furthermore, the Greek drachme which does not participate in the ERM is devalued by 15 per cent. Greece is granted a *Community loan* of ECU 1.75 billion.

9/9   First meeting of the IGC in Luxembourg, attended by the Foreign Affairs Ministers of the ten EC countries and Spain and Portugal. The conference is charged with the *amendment of the EEC Treaty* and the establishment of a Treaty on foreign policy and common security. President Delors of the Commission proposes an expansion of the competences of the Community in four areas: European market, technical competences, economic and social harmonization and 'a certain monetary competence'.

21/10   Second meeting of the IGC in Luxembourg. The *draft Treaty on political cooperation* is not yet discussed.

28/10   On the initiative of Delors, the Commission attempts to *incorporate the EMS into the EEC Treaty.* This would mean that the competence of the EC Institutions on community matters of a monetary nature would be confirmed and that the Commission would obtain the right of initiative with regard to the future development of monetary cooperation within the Community.

2-3/12   In Luxembourg, the European Council reaches an agreement in principle on the *revision of the Community institutions.* A limited revision of the EEC Treaty and a draft Treaty on European co-operation in the field of foreign policy is decided on. The internal market will be completed before 1 January 1993. The European Parliament will get a larger say, but the EC Council of Ministers will hold the decisive vote. References to EMU and EMS are included in the preamble to the amended EEC Treaty. The results of the conference on the amendment of the EEC Treaty and the text on political cooperation will possibly be presented by the Ministers in the form of one single Act.

16-17/12 During the third IGC meeting in Brussels the finishing touch is put to the *Single European Act (Acte Unique Européenne)*, which will be submitted for ratification by the Member States at the end of January 1986. It is the first time that both the development of the Community, due to a revision of the EEC Treaty, and the development of political cooperation are regulated in a single act. However, it proves impossible to incorporate the objective of EMU into this Act as a new Treaty obligation. The text finally agreed on stresses the need for cooperation in the economic and monetary areas. For institutional changes in economic and monetary policy, a new Treaty Amendment will be required. In the 'common provisions' (Title 1 of the European Act), the European Council has been institutionalized. Italy and Denmark accept the decisions made with reservation, while the United Kingdom maintains a reservation with regard to the social chapter.

1986

1/1   *Accession* of Spain and Portugal to the EC.

21/1   The Danish Parliament rejects the *Single European Act.* Subsequently, The Netherlands decides to postpone ratification.

17/2   The Ministers of Foreign Affairs of nine Member States sign the *Single European Act.* Denmark, Greece and Italy sign the Act on 28 February.

7/4   *Realignment* within the EMS: vis-à-vis the Deutsche mark and the guilder all other EMS currencies are devalued: the French franc by 6 per cent, the Belgian franc and the Danish crown by 2 per cent, the lira and the Irish pound by 3 per cent (ECU central rate of the guilder: 2.40935). With regard to economic policy, Belgium links up with Germany and The Netherlands.

21/5   The Commission accepts a notification on behalf of the EC Coun-
        cil of Ministers, setting a programme for the *liberalization of capi-
        tal transactions* in the Community. The creation of a homogeneous
        financial area is one aspect of the creation of the large *internal
        market*, which is to be realized by 1992 according to the objective
        set in the Single European Act.

26-27/6 European Council meeting at The Hague. The participants in-
        clude the Spanish and Portuguese Prime Ministers. The Council
        welcomes the proposals for *liberalization of capital transactions*
        put forward by the Commission and encourages the Council of
        Ministers to place these proposals high on the agenda.

4/8   *Realignment* within the EMS: the Irish pound is devalued by 8 per
        cent vis-à-vis the other EMS currencies (ECU central rate of the
        guilder: 2.37833).

17/11   The EC Council of Ministers approves the directive providing
        for the amendment of the First Directive of 11 May 1960 and
        the expansion of the community obligations in respect of the
        liberalization of capital transactions.

5-6/12 In London, the European Council takes note of the fact that the
        Member States which have not yet ratified the *Single European
        Act* intend to do so on time, so that the Act may enter into effect
        on 1 January 1987.

1987

12/1   *Realignment* within the EMS: vis-à-vis the Deutsche mark and the
        guilder, the Belgian franc is devalued by 1 per cent, the French
        franc, the lira, the Danish crown and the Irish pound are devalued
        by 3 per cent (ECU central rate of the guilder: 2.31943).

18/2   Commission President Delors presents a plan to the European
        Parliament for a *reorganization of the Community.* This notably
        concerns its financial structure, with a reduction of expenditure
        on agriculture from 70 to 50 per cent of the EC budget.

25/3   *Thirtieth anniversary of the EEC Treaty.* On occasion, the Chair-
        man of the EC Council of Ministers Tindemans notes that 'what
        the pioneers wanted to achieve, is still our objective'. He states
        that Europe continues to be a notion consisting of a multitude
        of elements which can be summarized into a certain identity.
        According to Tindemans, it goes without saying that this cultural,

political, economic and social scale of values must have a structure uniting the Europeans.

23/4   Publication of a report on the strategy for the development of the economic system of the EC by a group of independent experts under the chairmanship of Padoa-Schioppa. Recommendations in the report include *monetary policy coordination* and a considerable reinforcement of the mechanisms of the EMS. Both aspects are considered necessary if freedom of capital transactions and discipline in the exchange markets are to be maintained.

24/4   Request of Turkey to join the *EC*.

11/5   In its second report on the implementation of the *White Paper* regarding the completion of the internal market, the Commission considers the results disappointing, but not discouraging.

12/5   The Bank of Spain signs an official act as a result of which it becomes party to the *agreement on the EMS*. After depositing 20 per cent of its gold and foreign exchange reserves with the EMCF, Spain will hold a position similar to that of Greece and the United Kingdom, with the exception of its currency, the peseta, which is not yet included in the ECU.

19-20/6 In Brussels, the European Council feels that a number of concrete objectives with regard to the *internal market* should be agreed on now and that a procedure should be laid down to adopt, in the short term, decisions to realize this objective.

1/7   The *Single European Act* enters into force.

12/9   Informal meeting of the EC Council of Ministers in the Danish town of Nyborg. The Ministers approve the agreement reached by the Committee of Central Bank Governors to improve the functioning of the EMS without any institutional changes to the system. Pursuant to this *Basle/Nyborg Agreement*, adequate interest rate differentials will be implemented on time and the full bandwidth will be used in order to discourage speculative capital flows. In addition, mutual surveillance on the developments taking place within the EMS will be reinforced.

28/10   The Commission approves proposals for the final stage of the full *liberalization of capital transactions* within the Community. Earlier the protective measures in France and Italy were abolished. From this date, only Greece, Ireland, Portugal and Spain may maintain their restrictions on capital transactions.

10/11   By signing an official act, the Bank of Portugal becomes party to the *agreement on the EMS*. After a deposit of 20 per cent of its gold and foreign exchange reserves with the EMCF, the position of Portugal will be comparable to that of Greece, Spain and the United Kingdom, on the understanding that the escudo, like the peseta, is not yet included in the ECU basket.

17/12   Publication of a progress report on the EMS and the *liberalization of capital transactions* drawn up by the Commission on the request of the European Council at the end of 1985. According to this report, there is a close interdependence between the completion of the internal market, the EMS and the liberalization of capital transactions.

1988

16/3   Third report of the Commission on the completion of the *internal market*. So far, the Commission has submitted 208 out of the 300 proposals mentioned in the White Paper to the EC Council of Ministers.

20/5   Proposal by the Commission to come to an *integrated mechanism for medium-term financial assistance in support of the balance of payments* of the Member States. This proposal is a combination of the medium-term credit facility and the instrument of Community loans. The maximum contribution of the Member States to the medium-term mechanism (ECU 13.9 billion) remains unchanged.

13/6   *Interinstitutional agreement* (Council of Ministers, Commission and European Parliament) on budgetary discipline and the improvement of the budgetary procedure.

24/6   Regulation of the EC Council of Ministers to set up an integrated *mechanism for medium-term financial assistance in support of the balance of payments* of the Member States. Furthermore, a directive is issued to liberalize *capital transactions* between the EEC Member States.

27-28/6   In Hanover, the European Council decides to set up a *Committee, chaired by Delors*, whose task will be to examine concrete steps that may lead to EMU. The United Kingdom declares that neither a European Central Bank (ECB) nor a European currency are required for the establishment of EMU. Germany regards the ECB as the crown on progressing monetary cooperation.

15/11   Spain and Portugal join the *WEU*.

2-3/12   On Rhodes, the European Council stresses the *social dimension*. An undivided market cannot be considered a goal in itself. As traditionally incorporated in the history of Europe, the objective of the internal market is to ensure social progress and optimal well-being for all people in the Community.

1989

13/3   The EC Council of Ministers, commemorating the *tenth anniversary of the EMS*, underlines unanimously that the EMS has contributed to lower inflation, more stable exchange rates and thus to sound economic growth.

27/4   Publication of the *Delors Report*, describing the most important elements of EMU as well as the way in which EMU may be achieved within the EC. It is suggested to realize EMU in three stages: in stage one, emphasis is to be placed on convergence of economic developments and intensified policy coordination. Stage two is the transitional stage, which may start after the required Treaty amendments have been implemented. In stage three, the exchange rates must be fixed irrevocably. After some time, the national currencies may subsequently be replaced by the ECU.

19/6   Spain joins the *ERM* with a fluctuation margin of ± 6 per cent. The Greek drachme, the Portuguese escudo and sterling do not yet participate in the mechanism.

26-27/6 In Madrid, the European Council decides to start *stage one of EMU* on 1 July 1990. At the same time, the preparations for the following stages, which also comprise an IGC, will be started. The Council stresses the need to abolish material and fiscal restrictions in order to realize a market without internal frontiers by 31 December 1992 (according to article 8A of the Single European Act).

9-10/9   The EC Council of Ministers reaches agreement on the need to revise the Decision of 8 May 1964 regarding cooperation between the central banks of the Member States and the Decision of 18 February 1974 regarding *convergence of economic policies*.

21/9   The Spanish peseta and the Portuguese escudo are included in the *ECU basket*. As from this date, the weights in ECU are as follows: BFr 3.301, DKr 0.1976, DM 0.6242, GDR 1.440, Esc 1.393, FF 1.332, Hfl 0.2198, I£ 0.008552, LFr 0.130, Lira 151.8, Peseta 6.885 and £ 0.08784.

8/12   In Strasbourg, the European Council decides that stage one of EMU as described in the Delors Report may start on 1 July 1990. In addition, it is agreed that an IGC will be held before the end of 1990 which is to draw up amendments to the EEC Treaty with a view to the final stage of EMU. It is also decided to set up the *European Bank for Reconstruction and Development (EBRD)*. The EC and its Member States participate in its capital for 51 per cent.

1990

8/1   *Realignment* within the EMS. Italy returns to the narrow fluctuation margin of ± 2.25 per cent after a devaluation of the central rate of the lira by 3.68 per cent. This is the twelfth realignment since the start of the EMS in March 1979 (ECU central rate of the guilder: 2.30358).

28/3   Fifth Commission Report on the implementation of the *White Paper*. The Report confirms the irreversibility of the establishment of the internal market by 1992.

19/4   The French President Mitterand and the German Chancellor Kohl submit proposals to start political unity within the EC around 1 January 1993. The proposals comprise: expansion of democratic control in order to provide the political unity with a legitimate basis, improvement of the efficiency of EC institutions, insurance of economic, monetary and political harmonization of the EC and the determination of common foreign and security policies. Shortly afterwards, during a meeting of the European Council on 28 April, they call for an *IGC on political unity* before December 1990, which is to be held at the same time as the summit on Economic and Monetary Union.

28/4   In Dublin, an extraordinary meeting of the European Council results in unanimous agreement on a common approach to *German unification* and to the relationship with the countries of Central and Eastern Europe. Furthermore, agreement is reached on a working method for the preparation of proposals regarding the reinforcement of the *political union*.

21-23/5 The Treaty on *economic and monetary union between East and West Germany* is approved by the two German Parliaments. The Deutsche mark will be introduced as the common currency unit as from 1 July.

29/5   Signing of the memorandum of association of the *EBRD*, whose
            objective it is to finance industrial and economic development in
            the Eastern European countries by means of loans, guarantees and
            capital investments and to promote the transition towards a free
            market economy in these countries.

11/6   The Governor of the Deutsche Bundesbank Pöhl submits a pro-
            posal to the EC Council of Ministers to complete EMU in 'a
            process of two speeds'. His plan envisages a small number of
            low-inflation countries (Benelux, France, Germany) to participate
            in the *European System of Central Banks (ESCB)*. The other
            countries, which have not reached the same degree of economic
            convergence or which are not willing to give up sufficient autonomy
            are invited to join later.

18/6   The EC Council of Ministers (of General Affairs) approves guide-
            lines for negotiations between the EC and EFTA regarding the
            realization of the *European Economic Area (EEA)*.

19/6   The Agreement of 14 June 1985, signed at *Schengen*, is followed
            by a Convention on the Application of the Agreement.

20/6   The United Kingdom puts forward proposals for a gradual tran-
            sition to EMU by the introduction of a *parallel currency*, the so-
            called 'hard' ECU.

25-26/6   In Dublin, the European Council decides unanimously that the
            IGC on EMU will start on 13 December. The objective of the
            conference is to determine the final stage of EMU. Furthermore,
            the opening of a second *IGC on EPU* on 14 December is approved
            by unanimous vote.

1/7   The *German monetary union* enters into effect.
            Start of *stage one of EMU*.
            In most Member States, all *restrictions on capital transactions* are
            abolished. For Greece, Ireland, Portugal and Spain a derogation
            is effective giving them time to comply with the directive until the
            end of 1992.

12/7   The Greek Government announces its intention to join the *ERM*
            in 1993 if the tax measures of the Greek Government are imple-
            mented successfully.

21/8   Proposals of the Commission on EMU in preparation of the IGC
            of December in Rome. The proposals contain the recommendation

that *stage two of EMU* should be started on 1 January 1993 and that this stage should be 'as short as possible'.

8/9   The EC Council of Ministers fails to reach agreement on the *speed of integration*. Spain suggests that stage two be started on 1 January 1994 and that the transition towards stage three should not take longer than five to six years.

12/9   Signing in Moscow of the *Treaty on the German Reunification* by the two German States, France, the United States, the United Kingdom and the Soviet Union.

19/9   The Governor of the Bundesbank Pöhl imposes absolute demands on EMU. It must be based on an economic and financial attunement between the Member States, notably where anti-inflationary policy and the contractually enforced budgetary discipline are concerned. In the final stage of EMU which will be achieved via a *long-term transition process*, Governor Pöhl envisages that the independence of the ESCB will be guaranteed and that this institution will be authorized to impose sanctions on Governments which do not comply with the budgetary discipline.

3/10   The *Treaty on the German Reunification* enters into effect.

8/10   Sterling joins the *ERM* with a fluctuation margin of ± 6 per cent (ECU central rate of the guilder: 2.31643).

19/10   The Norwegian Government links the crown to the *ECU* and regards this as a step towards closer cooperation with the EC.

27-28/10 In Rome, during an extraordinary meeting of the European Council, all Member States, except the United Kingdom, agree to the start of *stage two* on 1 January 1994. With regard to EPU, the Council confirms that it gradually wishes to transform the Community by developing its political dimension.

27/11   Italy signs the *Schengen Treaty*.

6/12   France and Germany put forward proposals for the achievement of *political union*, notably where the development of common foreign and security policies are concerned. A clear organic relation will have to be developed between the WEU and the new political union with the WEU ultimately being incorporated into this union. The proposal is criticized by the Dutch Prime Minister Lubbers who holds the view that this will disturb the existing balance between the EC Institutions.

14-15/12 In Rome, the European Council agrees to continue playing an essential role as a political motor in important matters. It is stressed that the *expansion of the competences* of the Union should be attended by a reinforcement of the role played by the Commission. The question whether decision-making on the basis of majority voting may become the general rule within the EC Council of Ministers will also be investigated.

15/12   First session of the *IGC* in Rome. The European Council confirms that the two conferences will continue their activities independently of each other and that they will quickly and simultaneously present results so that both conferences may be rounded off before the end of 1992.

1991

8/1   The British Chancellor of the Exchequer Lamont presents detailed proposals on the creation of the 'hard' ECU as a *parallel currency* and on the way in which the issue of this currency will be regulated by a European Monetary Fund.

28/1   Second session of the *IGC on EMU*. Spain and Portugal submit proposals to 'harden' the existing ECU as the precursor to the final single currency instead of creating a thirteenth currency as proposed by the United Kingdom. Spain assumes that the monetary institution to be set up during stage two will be a clear precursor of a full ECB. France stresses the need for 'fully democratic management' which will be concentrated with the existing EC Council of Ministers to control a future ECB.

4/2   Second session of the *IGC on political union*. A plan by the French and German Ministers of Foreign Affairs (Dumas/Genscher) is discussed. This plan suggests that EMU should decide — provided that a unanimous decision may be made in this connection — which aspects of foreign policy will be included in the common policy. The EC Council of Ministers will subsequently decide on these issues by majority vote. Initially, the WEU (consisting of all Member States except Denmark, Greece and Ireland) may function as a link between EC and the North Atlantic Treaty Organization (NATO) established in April 1949. The proposals are rejected by the non-WEU countries, as well as by the United Kingdom and The Netherlands, which are both concerned about their relationship with the United States.

22/2   The EC Council of Ministers (Foreign Affairs and Defence) agrees
        to a provisional report, in which the *WEU* is regarded as a bridge
        between EU and NATO.

25/2   Within the EC Council of Ministers, a German *draft Treaty for
        monetary union* is received with criticism. In this Treaty, the
        establishment of an ECB is postponed to 1997 at the earliest and
        preference is given to the reinforcement of the existing ECU.

18/3   Parallel discussions on EMU and EPU by the EC Council of
        Ministers. Agreement is reached on the *political supervision of the
        ECB*. The agreement is based on a proposal by Luxembourg to let
        the EC Governments draw up general guidelines for exchange rate
        policy. However, the ECB will have to be consulted in advance
        so as to reach consensus in accordance with the objective of price
        stability. The proposal attempts to strike a balance between the
        German preference for a politically independent ECB with an
        obligation under its articles of association to conduct an anti-
        inflationary policy, and the preference of France and other coun-
        tries for greater Government control.

19/3   Before the European Parliament, the Governor of the Bundesbank
        Pöhl warns against the introduction of a *European currency* in case
        there is no greater economic convergence.

22/3   The French and German Ministers of Foreign Affairs (Dumas
        and Genscher) discuss the time schedule for the *various stages
        of EMU*. In a joint statement they propose to set up the ECB at
        the beginning of stage two. This means that the ECB may start its
        operations in January 1994. In stage three, the new independent
        central bank will hold 'sole responsibility for the implementation
        of monetary policy and the protection of the stability of the cur-
        rency'.

26/3   The EC Council of Ministers (of Foreign Affairs) discusses a *Dutch
        proposal regarding the European role in the field of security and
        defence* while maintaining 'a continued North American political
        and military obligation with respect to the security of Europe'.

8/4   Within the EC Council of Ministers, Germany, supported by The
        Netherlands, advocates that *stage two of EMU* should only be
        started on January 1994 in case the national economies, as agreed
        in October 1990, have converged to a sufficient degree, notably
        where inflationary control and balance-of-payments deficits are
        concerned.

9/4   The Committee of Central Bank Governors approves the draft version of the *Statute of the ECB.*

15-16/4   The Government of Luxembourg presents a *draft Treaty on EPU,* which indicates the objectives and advocates an expansion of the competences of the European Parliament.

11/5   During an informal meeting of the EC Council of Ministers and the Committee of Central Bank Governors, the President of the Commission Delors suggests that an *'opting out' clause* be included in the Treaty text on EMU allowing the United Kingdom to leave the decision on the ultimate goal of stage three to a future Parliament.

17/5   Link between the *Swedish crown and the ECU.*

4/6   Link between the *Finnish mark and the ECU.*

18-19/6   Compromise agreement between the EFTA and EC on the final establishment on 1 August of the stipulations of the *EEA* which will take effect in January 1993.

20/6   Proposal by the Government of Luxembourg for a *new draft Treaty on EPU,* comprising references to a 'federal objective', a possible joint defence policy, a slimmed down Commission and a European Parliament having a say in the EC Council of Ministers.

25/6   Spain and Portugal sign the *Schengen Treaty.*

28-29/6   In Luxembourg, the European Council discusses *EMU and EPU.* Final decisions on controversial matters are postponed until the European Summit at Maastricht.

1/7   Sweden formally applies for *membership of the EC.*

8/7   The EC Council of Ministers concludes that, in the last two years, no progress has been made on the way towards the required *convergence.*

24/9   The Netherlands publishes a *draft Treaty on political union.* It advocates more competences for the Commission and the European Parliament, which would have the right to veto decisions of the EC Council of Ministers by a majority of votes. Some countries, including the United Kingdom, consider this proposal too radical, while other countries, such as France, consider it not radical enough. Germany and Spain support the Dutch text.

9-10/12   The European Council meeting at Maastricht is the last IGC on EMU and EPU. Agreement is reached on a framework for a Treaty on EU, comprising the *EPU and EMU agreements*. This means that stage two will enter into effect on 1 January 1994. Under pressure from the United Kingdom, the chapter on social policy is left out of the Union Treaty. A special protocol allows this country and Denmark not to participate ('opting out') in stage three.

1992

7/2   The twelve Member States officially sign the Treaty concerning European Union (*Maastricht Treaty*). The EU Treaty stipulates that every European state with a democratic Government system may request accession to the Union. The Bundesbank urges the national Governments to work out the structure of the envisaged political union, which it considers essential for the success of EMU. Furthermore, the Bundesbank holds the view that meeting the convergence criteria formulated in the Treaty should not be linked to a time schedule.

18/3   Finland submits a request for *accession to the EC*.

6/4   Portugal joins the *ERM*. The fluctuation margin for the escudo is ± 6 per cent.

7/4   The European Parliament approves the *resolution on EU Treaty* by a 226 to 62 vote (31 abstentions).

2/5   Signing of the Agreement on the *EEA*. This agreement enables eighteen European countries to realize the free movement of goods, persons, services and capital on the basis of the existing EC legislation (*'acquis communautair'*) as developed in the past thirty years.

14/5   The EC Council of Ministers confirms its commitment to take the measures required for the achievement of the objective regarding the establishment of the *internal market* as at 31 December 1992 at the latest.

15/5   The British Prime Minister Thatcher warns that the problem of German supremacy has surfaced again. She advocates a looser and broader *confederation in Europe* instead of a centralized superstate.

2/6   Denmark rejects the *EU Treaty* in a referendum.

3/6   In France, President Mitterand announces that a referendum will be held on *ratification of the EU Treaty*. In the United Kingdom, ratification is suspended following the negative outcome of the Danish referendum.

18/6   In Ireland, the majority of the voters in the referendum say 'yes' to *ratification of the EU Treaty*.

23/6   In France, the Parliament approves the amendments of the constitution required to hold a referendum on *ratification of the EU Treaty*.

26-27/6 In Lisbon, the European Council expresses the view that the EEA agreement paved the way for the opening of *expansion negotiations* with the EFTA countries wishing to join the EU.

2/7   In Luxembourg, the Chamber of Representatives votes by majority in favour of the *ratification of the EU Treaty*.

17/7   In Belgium, the Second Chamber of Parliament votes by majority in favour of *ratification of the EU Treaty*.

22/7   In Spain, the Second Chamber of Parliament approves an amendment of the constitution paving the way for *ratification of the EU Treaty*. On 30 July, the First Chamber of Parliament approves the amendment.

31/7   The Greek Parliament, which only consists of one chamber, votes by majority in favour of the *ratification of the EU Treaty*.

8/9   *Currency crisis*. In the currency markets, speculation increases under the influence of the coming French referendum. Rumours spread when Finland announces that same day that it abolishes the link between the Finnish mark and the ECU.

13/9   *Realignment* within the EMS: the Italian lira is devalued by 3.5 per cent, the ten other currencies are revalued by 3.5 per cent (ECU central rate of the guilder: 2.29789).

16/9   *'Black Wednesday'*: the Italian lira, the peseta and sterling rock through the floor of the EMS. Sterling leaves the ERM (the interest rate in Sweden rises to 500 per cent).

17/9   Italy leaves the *ERM*, the Spanish peseta is devalued by 5 per cent (ECU central rate of the guilder: 2.29193).

20/9   From the French *referendum* it becomes evident that 51 per cent
        in favour of ratification of the EU Treaty.

8/10   In Germany, the Parliament approves the Treaty in the first read-
        ing, provided that it has the final say on the introduction of a
        single European currency to complete *EMU*.

9/10   In Denmark, the Government publishes a *White Paper*, in which
        it explains its viewpoints following the rejection of the EU Treaty.

16/10   In Birmingham, the European Council urges for rapid *ratification
        of the EU Treaty* without new negotiations.

27/10   In Denmark, seven out of eight Parliamentary parties reach a
        'national compromise' on additions to the EU Treaty, on the basis
        of which they will support a second referendum in 1993.

29/10   In Italy, the Second Chamber of Parliament approves the *ratifica-
        tion of the EU Treaty* by a majority of votes. The same happens
        in the Spanish Congress.

5/11   In Belgium, the First Chamber of Parliament approves the *ratifi-
        cation of the EU Treaty* by a majority of votes.

6/11   Greece signs the *Schengen Treaty*.

12/11   In The Netherlands, the Second Chamber of Parliament approves
        a bill on *ratification of the EU Treaty* by a majority of votes.
        Parliament imposes the condition that it is to be consulted with
        regard to the introduction of a single currency. On 15 December,
        the First Chamber also approves the bill.

19/11   Sweden decides to let the crown *float*.

22/11   *Realignment* within the EMS: the central rates of the peseta and
        the escudo are lowered by 6 per cent (ECU central rate of the
        guilder: 2.21958). Between June and December, the *interven-
        tions* of all European central banks (including the Scandinavian)
        denominated in Deutsche mark amount to 284 billion.

2/12   In Germany, the *Bundestag* approves the *ratification of the EU
        Treaty* by a majority of votes. In December, the *Bundesrat* does
        the same.

6/12   In a referendum, Switzerland says 'no' to the *EEA*.

10/12   Norway decides to let the crown *float*.

11-12/12 In Edinburgh, the European Council arrives at a compromise on the Danish problem with regard to the acceptance of the EU Treaty. Furthermore, it decides to set up a temporary *credit facility* of ECU 5 billion.

1993

1/1 The *Treaty on the EEA* enters into effect.
The *Single Market* has been nearly completed. This means that most Single Market legislation applies throughout the European Economic Area.

18/1 The EC Council of Ministers agrees to a loan of ECU 8 billion to Italy within the framework of the *mechanism for medium-term financial assistance in support of the balance of payments.*

1/2 *Realignment* within the EMS: the central rate of the Irish pound is devalued by 10 per cent (ECU central rate of the guilder: 2.20045).

22/3 In Belgium, the competences of the Government to check the decisions and tasks of the National Bank are amended by law. The Government Commissioner appointed at the Bank no longer has the right to prevent monetary or political decisions. Furthermore, *monetary financing of budget deficits* is prohibited.

11/5 The French Government submits a bill to Parliament on the new *Statute of the French central bank.*

14/5 *Realignment* within the EMS: the central rate of the peseta is devalued by 8 per cent and that of the escudo by 6.5 per cent (ECU central rate of the guilder: 2.19672).

18/5 In Denmark, 56.8 per cent of the votes in the referendum are in favour of the *EU Treaty.*

21-22/6 In Copenhagen, the European Council focuses on the fight against unemployment. The Commission is ordered to compile a White Paper on a medium-term strategy to promote growth, competition and employment. Within this framework, it is decided to temporarily raise the *credit facility* introduced in Edinburgh by ECU 3 billion and to extend it until the end of 1994 at the earliest. Furthermore, the Council agrees that the associated countries in Central and Eastern Europe, should they wish so, may join the EU, provided that they meet the required economic and political conditions.

23/6   In the United Kingdom, the majority of Parliament approves *ratification of the EU Treaty*, with the exception of the social paragraph.

2/8   Decision by the EC Council of Ministers and the Committee of Central Bank Governors on a *far-reaching revision of the ERM*. The maximum fluctuation of the central rate of all currencies is raised from ± 2.25 per cent and 6 per cent respectively, to ± 15 per cent. The exception is the bilateral agreement between Germany and The Netherlands to maintain the fluctuation margin of ± 2.25 per cent between their currencies.

12/10   The *German Constitutional Court* rules that the EU Treaty is not in conflict with the principle of sovereignty embedded in the German constitution. However, the Court holds the view that the Treaty is revocable, while reserving the decisive vote in case of conflicts between European regulations and legislation and the German constitution.

17/10   The *Schengen Treaty* is postponed. The Treaty was to take effect on 1 December 1993.

21/10   The Governor of the Dutch central bank Duisenberg declares himself openly against a rapid return to the former bandwidth within the ERM. *Fixed exchange rates* require a high degree of convergence, both of the economic 'fundamentals' and of political objectives.

22/10   In Luxembourg, the Government adopts an Act granting *greater independence* to the LMI as stipulated in the Maastricht Treaty.

29/10   In Spain, the majority of the Congress of Representatives approves the *ratification of the EU Treaty*. On 25 November, the Spanish Senate follows.
        In Brussels, the European Council confirms that 1 January 1994 will be the starting date of stage two of EMU. In this stage, the *European Monetary Institute (EMI)* will be established in Frankfurt as the precursor to the ECB.

1/11   The *Treaty on EU* takes effect. Pursuant to article 109 G of the Treaty the shares of the currencies in the ECU basket are determined at those of 21 September 1989 (since that date, the share of the 'hard' currencies has risen from 70.8 to 74.7 per cent).

26/11   The permanent *credit facility* offered by the Banca d'Italia to the Italian Treasury is terminated by law.

5/12   Publication by the Commission of a *White Paper* on growth, com-
            petitiveness and employment, drawn up at the request of the
            European Council during the meeting at Copenhagen.

10-11/12 In Portugal, the majority of the Assembly, which consists of one
            chamber, approves the *ratification of the EU Treaty*. With ref-
            erence to the Commission's White Paper, the European Council
            decides in Brussels to carry out *a plan of action* to fight unem-
            ployment in the longer term. Furthermore, the Council is pleased
            to note that all conditions have been met to actually start stage
            two of EMU.

                                    1994

1/1   Stage two of EMU enters into effect. The *EMI* is established,
            having its temporary seat in Basle. The EMI takes over the tasks
            of the EMCF. It will create the conditions for the transition to
            stage three by reinforcing monetary policy coordination so as to
            ensure price stability. As from the start of stage two, the prohibi-
            tion against monetary financing of Governments by central banks
            and the prohibition against privileged access of Governments to
            financial institutions become effective. The establishment of the
            EMI means the end of the Committee of Central Bank Governors.
            The *EEA* becomes effective. Switzerland does not participate.
            In France, the new *statute of the French national bank* becomes
            effective, guaranteeing a degree of independence comparable to
            that of the Bundesbank.

1/3   *Expansion of the EU*. Agreement is reached with Austria, Finland
            and Sweden to join the EU as from 1 January 1995, following rat-
            ification by the national Parliaments. Negotiations with Norway
            do not lead to any concrete results.

18/5   The Spanish Parliament approves a bill regarding greater *au-
            tonomy for the Spanish national bank*. By Act of 1 June 1994,
            the bank is assigned full responsibility for the formulation and
            implementation of monetary policy, with price stability being the
            primary objective.

12/6   In Austria, the majority of the population votes in favour of
            accession to the EU in a referendum.

24-25/6   On Corfu, the European Council decides to set up a discussion
            group to prepare the IGC of 1996. Furthermore, the *Acts of*

accession to the EU are signed by Austria, Finland, Norway and Sweden.

19/9   Decision by the EC Council of Ministers concerning *excessive public deficits* in Belgium, Denmark, Germany, France, Italy, The Netherlands, Portugal, Spain and the United Kingdom.

16/10   In Finland, the majority of the population votes in favour of *accession to the EU* in a referendum.

8/11   The EC Council of Ministers adopts the name of *Council of the European Union (EU Council)*.

13/11   In Sweden, the majority of the population votes in favour of *accession to the EU* in a referendum.

15/11   First meeting of the *EMI* in Frankfurt.

9-10/12 In Essen, the European Council urges for budget consolidation and strict observance of the *convergence criteria*, which are to result in the establishment of EMU.

1995

1/1   Austria, Finland and Sweden join the *EU*. They also participate in the EMS, but not in the ERM. Norway has rejected the EU Treaty in a referendum.

9/1   The Austrian schilling joins the *ERM*, but is not yet included in the ECU basket. The national bank deposits 20 per cent of its gold and foreign exchange holdings (to an amount of some 18 million schilling) with the EMI on a swap basis.

6/3   *Devaluation* of the peseta and the escudo by 7 per cent and 3.5 per cent respectively against the ERM currencies (ECU central rate of the guilder: 2.15214).

7/3   Publication of the first annual report of the EMI, strongly criticising the tendency towards increasing *budget deficits* which has been evident for years.

20/3   First application of the *excessive deficit procedure*. According to the EU Council, ten out of the former twelve Member States do not meet the required *convergence criteria* for public sector finance. In addition to Luxembourg, Ireland is not censured although Irish public sector debt (nearly 90 per cent of GDP) is well in excess of the reference value of 60 per cent of GDP.

26/3   The *Schengen Treaty* enters into effect between the Benelux, Germany, Portugal and Spain. France is granted a postponement until 27 June to meet the requirements of the Schengen Treaty. Italy and Greece have signed the agreement, but do not participate for the time being. The United Kingdom is the only EU country refusing to abolish passport controls.

9/4   During an informal meeting at Versailles, the EU Council discusses possible scenarios for the transition to stage three. The Ministers declare themselves in favour of the so-called *'delayed big bang'* *model*. This model is based on an adjustment term of three years after 1999, with the ECU initially being used in inter-central bank transactions, while in the Member States only the national currencies remain in circulation. After thorough preparations, the ECU will be used on a large scale in private payments on day x.

15/4   The Governor of the Bundesbank Tietmeyer does not consider the *target date* of 1997 for the transition towards stage three of EMU realistic. He explicitly stresses the political implications of monetary union.

28/4   Austria signs the *Schengen Treaty*.

31/5   *Green Paper* of the Commission on the establishment of EMU. The Commission agrees to the adjustment term of three years proposed in Versailles, which will start in 1999. However, during that period it wants the national currencies to continue in circulation concurrently with the ECU (*'mounting wave' model*). Where the use of the ECU is concerned, the Commission aims at building a 'critical mass', which comprises not only intra-bank transactions, but also retail transactions.

1/6   In Messina, a Committee (*Groupe de Réflexion*) is set up, which is to prepare the IGC of 1996 under the chairmanship of Spain.

12/6   The three Baltic states Estonia, Latvia and Lithuania enter into the *European agreements*, offering the possibility of free trade with and full membership of the EU. Consequently, these countries have obtained the same status as Bulgaria, the Czech Republic, Hungary, Poland, Slovakia and Rumania, with which the EU entered into European agreements earlier.

19/6   The EU Council voices its doubts of the *feasibility of EMU* in 1997.

26-27/6 In Cannes, the European Council decides to set up a final scenario for the transition to *stage three of EMU* before the meeting to be held in Madrid before the end of 1995. This decision implies that the European Heads of State and Government Leaders implicitly give up the objective of 1997 as the starting date of stage three. The scenario submitted by the Commission is classified as an 'informal exercise'. A group of experts is charged with an examination of the relationship between the EMU participants and the EU countries which will not yet be able or willing to join.

27/6   France states that, within the framework of the *Schengen Treaty*, it will abolish passport controls as soon as possible but no later than 1 December 1995.

10/8   According to the Italian Prime Minister Dini his country has managed to put an end to the 'perverse spiral' of ever-increasing budget deficits thanks in part to the reform of the pension system. Against this background, he urges for a rapid return of the lira to the *ERM*.

14/9   The German Minister of Finance Waigel insists on a more strict application of some *convergence criteria*. This notably concerns the budget deficit and the public debt ratio.

19/9   The French President Chirac announces that it is 'highly likely' that France will request the European partners to the *Schengen Treaty* to continue French border controls after 1 January 1996.

20/9   Finance Minister Waigel states that neither Italy nor Belgium will be part of the *core group* of countries forming part of EMU in 1999, thus causing unrest in the foreign exchange markets.

24-25/9 During the informal European Summit on Mallorca, held to discuss the *preparations for the IGC of 1996*, it becomes evident that there are serious doubts about the feasibility of EMU on the agreed date. After the informal discussions, Prime Minister Dini suggests that EMU should be postponed for two years. His proposal is a reaction to the statements made by Waigel.

25/9   According to Waigel the EU should not assign the highest priority to the target date of 1999 for the start of EMU, if that would be at the expense of the EMU *convergence criteria*. From Dresden, Governor Tietmeyer says that there are many uncertainties surrounding the establishment of EMU.

7/10   Informal meeting of the Ministers of Finance and the Central Bank Governors of the EU in Valencia during which the *convergence criteria* and the timetable from the Maastricht Treaty are confirmed unanimously. The proposal put forward by Thibault de Silguy (European Commissioner for Finance) that banks and enterprises effect all giro transactions in the single currency as soon as possible is rejected. The new currency will be brought into circulation in 2002 at the latest, and will replace the national currencies as legal tender within a period of six months. This means that, for a period of at most six months, the national currencies and the common currency will both have the status of legal tender. In January 1998 at the latest, it will be decided which countries qualify for participation in EMU on the basis of 'hard' figures of 1997.

9/10   According to Dini the re-entry of the lira into the *ERM* is not a matter of life or death. The IMF advises Italy to wait a while.

15/10   The former President of the European Commission Delors states that a common monetary policy conducted by the ECB should be attended by a *common fiscal and marcoeconomic policy*. According to Chancellor Kohl, monetary union should go hand in hand with political union.

24/10   In Germany, the six reputed Economic Institutions advocate a less rigid application of the *convergence criteria*. Waigel strongly opposes this proposal. Supported by the Bundesbank, he wants the common currency to be at least as 'hard' as the Deutsche mark. If necessary, he opts for the postponement of EMU.

25/10   President Chirac makes known that France will do its utmost to meet the *convergence criteria* for EMU on time. If Germany should so require, France will 'at all times' be willing to discuss far-reaching requirements for stability to be applicable after the entry into effect of EMU.

14/11   Publication of the *EMI Report on the changeover to the single currency*.
        The Governor of the Dutch central bank Duisenberg urges for a decrease of the public debt ratio by two percent annually so as to ensure that The Netherlands meets the *convergence criteria* for EMU.

27/11   The EU Council supports the *'stability pact'* proposed by Waigel. However, important issues, such as the date for the participation decision, the transitional period and the name of the new currency are postponed to the European Summit to be held in December.

4/12   During a meeting of the European Foreign Affairs Ministers, Estonia formally applies for *membership of the EU*. An association agreement with the EU was already signed in June (together with Latvia and Lithuania).

5/12   The Prime Ministers of Belgium, Luxembourg and The Netherlands agree to the German proposal to call the European single currency *Euro*.

13/12   The European Parliament approves of a *customs union between the EU and Turkey*. This means that, as from 1 January 1996, all trade barriers between EU Member States and Turkey will be abolished, with the exception of levies on agricultural products and steel.

15-16/12 In Madrid, the European Council agrees that (1) the European currency is called Euro, (2) the IGC will start March 1996, (3) in 1998 'as early as possible' it will be decided, on the basis of *'hard' figures* of 1997, which countries may participate in EMU, (4) no preferential treatment will apply to the countries in favour of EU membership.

BIBLIOGRAPHY

'All Saint's Day Manifesto' (1975), *The Economist*, 1 November.

Allen, P.R. (1976), *Organization and Administration of a Monetary Union*, Princeton N.J.: Princeton University Press.

Bakker, A.F.P. (1996), *The Liberalization of Capital Movements in Europe. The Monetary Committee and Financial Integration 1958–1994*, Dordrecht: Kluwer Academic Publishers.

Bamberger, L. (1874), *Die Zettelbanken vor dem Reichstag: Versuch einer gemeinverständlichen Darstellung*, Leipzig: Brockhaus.

Bamberger, L. (1885), *Die Schicksale des Lateinischen Münzbundes. Ein Beitrag zur Wirtschaftspolitik*, Berlin: Verlag von Leonard Simion.

Bainbridge, T. and A. Teasdale (1995), *The Penguin Companion to European Union*, Harmondsworth: Penguin Books Ltd.

Benni, A.S. (1927), 'L'Assainissement monétaire de l'Europe', *XXVe Rapport Annuel et Bulletin Périodique de la Société Belge d'Etudes et d'Expansion*, **25** (59), February, pp. 52–55.

Bergman, M. S. Gerlach and L. Jonung (eds) (1992), 'The Rise and Fall of the Scandinavian Currency Union 1873–1920', *European Economic Review Paper*, **37** (2/3), pp. 507–517.

Beyen, J.W. (1980), 'Over de Europese integratie' in P.M. Hommes (ed.), *Nederland en de Europese eenwording*, The Hague: Martinus Nijhoff, pp. 170–183.

Blaum, K. (1908), *Das Geldwesen der Schweiz seit 1798*, Strasbourg: Verlag von Karl J. Trübner.

Bordes, Ch. E. Girardin and J. Mélitz (eds) (1995), *European Currency Crisis and After*, Manchester: Manchester University Press.

Burkhardt-Bischoff, A. (1886), *Die Lateinische Münz-Convention und der Internationale Bimetallismus*, Basle: H. Georg's Verlag.

Casella, A. (1992), 'Participation in a Currency Union', *The American Economic Review*, **82** (4), pp. 847–863.

Cohen, D. (1988), 'The Costs and Benefits of a European Currency', in M. de Cecco and A. Giovannini (eds), *A European Central Bank: Perspectives on Monetary Unification after Ten Years of the EMS*, Cambridge: University Press, pp. 195–215.

Commission of the European Communities (1973), *Communication de la Commission au Conseil relative au bilan des progrès accomplis au cours de la première étape de l'Union économique et monétaire, à la répartition des compétences et des responsabilités entre les Institutions de la Communauté et les Etats membres que nécessite le bon fonctionnement de l'Union économique et monétaire et aux mésures à adopter au cours de la deuxième étape de cette Union*, Commission (73).

Commission of the European Communities (1990), 'One Market, One Money', *European Economy*, **44**, October.

Coombes, D. (1970), *Politics and Bureaucracy in the European Community: A Portrait of the Commission of the E.E.C.*, London: Allen & Unwin.

Council-Commission of the European Communities (1971), 'Resolution of the Council and of the Representatives of the Governments of the Member States of 22 March 1971, Realization by Stages of Economic and Monetary Union in the Community', Section I, *Official Journal of the European Communities*, C 28, 27 March.

De Cecco, M. and A. Giovannini (1989), 'Does Europe need its own central bank?' in M. de Cecco and A. Giovannini (eds), *A European Central Bank? Perspectives on Monetary Unification after Ten Years of the EMS*, Cambridge: University Press, pp. 1–12.

De Cecco, M. (1992), 'European Monetary and Financial Cooperation before the First World War', *Rivista di Storia Economica*, **9**, pp. 55–76.

De Cecco, M. and F. Giavazzi (1994), 'Italy's Experience within and without the European Monetary System: A Preliminary Appraisal', in J.O. de Beaufort Wijnholds, S.C.W. Eijffinger and L.H. Hoogduin (eds), *A Framework for Monetary Stability*, Dordrecht: Kluwer Academic Publishers, pp. 221–238.

De Grauwe, P. (1995), *Monetary Union and Convergence Economics*. Paper presented at the Tenth Annual Congress of the European Economic Association, Prague, September 1–4 (to be published).

De Nederlandsche Bank (1946–1993), *Jaarverslagen*, Amsterdam.

De Nederlandsche Bank/Beyen, J.W. (1953), Grondslagen voor het Nederlandse standpunt met betrekking tot het vraagstuk der Europese integratie.

De Nederlandsche Bank/Holtrop, M.W. (1949), Some Notes to the Report of the Chairman of the Council of the Benelux Customs Union and the Consideration of H.M. Hirschfeld with reference to the Report, 28 January, MAZ, Cabinet.

Delors Committee for the Study of Economic and Monetary Union (1989), *Report on the Economic and Monetary Union in the European Commu-*

nity, SEMU/14/89, Luxembourg.

Denzel, M.A. (1992a), 'Vom Schweizer Franken zum "schweizer Franken" (1798–1860)', in J. Schneider and O. Schwartz (eds), *Währungen der Welt I, Europäische und Nordamerikanische Devisenkurse 1777–1914*, Stuttgart: Steiner, pp. 72–81.

Denzel, M.A. (1992b), 'Die währungspolitische Einigung Italiens: Italienische Wechselplätze zwischen 1815–1861', in J. Schneider and O. Schwartz (eds), *Währungen der Welt I, Europäische und Nordamerikanische Devisenkurse 1777–1914*, Stuttgart: Steiner, pp. 82–104.

Deutsche Bundesbank (1957–1994), *Auszüge aus Presseartikeln*, Frankfurt am Main.

Deutsche Bundesbank (1976), *Währung und Wirtschaft in Deutschland 1876–1975*, Frankfurt am Main: Fritz Knapp GmbH.

Deutsche Bundesbank (1990), 'Die erste Stufe der Europäischen Wirtschafts- und Währungsunion', *Monatsberichte*, Frankfurt am Main, July, pp. 30–39.

Dornbusch, R. (1992), 'Monetary Problems of Post-Communism: Lessons from the End of the Austro-Hungarian Empire', *Wirtschaftliches Archiv*, **128** (3), Kiel, pp. 392–424.

Duisenberg, W.F. (1989), 'The President's Report', in *Annual Report*, Amsterdam: De Nederlandsche Bank.

Duisenberg, W.F. (1992a), 'The Transformation of Europe; on Trade and Exchange Rates', in B. Bremer (ed.), *Europe by Nature: Starting-Points for Sustainable Development*, Assen: Van Gorcum & Comp., pp. 149–157.

Duisenberg, W.F. (1992b), *Financial and Monetary Policy in a Europe ohne frontières*, Amsterdam: De Nederlandsche Bank.

Duisenberg, W.F. (1992c), 'Financial and Economic Integration in the Benelux', in *Quarterly Bulletin* (3), Amsterdam: De Nederlandsche Bank.

Duisenberg, W.F. (1993), 'The President's Report', in *Annual Report*, Amsterdam: De Nederlandsche Bank.

Duisenberg, W.F. (1995), 'From Latin Monetary Union to European Monetary Union', in M.M.G. Fase, G.D. Feldman and M. Pohl (eds), *How to Write the History of a Bank*, Aldershot: Scolar Press, pp. 1–10.

Duroselle, J.B. (1957), 'Europe as a Historical Concept', in C. Grove Haines (ed.), *European Integration*, Baltimore: The Johns Hopkins Press, pp. 11–20.

Egner, E. (1925), *Der Lateinische Münzbund seit dem Weltkriege*, Leipzig: Akademische Verlagsgesellschaft mbH.

Eichengreen, B. (1993), 'European Monetary Unification', *Journal of Economic Literature*, **31** (3), pp. 1321–1357.

European Monetary Institute (1995), *The Changeover to the Single Cur-*

rency, Frankfurt am Main, November.

Fisher, I. (1911), *The Purchasing Power of Money*, New York: MacMillan.

Friedman, M. (1990), 'Bimetallism Revisited', *Journal of Economic Perspectives*, **4** (4), pp. 85–104.

Gallarotti, G.M. (1993), 'The scramble for gold: monetary regime transformation in the 1870s', in M.D. Bordo and F. Capie (eds), *Monetary Regimes in Transition*, Cambridge: University Press, pp. 15–68.

Gibbs, H.H. and H.R. Grenfell (1886), *Bimetallic Controversy*, London: Effingham Wilson, Royal Exchange.

Goodhart, C. (1989), 'Discussion', in M. de Cecco and A. Giovannini (eds), *A European Central Bank? Perspectives on Monetary Unification after Ten Years of the EMS*, Cambridge: University Press, pp. 280–285.

Goodhart, C. (1991), 'An Assessment of EMU', *The Royal Bank of Scotland Review*, (170), pp. 3–25.

Goodhart, C. (1995), *European Monetary Integration*, LSE Financial Markets Group, Special Paper Series, (73).

Greul, R. (1926), *Die Lateinische Münz-Union: eine völkerrechtliche Studie*, Berlin: Ferd. Dümmlers Verlagsbuchhandlung.

Griffiths, R.T. (1992), 'De Benelux-landen en het Schuman-plan', in E.S.A. Bloemen (ed.), *Het Benelux-effect*, Amsterdam: NEHA, pp. 71–89.

Haberler, G. (1970), 'The International Monetary System: some recent developments and discussions' in C.F. Bergsten, G.N. Halm and F. Machlup (eds), *Approaches to Greater Flexibility of Exchange Rates*, Princeton N.J.: Princeton University Press, pp. 115–123.

Hagen, J. von (1995), 'Monetäre, fiskalische und politische Integration: Das Beispiel der USA', *Auszüge aus Presseartikeln*, (76), Frankfurt am Main: Deutsche Bundesbank, pp. 13–20.

Halkema-Kohl, J.F. (1932), 'Belgisch-niederländisch-luxemburgische Wirtschaftskooperation, der Vertrag von Ouchy vom 18. Juli 1932', *Weltwirtschaftliches Archiv, Zeitschrift des Instituts für Weltwirtschaft und Seeverkehr an der Universität Kiel*, **36** (2), pp. 620–629.

Hartog, F. (1951), 'Moeilijkheden op weg naar een economische eenheid van Europa', The Hague: Ministry of Economic Affairs (Pierson Foundation, integration) 325/I '51.

Helfferich, K. (1894), *Die Folgen des Deutsch-Oesterreichischen Münz-Vereins von 1857. Ein Beitrag zur Geld- und Währungs-Theorie*, Strasbourg: Karl J. Trübner.

Henderson, W.O. (1957), 'A Nineteenth Century Approach to a West European Common Market', *Kyklos*, **11**, pp. 449–459.

Holtfrerich, C.-L. (1989), 'The Monetary Unification Process in 19th-Century Germany: Relevance and Lessons for Europe Today', in M. de Cecco and A. Giovannini (eds), *A European Central Bank? Perspectives on*

Monetary Unification after Ten Years of the EMS, Cambridge: University Press, pp. 216–243.

Holtfrerich, C.-L. (1993), 'Did Monetary Unification Precede or Follow Political Unification of Germany in the 19th Century', *European Economic Review*, **37** (2/3), pp. 518–524.

Ingram, J.C. (1973), *The Case for European Monetary Integration*, Princeton N.J.: Princeton University Press.

Ishiyama, Y. (1975), 'The Theory of Optimum Currency Areas: A Survey', in *Staff Papers*, International Monetary Fund, **22** (2), Washington, pp. 344–383.

Jacobsson, E.E. (1979), *A Life for Sound Money. Per Jacobsson, His Biography*, Oxford: Clarendon Press.

Jong Edz., Fr. de (1980), 'De historische ontwikkeling van het thema der Europese integratie', in P.M. Hommes (ed.), *Nederland en de Europese eenwording*, The Hague: Martinus Nijhoff, pp. 7–18.

Kersten, A.E. (1992), 'Oorsprong en inzet van de Nederlandse Europese integratiepolitiek', in E.S.A. Bloemen (1992), *Het Benelux-effect*, Amsterdam: NEHA, pp. 1–13.

Krämer, H.R. (1971), 'Experience with Historical Monetary Unions', in O. Emminger, H. Giersch and W. Hankel (eds), *Integration durch Währungsunion?*, Institut für Weltwirtschaft an der Universität Kiel, Tübingen, pp. 106–119.

La Malfa, U. (1957), 'The Case for European Integration: Economic Considerations', in C. Grove Haines (ed.), *European Integration*, Baltimore: The Johns Hopkins Press, pp. 64–80.

Lansburgh, A. (1928), 'Münzunionen', *Die Bank: Monatshefte für Finanz- und Bankwesen*, (12), pp. 731–735.

Lansburgh, A. (1932), 'Europa-Währung', *Die Bank: Wochenhefte für Finanz- und Bankwesen*, **50** (42), pp. 1455–1460.

Läufer, Th. (1993), *Europäische Gemeinschaft–Europäische Union, Die Vertragstexte von Maastricht*, Bonn: Europa Union Verlag GmbH.

Le Trocquer, Y. (1929), 'L'Union Douanière Européenne. Est-elle désirable – Est-elle réalisable?', *Bulletin Périodique de la Société Belge d'Etudes et d'Expansion*, **27** (70), pp. 172–183.

Le Trocquer, Y. (1932), 'La convention d'Ouchy, Première étape vers l'Union Douanière Européenne', *Bulletin Périodique de la Société Belge d'Etudes et d'Expansion*, **30** (86), pp. 283–287.

Ludlow, P. (1982), *The Making of the European Monetary System: A Case Study of the Politics of the European Community*, London: Butterworth Scientific.

Lusser, M. (1990), 'Die EG auf der Suche nach der monetären Integration–Parallelen zur schweizerischen Währungsgeschichte', *Geld, Währung und*

Konjunktur (3), Schweizerische Nationalbank, pp. 239–246.

Machlup, F. (ed.) (1976), *Economic Integration: Worldwide, Regional, Sectoral,* Proceedings of the Fourth Congress of the International Economic Association held in Budapest, London: MacMillan.

Machlup, F. (1979), *A History of Thought on Economic Integration,* London: The MacMillan Press Ltd.

Masera, R.S. (1988), 'Panel Discussion: the Prospects for a European Central Bank', in M. de Cecco and A. Giovannini (eds), *A European Central Bank? Perspectives on Monetary Unification after Ten Years of the EMS,* Cambridge: University Press, pp. 337–343.

Menger, C.M. (1895), *Beiträge zur Währungsfrage in Oesterreich-Ungarn,* Jena: Fischer.

Mertens, J.E. (1944), 'L'Union Latine', in *La Naissance et le Développement de l'Etalon-Or,* Paris: Presses Universitaires de France, pp. 257–276.

Müller-Ohlsen, L. (1954), 'Die Währungsprobleme der wirtschaftlichen Integration Europas', *Weltwirtschaftliches Archiv,* **72** (1), pp. 106–154.

Mundell, R.A. (1961), 'A Theory of Optimum Currency Areas', *American Economic Review,* **51** (4), pp. 657–665.

Nationale Bank van België (1957), 'Bijdrage tot de studie van het statuut der buitenlandse munten', *Tijdschrift voor Documentatie en Voorlichting,* **32**, September, pp. 189–204, October, pp. 264–283.

Nationale Bank van België (1957), 'Het muntstatuut van België', *Tijdschrift voor Documentatie en Voorlichting,* **32**, June, pp. 437–456.

Nielsen, A. (1927), 'Zum Problem der nordischen Münzunion', *Weltwirtschaftliches Archiv,* **26** (2), pp. 293–304.

Nielsen, A. (1933), 'Monetary Unions', in E.R.A. Seligman (ed.), *Encyclopaedia of the Social Sciences,* X, pp. 595–601.

Pesmazoglou, G.J. (1931), 'De l'Union Monétaire Balkanique', *Bulletin périodique de la Société Belge d'Etudes et d'Expansion,* (79), pp. 48–50.

Pierson, N.G. (1912), 'De voornaamste muntstelsels', in *Leerboek der staathuishoudkunde,* I, Haarlem: De Erven F. Bohn, 3rd ed., pp. 444–490.

Pohl, M. and S. Freitag (eds) (1994), *Handbook on the History of European Banks,* Aldershot: Edward Elgar Publishing Ltd.

Posthuma, S. (1982), 'De Latijnsche Muntunie: 1 Januari 1866–31 December 1926', in *Analyses en beschouwingen in retrospect: een selectie uit de gepubliceerde werken,* Leyden: Stenfert Kroese, pp. 177–182.

Pryce, R. (1980), 'Historical Development (of the EC)', in P.M. Hommes (ed.), *Nederland en de Europese eenwording,* The Hague: Martinus Nijhoff, pp. 35–62.

Raalte, E. van (1931), *De Volkenbond en de Vereenigde Staten van Europa,* The Hague: Martinus Nijhoff.

Redish, A. (1993), 'The Latin Monetary Union and the Emergence of the International Gold Standard', in M.D. Bordo and F. Capie (eds), *Monetary Regimes in Transition*, Cambridge: University Press, pp. 68–85.

Ritzmann, F. (1964), 'Die Entwicklung des schweizerischen Geld- und Kreditsystems', *Schweizerische Zeitschrift für Volkswirtschaft und Statistik*, **100** (1/2), pp. 235–272.

Ritzmann, F. (1973), *Die Schweizer Banken: Geschichte, Theorie, Statistik*, Bern: Haupt.

Sannucci, V. (1989), 'The Establishment of a Central Bank: Italy in the 19th Century', in M. de Cecco and A. Giovannini (eds), *A European Central Bank? Perspectives on Monetary Unification after Ten Years of the EMS*, Cambridge: University Press, pp. 244–289.

Schwartz, H.P. (1980), 'Federating Europe — but how?', in P.M. Hommes (ed.), *Nederland en de Europese eenwording*, The Hague: Martinus Nijhoff, pp. 83–152.

Smith, V.C. (1936), *The Rationale of Central Banking*, London: King & Son.

Spinelli, A. (1957), 'The Rationale of European Integration', in C. Grove Haines (ed.), *European Integration*, Baltimore: The Johns Hopkins Press, pp. 37–64.

Sprenger, B. (1991), *Das Geld der Deutschen: Geldgeschichte Deutschlands von den Anfängen bis zur Gegenwart*, Paderborn: Verlag Ferdinand Schöningh.

Stoel, M. van der (1976), 'Europese eenwording: de Nederlandse waardering van idealen en werkelijkheden', *Internationale Spectator*, **30** (1), pp. 39–48.

Szász, A. (1989), *The politieke economie van de Europese munt*, Rotterdamse Monetaire Studies (37), Rotterdam: Erasmus Universiteit.

Szász, A. (1993a), 'Towards a Single European Currency: Ecu, Franc-Fort, Question-Mark', in D.E. Fair and R.J. Raymond (eds), *The New Europe: Evolving Economic and Financial Systems in East and West*, Dordrecht: Kluwer Academic Publishers, pp. 217–235.

Szász, A. (1993b), 'Monetair Europa na Maastricht: op weg naar een brede en evenwichtige basis', *Internationale Spectator*, **47** (3), pp. 146–151.

Theurl, T. (1992), *EINE gemeinsame Währung für Europa, 12 Lehren aus der Geschichte*, Innsbruck: Oesterreichischer Studien Verlag.

Tietmeyer, H. (1993), 'The European Monetary Agenda', *Auszüge aus Presseartikeln*, (83), Frankfurt: Deutsche Bundesbank, pp. 2–4.

Tindemans, L. (1982), 'Europese Raad. Herdenking 25 jaar EG', in *Keesings Historisch Archief*, 23 April, pp. 265–267.

Tindemans, L. (1995), *De Europese Unie. Verslag aan de Europese Raad*, Brussels, December.

Toniolo, G. (1989), 'Discussion', in M. de Cecco and A. Giovannini (eds), *A European Central Bank? Perspectives on Monetary Unification after Ten Years of the EMS*, Cambridge: University Press, pp. 285–289.

Tower, E. and Th.D. Willet (1976), *The Theory of Optimum Currency Areas and Exchange Rate Flexibility*, Special Papers in International Economics (11), Princeton N.J.: Princeton University Press.

Tromp, B.A.G.M. (1994), 'De Europese mythe', *HP De Tijd*, 21 January, pp. 60–65.

Vanthoor, W.F.V. (1991), *Een oog op Holtrop. Grondlegger van de Neder-landse monetaire analyse*, Amsterdam: NIBE.

Vanthoor, W.F.V. (1994), *De Europese monetaire eenwording in historisch perspectief*, Amsterdam: NIBE.

Vanthoor, W.F.V. (1996) 'The Age of (Western) European Integration: A History of Trial and Error', *De Economist*, **144** (2), pp. 137–164.

Verwilst, H. and M. Quintyn (1982), 'De Belgisch-Luxemburgse Econo-mische Unie in opspraak?', *Maandschrift Economie*, **46** (5), Tilburg, pp. 195–206.

Walré de Bordes, J. van (1924), *The Austrian Crown: its Depreciation and Stabilization*, London: P.S. King & Son.

Wee van der, H. and K. Tavernier (1975), *De Nationale Bank van België en het monetaire gebeuren tussen de twee wereldoorlogen (1918–1940)*, Brussels: Nationale Bank van België.

Werner, P. (1971), 'Floating and Monetary Union — Without Monetary Union there is no Political Integration', *Intereconomics*, **6** (8), Hamburg.

Werner Report (1970), 'Report to the Council and the Commission on the Realization by Stages of Economic and Monetary Union in the Com-munity', in *Bulletin van de Europese Gemeenschappen*, Supplement II, October, Luxembourg.

Willis, H.P. (1901), *A History of the Latin Monetary Union*, Chicago: The University of Chicago Press.

Witteveen, H.J. (1970), *Munt slaan uit de Europese eenheid*. Address to the Dutch Organization for the International Chamber of Commerce on 26 May, Amsterdam.

Wouters, V. (1953), 'De positie van de Belgisch-Luxemburgse Economische Unie in de Europese Betalingsunie tussen 1952 en 1953', *Economisch-Statistische Berichten*, **38** (1900), pp. 870–872.

Zellfelder, F. (1992), 'Der Lateinische Münzbund: Grundlagen, Entstehung und Scheitern', in J. Schneider and O. Schwartz (eds), *Währungen der Welt I, Europäische und Nordamerikanische Devisenkurse 1777–1914*, Stuttgart: Steiner, pp. 105–122.

Zellfelder, F. (1992), 'Die Währungsprobleme der Donaumonarchie', in J. Schneider and O. Schwartz (eds), *Währungen der Welt I, Europäische und Nordamerikanische Devisenkurse 1777–1914*, Stuttgart: Steiner, pp. 122–135.

Zottman, A. (1963), 'Europäische Unionsbewegungen', in *Handwörterbuch der Sozialwissenschaften* III, Stuttgart, pp. 399–404.

INDEX